Art in Chemistry;
Chemistry in Art

Art in Chemistry; Chemistry in Art

Barbara R. Greenberg

Dianne Patterson

1998
Teacher Ideas Press
A Division of
Libraries Unlimited, Inc.
Englewood, Colorado

*Dedication to Dick and Bob
in appreciation of their
support, cooperation, and sense of humor.*

TEACHER IDEAS PRESS / Libraries Unlimited
A member of Greenwood Publishing Group, Inc.
88 Post Road West,
Westport, CT 06881
www.lu.com

Production Editor: Kevin W. Perizzolo
Copy Editor: Jason Cook
Proofreader: Felicity Tucker
Indexer: Nancy Fulton
Typesetter: Kay Minnis

Library of Congress Cataloging-in-Publication Data

Greenberg, Barbara R.
    Art in chemistry; chemistry in art / Barbara R. Greenberg, Dianne Patterson.
    xiv, 259 p. 22x28 cm.
    Includes bibliographical references and index.
    ISBN 1-56308-487-2
    1. Chemistry--Study and teaching (Secondary) 2. Art--Study and teaching (Secondary) I. Patterson, Dianne. II. Title.
QD40.G73   1998
540'.71'2--dc21   98-18796
                                                           CIP

Contents

4—THREE-DIMENSIONAL WORKS OF ART: Playing with Clay 86

5—SCULPTURE AND ORGANIC CHEMISTRY: Macroscopic and Microscopic Sculpture 116

Preface

Art in Chemistry; Chemistry in Art was born around 1985 when we were teaching introductory art and general, honors, and A.P. chemistry as separate subjects. Chemistry students were sometimes bored or turned off by a traditional approach to chemistry. The art students were a mixed group: Some were enthusiastic about art; others were not so enthusiastic. We recognized that chemistry is an integral part of art and that the combination of the two subjects would result in a meaningful, relevant, and interesting way of approaching art and chemistry, adding a new dimension to each subject.

We wrote a skeleton curriculum during the summer of 1985 as a project authorized by Willowbrook High School, Villa Park, Illinois, and taught segments of the course to introductory art students and general chemistry students. It was an immediate success. Student interest and alertness increased. Chemistry students expressed atomic theories as works of art and art students were quite adept at preparing developers for photography for their artistically created photograms. The learning of chemistry came painlessly when associated with artwork, and art assignments had a new and deeper meaning.

In 1988, the philosophy and curriculum was presented in the *Journal of Chemical Education*. Nationwide response was immediate: Requests for the curriculum came from high schools, colleges, and even museums. When the *Journal* was published overseas, requests for the curriculum came from around the world. As recently as 1996, a request for a copy of the curriculum was received from Italy. This was a book that was waiting to be written.

The course in this book is designed for high school students in grades 10–12. However, the curriculum can be adapted for use at many levels. A simplified version of the material has been taught to eighth-grade students with great success. Also, at the college level, difficult topics such as equilibrium and specific heat can be extended to include more challenging quantitative relationships. The abstract nature of chemistry can be explored at any level. Students are able to express abstractions through art projects. For instance, the abstract idea of what constitutes an atom according to various atomic theories can be expressed by the student in an art project emphasizing center of interest. There is a tremendous value to this approach. By examining the art project, the teacher can gain a new insight about student visualization and understanding of the atomic theory.

The scope of the art and chemistry material in this resource book is extensive. It includes most of the material found in a traditional introductory art course and in a general chemistry curriculum. *Art in Chemistry; Chemistry in Art* covers the nature of color and its psychological significance, the elements of design and principles of good composition; pigment and light primaries; color systems and color wheels; warm and cool colors; the properties of color; color relativity; proper use of various paints and papers; pen-and-ink techniques; three-dimensional and relief construction, including ceramics and plaster sculpture; metalworking and jewelry making; photography; perspective; and an investigation of art forgeries, art conservation, and art restoration. Also included is information about how artists can protect themselves from harmful art materials. This information is supplemented by lists of suggested, representative artwork created by significant artists.

Discussed within these art topics are the following chemical principles: Electromagnetic radiation; atomic theory and structure; electron configuration; chemical and physical properties; chemical and physical change; classification of matter; solution preparation and concentration; the mole concept; chemical formulas; chemical equations; ions and molecules; elements; compounds and mixtures; the periodic table; types of solids; crystals vs. glasses; relative weights; ionic, covalent, and polar covalent bonding; shapes of molecules; organic chemistry; catalysts; specific heat; the heat of a reaction; metals, nonmetals, and metalloids; electrochemical cells; electrolytic cells; electronegativity; oxidation-reduction; acids and bases; equilibrium; qualitative analysis; nuclear equations; spectroscopy; half life; and radioactive dating. There is enough material in *Art in Chemistry; Chemistry in Art* to teach art and chemistry as a two-year curriculum. Most importantly, the chemistry is taught with relevance to art topics. Art and chemistry are truly integrated into one subject.

We wish to acknowledge the eighth-graders and their principal, Mrs. Lynn Mills of Our Lady of Mount Carmel School in Melrose Park, Illinois, who welcomed us into their school and were so receptive to our art-in-chemistry curriculum. It was a great pleasure to work with these eighth-graders and experience their joy of learning chemistry through art.

Supplies for *Art in Chemistry; Chemistry in Art* can be obtained from:

Kemtec Educational Services
9889 Crescent Park Drive
West Chester, Ohio 43069
1-800-733-0266

Kemtec Educational Services will supply individual chemistry and art materials and also kits for the activities and demonstrations.

Introduction

We have become a society of specialists. Doctors specialize in specific areas of medicine such as ophthalmology or gynecology. Lawyers specialize in specific areas of law such as personal injury or real estate law. A specialist, while trying to solve a problem, might focus on a narrow theme and lose sight of the whole picture.

In most secondary schools, individual subjects are taught by teachers who specialize in a certain area. There is little subject matter integration. Therefore, students fail to grasp interconnections between disciplines. However, problem solving associated with life experiences requires information that crosses several subject areas.

This book is designed to integrate visual art with chemistry. Most of the concepts found in a basic chemistry course are introduced within a framework of introductory visual art.

In the first chapter, color is defined in terms of electromagnectic radiation and how this radiation interacts with atoms, molecules, and ions. Color from visible light is compared with color from mixing paints. Color is related to the arrangement of elements in the periodic table. The elements of color and of design are studied. The psychology of color is related to the physical properties of colored flames.

Paint is the topic in Chapter 2. Classes of matter are related to paint types. Students examine saturated, unsaturated, and supersaturated solutions and their relationship to paint composition.

In Chapter 3, grounds such as paper and gesso are introduced. Students use their prepared paints to paint on their handmade grounds. For paper grounds, students consider the function of acids and bases in paper production and the use of oxidizing agents as paper whiteners.

Chapter 4 examines three-dimensional clay works of art as related to the crystalline structure of solids. Chemical bonding is studied in connection with these solid structures. Students prepare clay glazes while studying the mole concept. Information concerning the periodic table is expanded.

In Chapter 5, organic molecules are considered to be microsculptures. Microsculptures are compared to macrosculptures regarding composition. Kinetic sculpture movements are related to molecular motions.

Jewelry making is studied in Chapter 6. Emphasis is placed on metals, alloys, and electrochemistry.

Chapter 7 relates two- and three-dimensional works of art to molecular shapes.

In Chapter 8, photography—developing, printing, and composing the photo—provides a vehicle for examining chemical equilibrium and oxidation reduction reactions.

An introduction to methods of detecting an art forgery is provided in Chapter 9. Students perform a qualitative analysis of a paint chip to find whether or not a painting is "forged."

A discussion of chemical hazards in art, in Chapter 10, helps an artist use chemical materials in a safe manner.

This book is designed for all teachers who wish to integrate art with chemistry and also present students with the fundamental principles of both subjects. The book is sequenced in a logical order that will provide an entire course in basic chemistry and introductory art. In the alternative, the activities and demonstrations can be used to complement an ongoing course. Activities and some demonstrations challenge students of all levels of competence. Students can start at level one with basic material and continue to level two for a more in-depth look at the material. These extensions of the activities and demonstrations serve to enrich and challenge advanced students. Tenth, eleventh, and twelfth grade students should be able to understand the basic material as presented. The material can be modified for eighth and ninth grades and also for college students. Also, the activities and demonstrations can be used in museum programs.

Note

It should be understood that the authors and publisher can take no responsibility for the use or misuse of any information provided herein. Readers should use common sense and seek advice from the medical profession, regulation agencies, and associated professionals concerning specific hazards and problems.

Always review with students proper handling procedures when dealing with sharp instruments such as X-ACTO blades, knives, etc.

1

Colors Do Matter

How Do We See Color?

INTRODUCTION

When a small child asks mom the question, "Why is the sky blue?" mom may be headed for trouble because there is no simple answer to this difficult question. To understand why the sky is blue, it is necessary to understand the nature and properties of matter and electromagnetic radiation and see the connections between matter, electromagnetic radiation, and color. We look to both art and chemistry for enlightenment.

In the study of chemistry, the properties and composition of matter are investigated, along with the nature of electromagnetic radiation and how it affects matter. Electromagnetic radiation is radiant energy that exhibits wave properties and travels at the speed of light (when in a vacuum). Matter is made of particles. Some particles are atoms that contain subatomic particles called electrons, protons, and neutrons; other particles are molecules that are made up of atoms. If all the atoms in a particular substance have the same electron configuration (i.e., if they have the same number and arrangement of electrons), the substance is an element. An atom is the smallest particle of an element that can exist alone or in combination with particles of the same or a different element. Each atom of a particular element has the same number of protons in its nucleus. An element cannot be broken down by ordinary chemical means, such as burning, heating, or simply combining with other substances. Some elements are colored; others are colorless. Why? In order to answer this difficult question, we will examine the internal structure of atoms and also investigate the three-dimensional patterns of atoms in molecules. When atoms of the same or different elements bond, they form molecules. A compound is a substance made of molecules that are all the same. Certain compounds are colored; others are not. Why? We can answer these questions when we understand the effect of electromagnetic radiation on matter.

In the study of art, design is the basis of an artistic arrangement, and color is one element of design. The design of a work of art includes not only color but also line, texture, light and dark contrast, and shape. However, color is the element of design that arouses the most appreciation and is the element to which we are most sensitive. Even one who is puzzled by "modern art" usually finds its color exciting and attractive. One may question the use of distortion of shape but will seldom object to the use of color, and may like a work of art solely for its use of color. A small child sees the world as a work of art and questions the color scheme: "Why is the sky blue?" In Chapter 1, we will seek an answer to this question.

THE NATURE OF COLOR

Color is one of the most expressive elements of design because its quality affects our emotions directly and immediately. For example, red signifies energy (among other things) and blue is often associated with wisdom. In China, red is attributed to the living and blue to the dead.

1.1

The Psychology of Color

Objectives

1. Students will examine the emotional effects of color.
2. Students will interpret the meanings of particular colors from a personal point of view.
3. Students will relate symbolic colors for atoms to emotional feelings about the elements.

Materials

Pencil, paper, atomic model kits.

Time

60 minutes

Procedure

1. Ask students to describe emotions associated with yellow, purple, and red.
2. Ask students to describe, either orally or in writing, examples from their experiences in which these colors are used to express emotions.
3. Using an atomic model kit, have students make a list of the names of the elements represented in the kit along with each color used to represent each element.
4. Next to the name and color, have the students list each element's properties. For example, oxygen is a colorless gas. It supports the burning of other elements.
5. Using student suggestions, create a list of emotional feelings such as happiness, anger, boredom, confusion, warmth, and surprise.
6. Considering their generated list, have the students list their emotional feelings about each element color. Have them discuss whether or not their feelings about the element colors are representative of the element's properties.

A colorless world would be a drab one. The fictional story *The Giver* by Lois Lowry describes an Orwellian society in which every member is assigned a specific, lifelong task. No one has a choice. All originality is lost. The world is colorless until one young man breaks out of the mold. As he rebels, objects take on a new appearance. He sees a *red* apple! As the young man begins to see more and more colored objects, there is no turning back to a colorless world.

With a sense of color, people can see more aspects of their world, in more detail. Without color, with only black and white and gray, the eye can see a mere dozen or so different tones. With color, the eye can see thousands of distinctions, which not only look different than one another but also convey different feelings and associations. Psychologically, gray is dull and negative. With color, warmth and coldness, excitement and stimulation, and countless other human expressions are conveyed.

1.2
Color vs. Black and White

Objectives

1. Students will examine how color expresses emotion.

2. Have students create a black-and-white picture that tells a story, then rework the same picture in color.

3. Have students evaluate each of their pictures for emotional significance and storytelling effectiveness.

4. Have students watch the portion of *The Wizard of Oz* in which the film changes from black and white to color. Ask students to explain why they think the film was made in this manner. Discuss the use of black and white and color in other films they have seen (e.g., why do they think that *Schindler's List* was filmed in black and white and later filmed in color?).

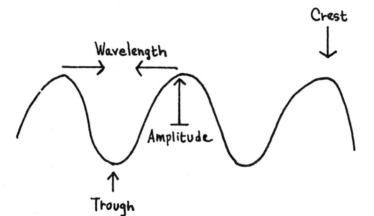

Figure 1.1. Wave Properties.

Light As a Source of Color:
The Electromagnetic Spectrum

Color begins with and is derived from light, either natural or artificial. Where there is little light, there is little color; where the light is strong, the color is likely to be particularly intense. We notice at such times as dusk or dawn, when the light is weak, that it is difficult to distinguish one color from another. Under bright, strong sunlight, such as in tropical climates, colors have more intensity. All light from the sun comes to us in the form of waves that transfer, or radiate, energy. Waves from the sun are disturbances that carry energy through space. All these waves travel at the same speed through a vacuum, the speed of light, but they differ in wavelength, the distance from crest to crest, and frequency, the number of waves that pass a point in a certain period of time. Some waves from the sun are not visible to the human eye. Together, these visible and invisible waves are called *electromagnetic radiation*. The three characteristics of waves that will be discussed here are wavelength and frequency (defined above) and amplitude, half the distance from the crest of a wave to its trough.

In the electromagnetic spectrum, the waves with the shortest wavelength and, correspondingly, the greatest energy and highest frequency are called gamma rays. The waves with the longest wavelength, least energy, and lowest frequency are called radio waves. As shown in Figure 1.2, the visible range is very narrow compared to the entire range of electromagnetic radiation. We only see a narrow range of the vast amount of radiation that surrounds us. How would the world look if every wave of the electromagnetic spectrum became visible to our eyes? We would see colors beyond our wildest imagination. When we use a prism to separate sunlight, visible light, into its component wavelengths, we see the colors of the rainbow. This is a very small sample of what might appear if gamma rays, X-rays, microwaves, and radiowaves were visible to our eyes.

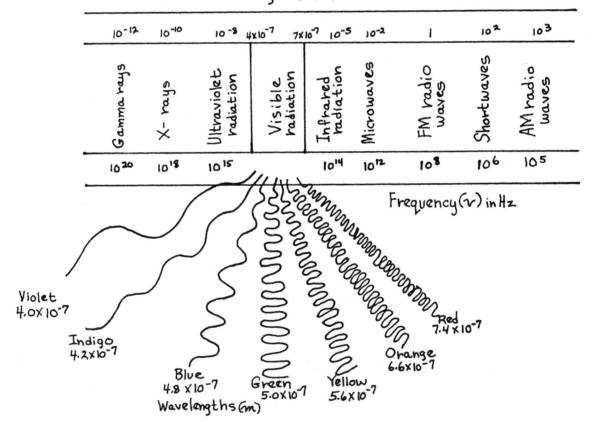

Figure 1.2. The Electromagnetic Spectrum.

1.3

The Rainbow—A Chorus of Waves

Objectives

1. Students will define the waves in the electromagnetic spectrum in terms of their wavelengths and frequencies.

2. Students will make a diagram identifying the following characteristics of a wave: Crest, trough, wavelength, and amplitude.

3. Students will use a prism to see the colors of the waves present in the visible range of the electromagnetic spectrum.

4. Students will make a poster of the electromagnetic spectrum.

5. Students will describe the relationships among wavelength, frequency, and energy of waves in the electromagnetic spectrum.

6. Students will describe and explain the differences between the spectrum created by white light leaving a prism and the spectrum created by plant grow-light leaving a prism.

Materials

Figure 1.2, prism, incandescent light or sunlight, sheet of white paper, plant grow-light, colored pencils or markers, 1-x-5-foot sheet of shelf paper.

Time

60 minutes

Procedure

1. Have students make a diagram of a wave and label the crest, trough, wavelength, and amplitude (see Fig. 1.1). This diagram can be included on a separate space on the poster used to draw Figure 1.2 in step 2 below.

2. Have students, working in groups of four to six, copy Figure 1.2 onto a 1-x-5-foot sheet of shelf paper. As shown in Figure 1.2, add waves in the visible range of the spectrum, using the correct colors and relative wavelengths for each visible wave (the red wave should have the longest wavelength; the violet wave should have the shortest wavelength). Use colored pencils or markers to represent the colors of the visible waves and to make the poster attractive. Save room on the poster to include the wavelengths observed in step 6 below.

3. Hang the poster on the wall.

4. Allow incandescent light or sunlight to pass through a prism at an angle that projects a rainbow, sometimes referred to as a spectrum, onto a sheet of white paper.

5. Repeat step 4, using a plant grow-light.

6. Have students make colored drawings of the spectra produced from incandescent light or sunlight, and from a plant grow-light, using relative wavelengths. The drawings should be sized to fit on the poster of the electromagnetic spectrum.

7. Place the drawings on the poster (be sure that the color of the longest wavelength, red, is oriented beside the infrared wave group, and that the color of shortest wavelength, violet, is oriented beside the ultraviolet wave group).

Questions and Conclusions

Level One

1. Which waves in the electromagnetic spectrum carry the greatest energy? The lowest energy? (The common names for the wave groups indicate the amount of energy associated with a particular wave group.)

2. What color was the light that entered the prism? What colors of light left the prism? What waves are present in white light?

3. Compare the spectrum from the incandescent light or sunlight to the spectrum from the plant grow-light. Make a list of any differences and explain why they occur.

Level Two

1. As the energy of a wave increases, what happens to its frequency? To its wavelength?

2. As the wavelength of a wave increases, what happens to its frequency?

3. Speed is defined as distance traveled in a period of time. All waves in the electromagnetic spectrum travel at the same speed, the speed of light. What is this speed?

In Activity 1.4, the component waves of white light having wavelengths in the range of 7.4×10^{-7} m (red) to 4.0×10^{-7} m (violet) are separated by a prism into individual wavelengths representing red, orange, yellow, green, blue, indigo, and violet. Because sunlight is made of all these waves, we would expect the sky to be white. The question "Why is the sky blue?" remains.

1.4
Color and Energy

Objectives

1. Students will learn how to calculate the frequency of a wave when its wavelength is known, and its wavelength when its frequency is known.

2. Students will relate wave energy to frequency and wavelength.

3. Students will experimentally examine the difference in the temperature of a blue flame compared to a yellow flame, then they will examine the psychological effects of these colors.

Materials

Two Bunsen burners, matches.

Time

10 minutes

Procedure

1. Light two Bunsen burners, adjusting the air inlets so one flame is yellow and the other is blue.

2. Simultaneously, place a match into each flame.

3. Have students note the time it takes for the matches to light and record their observations. (The match in the blue flame will light more quickly than the match in the cooler yellow flame.)

Questions and Conclusions

Level One

1. Use Figure 1.2 to find the wavelength and frequency of blue and yellow waves:

	Wavelength	Frequency
Blue	4.8×10^{-7} m	6.2×10^{14} Hz
Yellow	5.6×10^{-7} m	5.4×10^{14} Hz

2. Compare yellow and blue waves for each of their three wave characteristics: Wavelength, frequency, and energy.

3. Compare the energy of blue and yellow waves to the sense of temperature evoked by these colors. Was your sense of temperature confirmed in Activity 1.4?

Level Two

1. Calculate the frequency of blue and yellow waves by dividing the speed of light (2.9979×10^8 m/sec) by wavelength in meters, and compare these answers to the values given in Figure 1.2.

2. Explain how to calculate the frequency of a wave when the wavelength is known, and how to calculate the wavelength of a wave when the frequency is known. (Frequency and wavelength are inversely related.)

From Activity 1.4, it can be seen that blue waves carry more energy than yellow waves (a blue flame is hotter than a yellow flame). Yet, we often think of blue as being cool and yellow as being warm—blue jeans are cool; the sun is warm. There is little relationship between the energy of visible waves and the psychological significance of their colors.

THE PSYCHOLOGICAL SIGNIFICANCE OF COLOR

Each color has its particular traditional significance. Partly because of its direct emotional effect upon us and partly because of its associations with various experiences, each color has acquired a symbolic significance. Color conditioning through the centuries has had a strong influence on our lives. Usually, each color has positive and negative connotations. For example, we use expressions such as "black-hearted," "green with envy," and "red-hot." Many of our associations with colors are a result of the manner in which we have been taught to think of them since we were children. Consider the following color combinations: Orange and black; red and green. Do Halloween and Christmas come to mind? On what holiday do we see red? We hope to see red on Valentine's Day. It would be hard for us to send an orange-and-yellow valentine or decorate our house in red and green for Halloween. How many people do you know who think pink is for boys and blue is for girls?

Color: Get the Meaning

White. White stands for purity and light, innocence and spiritual joy, as in "whiter than snow." Negatively, white is sterile, blank, and ghostly.

Black. Black represents the absence of light. It often stands for the power of darkness. It has a strong, solid feeling about it. Objects made of black often appear smaller than the same object made of white. Black is usually associated with mourning and is symbolic of evil, death, and despair.

Yellow. Yellow is the lightest color after white. It usually suggests light. It is also associated with gold and suggests power and wealth. It is a symbol of happiness or cheerfulness. In China, it is the imperial color. Negatively, yellow suggests cowardice ("to have a yellow streak"), sickness, and decay.

Red. Red is the most vibrant color, which is why the eye is drawn to it. Traditionally, it stands for love, energy, strength, and courage. Red means "stop" all over the world (except in China, where green means "stop" and red means "go"). Red also means danger ("red alert"), cruelty, and sin.

Blue. Blue is a favorite color of many people, as is evidenced by the prominence of blue in clothing. Blue suggests truth and loyalty ("true blue"). In China, blue is attributed to the dead, signifying divine eternity and immortality. It is a cool, relaxing color. It is also associated with wisdom, reliability, and justice. Negatively, blue suggests melancholy and sadness ("feeling blue").

Violet (Purple). Violet is the royal color, suggesting wealth and power, passion and luxury. The Phoenicians obtained a purple dye from oysters and it was reserved for royalty because of its rarity. Negatively, violet indicates mourning and sadness, but a sadness not as deep as that indicated by black.

Green. "Having a green thumb" is a familiar phrase. The word *green* brings to mind growth, life, and continuation. It is a quiet color often suggesting restfulness. It also symbolizes a tender, unripe state or lack of experience. Green also suggests jealousy.

Orange. Orange suggests glory, heat, a sense of plenty, and happiness, and has few negative associations. Because the eye is attracted to it, it has visibility and is especially useful in identifying important areas.

1.5

Color Psychology I

Objectives

1. Students will observe the effects of color on individuals in specific situations.
2. Students will apply the principles of good composition and the creative process to an original work.

Materials

Paper; pencils (level one); colored pencils, markers, or paints and paintbrushes (level two and level three only).

Time

15 minutes (Level One); 50 minutes (Level Two); 30 minutes (Level Three)

Procedure

Level One

1. Have students make a list of specific situations in which color plays a psychologically expressive role.

Level Two

1. Have students draw and then color an original composition based on a holiday celebrated with nontraditional colors. Or, students may draw and then color a scene or a single object using atypical or unexpected colors (e.g., a green hamburger in a blue bun, or a forest of blue and pink trees).

Level Three

1. Have students interpret, in picture form, a phrase using a specific color (e.g., "green with envy," "yellow streak," or "true blue").
2. At this point, a brief discussion of how to arrange a work of art would be appropriate.

THE PRINCIPLES
OF GOOD COMPOSITION

When planning a work of art, good composition is important. An interesting, orderly arrangement of line, texture, light-and-dark contrast, shape, and color (the elements of design) will help create an interesting work of art. In Chapter 7 (p. 177), the elements of design and the principles of composition will be addressed in greater depth; for now, a brief introduction to good composition is appropriate.

All the Pieces Are in Place

We have all had a chance to assemble a jigsaw puzzle. After emptying the puzzle box, we have a jumble of odd-shaped pieces that we must assemble into a meaningful whole. Good composition is much the same: The pieces of this puzzle are the elements of design: Line, texture, light-and-dark contrast, shape, and color. Any composition, whether two- or three-dimensional, should use the elements of design to achieve the following:

1. Strong center of interest or focal point

    This is the point or spot that first attracts the viewer's attention, which can be achieved by a variety of means:

    a. A light center of interest against darker areas, or vice versa

    b. A bright or intense (full strength) color as the center of interest against duller areas, or vice versa

    c. A group of small objects against a background of larger shapes, or vice versa

    d. A complex or detailed area set against areas of less complexity

    This contrast of focal point against the remainder of the composition is known as the effect of dominance and subordination

2. Movement of the eye through the composition

    Once the center of interest has been established, the rest of the composition should be arranged so that the eye of the viewer will move in a predetermined direction through it. This movement should follow a direction, such as around, back and forth, up and down, or diagonally, which can be indicated by various means:

    a. Repetition of a single color in different amounts

    b. A line or lines

    c. A shape or shapes

    d. Repetition of a texture, line, or shape in various sizes

3. Balance of parts

    The focal point need not be placed at the center of the picture. Frequently, the focal point is moved off-center to create an interesting effect. In a good composition, the balance of all parts is important. There are two types of balance: Formal balance (or symmetrical balance) and informal balance (or asymmetrical balance). In symmetrical balance, the subject is centered and other elements are placed on either side of an imaginary center line to achieve a balanced presentation. In asymmetrical balance, objects of one type or size on one side of a center line are visually balanced by objects of a different type or size on the opposite side of the line.

4. Interesting negative and positive space

    This will be addressed in greater detail in Chapter 5; for now, it is sufficient to say that the artist should be aware of not only the shapes and sizes of the subject matter but also of the negative space, or remaining space in the background. Too much negative space can overpower the subject matter, detracting from it rather than complementing it.

5. Unity and harmony

Finally, the composition should possess unity and harmony if all the elements of design—line, texture, light-and-dark contrast, shape, and color—fit together successfully. Regarding art, the word *unity* does not necessarily mean "sameness." Therefore, within unity variety of size, shape, and color are important to a successful composition. The puzzle is then complete!

Examples of Good Composition

Focal Point

Woman Weighing Gold, Jan Vermeer, 1664
The White Girl, James Abbott McNeill Whistler, 1862
Fighting Forms, Franz Marc, 1914
A Ballet Seen from an Opera Box, Edgar Degas, 1885

Movement

The Starry Night, Vincent van Gogh, 1889
Dutch Interior II, Joan Miro, 1928
Three Dancers, Pablo Picasso, 1925
The Assumption of the Virgin, Peter Paul Rubens, 1626

Balance: Symmetrical

Portrait of a Man in a Tall Hat, Rembrandt van Rijn, 1662
The Sisters, Berthe Morisot, 1869
Vase of Chrysanthemums, Claude Monet, 1880
Beasts of the Sea, Henri Matisse, 1950

Balance: Asymmetrical

Four Dancers, Edgar Degas, 1899
Breezing Up, Winslow Homer, 1876
Persistence of Memory, Salvador Dali, 1931
The Starry Night, Vincent van Gogh, 1889

Interesting Negative and Positive Space

Equatorial Jungle, Henri Rousseau, 1909
Portrait of an Elderly Lady, Mary Cassatt, 1887
Woman with Red Hair, Amedeo Modigliani, 1917
A Young Girl Reading, Jean Honore Fragonard, 1776

COLOR IN COMMERCIAL USE

People connect more immediately with color than with words or pictures. This is clearly evidenced in street signs and traffic signals: Red means "stop," green means "go," and yellow means "caution." Some colors symbolize meanings more clearly than others; some combinations are more easily seen than others. The best and most easily seen combination is black on yellow, followed by green on white, then red on white. The least effective combination is red on green. Strongly contrasting color combinations are used on automobile license plates, road signs, billboards, packaged goods in grocery stores, book and magazine covers, and myriad other objects for clarity, visibility, and attractiveness. The primary colors (red, yellow, blue) and the secondary colors (orange, green, violet) in full strength plus black or white are most often used because these combinations are the easiest to identify. In the world of advertising, companies use color to imprint a product in the memory of the consumer (a combination of red and yellow is often associated with McDonalds; a combination of red and white is often associated with Coca-Cola).

The following list includes artists who have used color in an unusual way to evoke emotions and imprint an image in the viewer's memory:

Franz Marc, *Blue Horse*, 1911
Henri Matisse, *Green Stripe (Madame Matisse)*, 1905
Marc Chagall, *The Green Violinist*, 1918
Andy Warhol, *Marilyn Monroe Series*, 1970s
Pablo Picasso, any painting from his blue period, 1901–4

1.6

Color Psychology II

Objectives

1. Students will analyze the effectiveness of color in conveying a specific emotion.

2. Students will explore the role of color in advertising.

3. Students will apply the principles of good composition and the creative process to an original work.

4. Alternatively, students will explain chemical concepts involved in advertising slogans.

Materials

Paper; colored pencils, markers, or paints and paintbrushes.

Time

50 minutes

Procedure

LEVEL ONE Have students make a list of specific emotions and the colors that evoke them, including situations in which the colors play a significant role.

LEVEL TWO Have students prepare an advertisement using color to evoke an emotion. For example, a travel advertisement might use blue and green to represent relaxation; an advertisement for children's clothes might emphasize red, yellow, and blue, the pigment primaries to represent youth and activity. Students should apply the principles of good composition to their advertisements.

LEVEL THREE Alternatively, prepare a list of advertising slogans based on chemical concepts, such as "Use Fluoride Toothpaste for Strong Teeth" or "Alpha Hydroxy Skin Cream Removes Wrinkles." Have students draw advertisements using color to evoke emotion, as discussed above, but also have them explain the chemical concepts involved in the slogans. Students should apply the principles of good composition to their advertisements.

THE CONNECTION BETWEEN LIGHT AND COLOR

Light Primaries

To see color, light must enter the eye through the iris and focus on the retina, which contains rods for night vision when there are few light waves, and cones to detect color during the day when more light waves are present. Some cones absorb mostly red and some yellow waves; other cones absorb mostly green and some yellow waves; and a third variety of cones absorb mostly blue and some violet waves. Red, green, and blue are the primary colors of light, which when mixed in various proportions produce all other colors. When the three primary colors are mixed in equal proportions, white light is produced. When equal portions of red and green light are mixed, yellow light will be observed. If equal portions of blue and red light are mixed, magenta light results and blue and green light produce cyan. Try it.

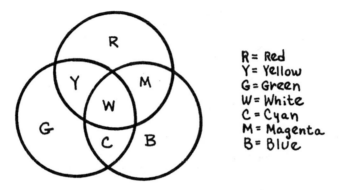

R = Red
Y = Yellow
G = Green
W = White
C = Cyan
M = Magenta
B = Blue

Figure 1.3. Mixing Primary Colors of Light.

Now we can re-address the question "Why is the sky blue?" We know that the sun brings us light that contains all the colors of the rainbow, or visible spectrum, not just blue. If all waves are reaching our eyes, the sky should be white. We need still more information to explain why the sky is blue.

ATOMS AND "NEON" SIGNS: AN ARRAY OF COLORED LIGHT

New York City's Times Square and Las Vegas, Nevada have something in common: High electric bills! At night, both places glow with colored lights, many of which are electrified gas-tube signs that light up the sky. Obviously, this is not light sent from the sun. To understand the source of the spectacularly colored signs of Times Square and Las Vegas, we must examine the structure of atoms.

Atomic Theory:
An Historical Perspective

In 400 B.C., the Greeks explained that all matter was made of fire, earth, water, and air. A Greek philosopher, Democritus, reasoned that matter was made of small, indivisible particles called *atomos*. Though the Greeks did not use experiments to test their ideas, the following scientists did, basing their atomic theories on experimental data:

John Dalton (1766–1844) stated that each element was made of tiny, indivisible particles called atoms, and that the atoms of one element were different from the atoms of another element.

 J. J. Thomson (1856–1940), an English physicist, proposed a "plum pudding" model of the atom in which the atom was a diffuse cloud of positive charge (the pudding); negatively charged electrons (the raisins) were embedded randomly in the cloud.

Ernest Rutherford (1871–1937) said that the atom was mostly empty space. He proposed a nuclear atom with a dense, positively charged center, the nucleus, and negatively charged electrons moving around the nucleus, at a relatively great distance from the nucleus.

Neils Bohr (1885–1962) proposed an orbital model of the nuclear atom in which electrons in an atom moved around the nucleus, just as planets move around the sun.

Erwin Schrodinger (1887–1961) and others considered the wave properties of electrons and proposed that electrons were not orbiting around the nucleus in an atom but were in electron-cloud probability areas outside the atomic nucleus. These probability areas were designated as energy levels.

Today, we recognize the atom as having negatively charged electrons outside the nucleus and positively charged protons and uncharged neutrons inside the nucleus. The mass of an electron is about one two-thousandth the mass of a proton or neutron, a neutron being slightly heavier than a proton.

1.7

Create Your Own Atom

Objectives

1. Students will demonstrate their understanding of the five basic atomic theories—the Dalton atom, the Thomson atom, the Rutherford atom, the Bohr atom, and the Schrodinger electron cloud model.

2. Students will use principles of good composition to achieve a strong focal point when illustrating their conception of an atom.

Materials

Colored pencils, paper.

Time

45 minutes

Procedure—All Levels

1. Have students make a drawing of an atom or atoms based on the atomic theories discussed previously. Students should use principles of good composition to achieve a strong focal point, and use colors that convey the emotions they want their drawings to evoke. The drawings should contain detailed visual information about atomic structure (including depiction of subatomic particles), and students should feel free to let their imagination run wild (e.g., a drawing of "The Atom That Ate New York" would be interesting).

Questions and Conclusions

Level One

1. Explain the relationship of your drawing to the particular atomic structure, as well as your choice of design elements, particularly color.

Level Two

1. Explain your depiction of subatomic particles, pointing them out while discussing the theory on which the drawing is based.

Atoms and "Neon" Signs: What's the Connection?

Not all electrified, tubular glass signs—"neon" signs—contain neon gas. Neon is just one of several gaseous elements used in sign creation. Helium gas, argon gas, mercury vapor, and sodium vapor are also used to make brightly colored signs. Electrified gas tubes are also used to make works of art.

Each of these gases glows in a characteristic color, which never changes. When no electrical energy is present, all these elements are colorless in the gas phase. When electricity is added, these elements release energy with wavelengths in the visible range of the electromagnetic spectrum.

Neon Gas	Red	Mercury Vapor	Purple-Blue
Helium Gas	Violet	Sodium Vapor	Orange
Argon Gas	Violet		

When atoms of these elements are bombarded with electricity and some of this electrical energy is absorbed, we say that the atoms become "excited." These atoms are having a party, and they turn color with excitement! Actually, the electrons outside the nucleus of the atom are affected. The excited electrons move to specific levels of greater energy, farther from the nucleus. Before the electrical energy is added, we say the electrons are in the "ground" state, having no fun. When the electrons move to higher energy levels, their configuration becomes very unstable. They fall back to lower energy levels closer to the atomic nucleus and release packages of energy, previously absorbed, in the form of light waves. For each of these elements, the light waves released from its electrons when electricity is added are always from the same range of wavelengths. For gaseous neon atoms, the energy released is mostly in the range of red wavelengths; therefore, neon signs appear red.

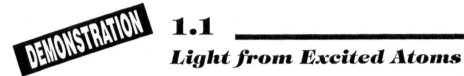

1.1

Light from Excited Atoms

Objectives

1. Students will explain how energy is emitted from atoms when the atoms are stimulated with an electrical charge.

2. Students will explain the electron cloud model of the atom and the significance of energy levels for electrons.

3. Students will calculate the energy emitted or absorbed when electron transitions occur.

4. Students will explain why an atom's spectral lines are called the "fingerprints" of the atom.

5. Students will make a drawing using spectral lines and color to convey an emotion.

Materials

Spectroscopes; gas discharge tubes, one filled with hydrogen, one with neon, and one with argon; a source of high-voltage direct current; colored pencils or paints and paintbrushes; paper; spectral line charts for hydrogen, neon, and argon.

Time

15–30 minutes

Procedure

1. Send high-voltage direct current through each gas discharge tube.

2. Have students view each electrified gas discharge tube through a spectroscope.

3. Have students draw and color or paint the lines observed through the spectroscope. These lines are called spectral lines; each element produces a particular pattern of spectral lines, which can be used to identify the element. The spectral lines represent specific waves of energy released when electrons in atoms fall back to lower energy levels.

4. Have students make a drawing using spectral lines as the theme. Colors having desired emotional significance should be used in the drawing.

Questions and Conclusions

Level One

1. Find charts showing spectral lines of several elements (try chemistry books). Students should draw and color the spectral lines of three elements.

2. Compare and contrast the spectral lines of the three elements and explain why elements have different spectral lines.

3. The ground state for electrons in an atom is when they are as close to the atomic nucleus as possible and have not moved to higher energy levels, farther from the nucleus. When electrons absorb energy and move away from the atomic nucleus, they are in the excited state. In which state—ground state or excited state—does an electron have more energy?

Level Two

1. Examine the spectral lines for hydrogen and determine the following:

   a. The energy of a mole (6.02×10^{23}) of hydrogen atom electrons at the second and third energy levels. Use the equation:

   $$E = -\frac{1312}{n^2} \text{ kj/mole}$$

   (n is a quantum number that has a positive integer value corresponding to an electron's energy level. In these calculations, n = 2 and n = 3. 1312 kj is the amount of energy needed to remove a mole of hydrogen atom electrons at the ground state, n = 1, completely away from the atoms.)

   $$E_2 = -\frac{1312}{2^2} \text{ kj/mole} \qquad E_3 = -\frac{1312}{3^2} \text{ kj/mole}$$

   (Answers:

   $$E_2 = \frac{-1312 \text{ kj/mole}}{4} = -328.0 \text{ kj/mole}$$

   $$E_3 = \frac{-1312 \text{ kj/mole}}{9} = -145.8 \text{ kj/mole})$$

   b. Calculate the wavelength of the energy released when a mole of hydrogen atom electrons drop from the third energy level to the second energy level. Use the following equation:

   $$\text{wavelength} = \frac{1.196 \times 10^5}{E_3 - E_2} \text{ kj/nm}$$

   (Answer: 656.4 nm or 6.6×10^{-7} m, an orange wave in the visible spectrum.)

   c. Determine whether the wavelength calculated places the energy emitted from an electron drop from the third energy level to the second energy level in the visible spectrum. If the wavelength corresponds to energy in the visible spectrum, students should identify the color associated with the wavelength and check to see if the hydrogen atom has a spectral line of that color. Students can refer to Figure 1.2 to verify the color that corresponds to their calculated wavelength.

1.2

More Excitement in Atoms— A Fireworks Display

Objectives

1. Students will research simple equations for the chemical changes observed in this activity.

2. Students will explain how energy is released in a chemical change and research the types of electromagnetic radiation that can be released.

3. Students will explain how colorless compounds produce colored light in a chemical change.

Materials

$Sr(NO_3)_2$ (strontium nitrate) or $SrCO_3$ (strontium carbonate); CH_3OH (methyl alcohol); $(NH_4)_2Cr_2O_7$ (ammonium dichromate); two Petri dishes; distilled water; matches; 10 ml graduated cylinder; centigram balance.

Time

30 minutes

■ *Warning!*
This demonstration should be performed behind a protective shield.

Procedure—All Levels

1. The teacher should dissolve about five grams of either $Sr(NO_3)_2$ or $SrCO_3$ in a Petri dish using a small amount of distilled water and then add 10 ml CH_3OH (methyl alcohol) to the solution. Ignite the solution—a bright-red fireworks display will ensue: Electrons falling back to the ground state emit energy with wavelengths of about 6.5×10^{-7} m, in the red orange range.

2. The teacher should place about five grams of $(NH_4)_2Cr_2O_7$ in a Petri dish and ignite it. Orange, red, and yellow colors will be produced.

■ *Note:*
In this demonstration, chemical changes occur. With the addition of heat, reactants change into products. New substances are formed with new physical properties. Chemistry is the study of chemical change.

Questions and Conclusions

Level One

1. Explain how colors appear when some chemicals are ignited. Include electrons in the ground state and electrons in the excited state in your explanations.

2. Consider the colors observed during the demonstration and record your emotional response to the colors.

3. Define *chemical change* and explain why the reactions in this demonstration resulted in chemical changes.

Level Two

1. Research the chemicals used in this demonstration and determine what chemical products were produced. Students should find equations that express the chemical changes that occurred in the demonstration. (Answers: $2Sr(NO_3)_{2(s)} \rightarrow 2SrO_{(s)} + 4NO_{2(g)} + O_{2(g)}$; $(NH_4)_2Cr_2O_{7(s)} \rightarrow Cr_2O_{3(s)} + N_{2(g)} + 4H_2O_{(g)}$; $2SrCO_{3(s)} \rightarrow 2SrO_{(s)} + 2CO_{2(g)} + 3O_{2(g)}$.)

2. Research whether or not all chemical changes result in a release of energy.

3. Research the following question: If energy is released in a chemical change, is it always energy in the visible range of the electromagnetic spectrum? If you find the answer to be no, provide examples of the types of electromagnetic radiation that can be released in a chemical change.

4. Compare the colors of the original compounds to the colors of the energy that were released during this demonstration and explain how colorless compounds produced colored light.

Considering our understanding of excited atoms, we can now propose a theory about why the sky is blue: Perhaps atoms in the earth's atmosphere are absorbing blue wavelengths of light from the sun's electromagnetic radiation, and these atoms are releasing blue light waves when their electrons fall back to the ground state. However, oxygen (O_2), about 20% of the earth's atmosphere, absorbs radiation with wavelengths between 1.0×10^{-7} m and 2.4×10^{-7} m, waves of much shorter wavelengths than blue light waves, which are 4.8×10^{-7} m. (Figure 1.2 shows that blue light waves are of 4.8×10^{-7} m in length.) Also, nitrogen (N_2), about 79% of the earth's atmosphere, absorbs wavelengths of less than 1.0×10^{-7} m in length. It is not likely that excited atoms of the atmospheric gases release blue waves of light. We must still ask, "Why is the sky blue?" (Scientists do believe that the northern lights are the result of sun-storm radiation producing a variety of excited atoms and, thus, the colorful displays in the northern night skies during periods of sun storms.)

THE CONNECTION BETWEEN PIGMENT COLORS AND LIGHT COLORS

We have discussed light wavelength stimulation of retina cones, which the brain translates into color, but there is more to understand when examining the nature of color. Most pigments, whether they are made of atoms or molecules (two or more atoms bonded together) selectively absorb, transmit, or reflect certain wavelengths of light. Basic pigment colors are magenta (red), yellow, and cyan (blue), usually referred to as red, yellow, and blue. They are identified as primary pigments because no other colors can be mixed to produce these colors. A primary pigment's color depends on the color of light it reflects. The following table summarizes the colors absorbed and reflected by the primary pigments:

Primary Pigment	Color Absorbed	Colors Reflected
Red	Green	Red-Orange, Violet
Yellow	Blue	Red-Orange, Green
Blue	Red, Red Orange	Green, Violet

1.8
Mixing Primary Pigments

Objectives

1. Students will learn the proper procedure for mixing secondary colors from primary pigments.

2. Students will observe the results of mixing two primary colors.

Materials

Red, yellow, and blue poster paints; paintbrushes; paper; mixing trays; paper towels; water containers.

Time

30 minutes

Procedure

1. Have students mix the following pigments in equal proportions:

   a. Red and yellow: The result will be orange or red orange. (This is because red pigment absorbs green waves and yellow pigment absorbs blue [violet], leaving red orange waves for us to observe.)

   b. Red and blue: The result will be violet. (This is because red pigment absorbs green waves and blue pigment absorbs red and red orange waves, leaving violet for us to observe.)

   c. Yellow and blue: The result will be green. (This is because yellow pigment absorbs blue waves and blue pigment absorbs red and red orange waves, leaving green for us to observe.)

   d. Yellow, red, and blue: The result should be black but will probably be a muddy color. (This is because all waves are absorbed, leaving no waves for us to observe.)

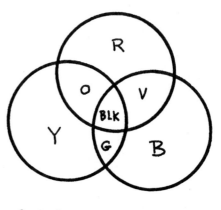

R = Red   O = Orange
Y = Yellow   G = Green
B = Blue   V = Violet
                BLK = Black

Figure 1.4. Mixing Primary Pigments.

Questions and Conclusions

1. What accounts for the difference? (When light waves are mixed, none of the waves are absorbed. They enter the eye and all the waves stimulate the cones in the retina. When pigments are combined, each pigment molecule or atom absorbs certain light wavelengths and reflects others. When all three pigment primaries are combined, all light wavelengths are absorbed and no waves reach the retina, so that no color message is sent to the brain: We "see" black.)

2. Why do you think the mixture of all three pigment primaries is a muddy color instead of black? (Answer: *Precisely equal amounts* of pure pigment primary colors must be mixed to achieve a true black.)

COLOR SYSTEMS AND COLOR WHEELS: A RIDE THROUGH COLOR

Color wheels take us on a sensational, visual ride. These wheels are color systems used to display colors in a systematic fashion and to illustrate a property of color called hue. Value and intensity, two other properties of color, are sometimes also illustrated in these color systems.

Color: An Historical Perspective

Through the years, many systems of color have been developed. Early theories about the nature of color existed in many countries of the ancient world. An interest in color was expressed by the Babylonians as early as 1900 B.C. Most early theories assumed that color was one of the properties of matter, such as density or mass. These theories were correct in identifying some physical properties of matter. Color and density are extensive physical properties. They remain constant regardless of amount. Mass, on the other hand, is an extensive physical property of matter. It changes with amount.

During the seventeenth century, Sir Isaac Newton, an English scientist, discovered the visible spectrum by projecting a beam of sunlight through a glass prism, separating the sun's electromagnetic radiation of visible wavelengths into the colors seen in a rainbow. Newton chose seven basic colors—red, orange, yellow, green, blue, indigo, and violet—and compared them to the seven major notes of the musical scale. He was looking for regularity: Repeating patterns to explain natural phenomena. Since the time of Newton, many scientists and artists have developed color theories.

Just about a century after Newton, about 1766, Moses Harris, 1731–1785, an English engraver and authority on insects, published the first known example of a color circle in full hue. This circle had primaries in red, yellow, and blue, and secondaries in orange, green, and purple (or violet).

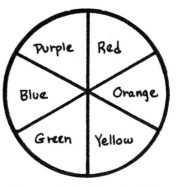

Figure 1.5. Harris Color Wheel.

Harris began a tradition for color order that is favored in art and color education today.

In modern times, the greatest American color theorist was Albert H. Munsell (1858–1918). About 1900, he designed and invented a color circle and color solid that has today become one of the most outstanding color order systems in existence. Munsell chose five basic colors: red, yellow, green, blue, and purple; and five intermediate colors: yellow-red (orange), green-yellow, blue-green, purple-blue, and red-purple. He described color in terms of hue, a simple color, value for lightness and darkness, and chroma for color purity, intensity, or saturation. Today, the Munsell

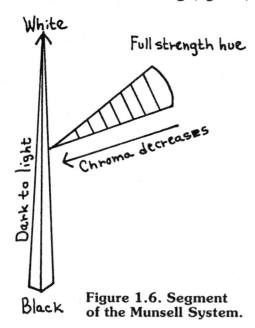

Figure 1.6. Segment of the Munsell System.

system is widely used as a standard for color identification and is so recognized in the fields of science and industry.

Another great modern theorist was Wilhelm Ostwald (1853–1932) of Germany, a Nobel Prize winner in chemistry. Ostwald developed the process for converting ammonia and oxygen to nitric acid. His color system, devised about 1915, had four primaries: Red, yellow, sea-green, and blue; and four secondaries: Orange, purple, turquoise, and leaf-green. Ostwald accepted a triangular order of color, with pure color at one angle, white at a second angle, and black at a third angle, intermixtures being within the triangle. Today, this system is commonly used by artists, designers, and stylists to achieve interesting color effects.

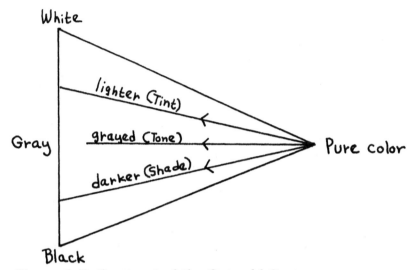

Figure 1.7. Segment of the Ostwald System.

The color wheel that we will be studying uses the colors as they appear in the rainbow, bent into a circle and connected together with the color red-violet. The color wheel consists of 12 main divisions, or sections. Three categories of color are represented in the hues of the wheel, and all appear in full strength; a fourth category, neutrals, is not part of the color wheel. To review information about color with the students, Handout 1.1 (following the discussion below) may be distributed.

Primary Colors. Red, yellow, and blue are called primary because no combination of other colors will produce any of these colors. From the three primary colors, all the remaining colors are produced.

Secondary Colors. Orange, green, and violet (or purple) are second in importance. Each is made by combining two primary colors in equal amounts.

Intermediate Colors. There are six intermediate colors, each made by combining adjoining primary and secondary colors in equal amounts. The intermediate colors are red-orange, red-violet, blue-violet, blue-green, yellow-green, and yellow-orange.

Neutrals. Black, white, and gray are the three neutrals or non-colors, which are not part of the color wheel. A neutral, when used beside a color, intensifies the color. Black and white, if not used properly, can dominate a composition. We "see" black when no electromagnetic radiation reaches our eyes; we see white when all the wavelengths in the electromagnetic spectrum reach our eyes.

Handout 1.1

Color

Figure. 1.8.

Name: _____

A prism is used to separate white light waves into separate wavelength bands that we call the colors of the rainbow. The flat band of colors formed in this way is called a spectrum.

These colors, in the same order as in a rainbow, can be bent into a circle. In the circular form, they are called a _____ _____. If you know the arrangement of the colors and their places on the _____ _____ , you will be able to mix and identify colors more easily.

There are twelve colors on the color wheel that we are using. They are divided into three groups:

Primary Colors. Three colors: Red, yellow, and blue.

Secondary Colors. Three colors: Orange, green, and violet (or purple). Each secondary color is a mixture of equal amounts of the two primary colors on either side of it on the color wheel:

    red + blue   = _____
    blue + yellow   = _____
    yellow + red   = _____

Intermediate Colors. Third in importance are the six remaining colors on the color wheel, which are combinations of equal amounts of the colors on either side of them on the wheel:

    red-orange   = _____ + _____
    red-violet   = _____ + _____
    blue-violet   = _____ + _____
    blue-green   = _____ + _____
    yellow-green   = _____ + _____
    yellow-orange = _____ + _____

The name of the primary color always appears first. There could be many more than 12 divisions on the color wheel, but we will only use 12.

1.9
Creating a Color Wheel

Objectives

1. Students will learn the proper procedure for mixing secondary and intermediate colors.

2. Students will learn the proper sequence of colors as they appear on the color wheel.

Level One:
Creating a Simple Color Wheel

Materials

Rulers; compasses; pencils; red, yellow, and blue poster paints; small paintbrushes; white paper suitable for paint; water containers; paper towels; black markers.

Time

100 minutes

Procedure

1. Have students use a compass to draw a circle with a radius of 4 inches.

2. Divide the circle into four equal parts.

3. Divide each of the four parts into three equal parts.

4. Paint in the primary colors as indicated on Handout 1.1.

5. Paint in the secondary and intermediate colors by mixing appropriate primary and secondary colors.

6. When dry, accent the circle and its divisions by outlining with a black marker.

Level Two:
Creating a More Elaborate Color Wheel

Materials

Same as level one, with the addition of heavy paper for making a pattern, a second sheet of paper for mounting the color wheel, and glue or rubber cement.

Time

200 minutes

Procedure

1. Have students follow step 1 though 5 for level one.

2. When the color wheel is complete, have students design a motif or pattern of their own choice (see Fig. 1.9 for an example) on the heavy paper. The motif should be large enough to cover the majority of a single pie-shaped section of the color wheel.

3.   Trace the motif onto each of the 12 sections of the color wheel; cut out the shapes and arrange them on the second sheet of paper in the same order, creating a color wheel of original design. Outline each section with marker.

4.   Glue the sections into place.

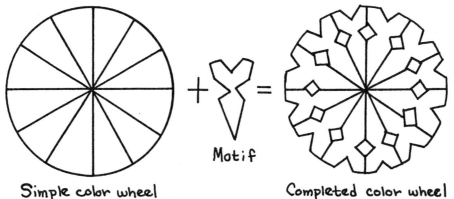

Simple color wheel

Figure 1.9.

Motif

Completed color wheel using the motif design

Level Three:
Creating a Color Design

Materials

Same as level one, with the addition of 12-x-12-inch white, heavy paper suitable for painting.

Time

200 minutes

Procedure

1.   On a sheet of white, heavy 12-x-12-inch paper, have students create an original, non-objective, symmetrical design of geometric shapes. The composition should have a minimum of 12 different shapes radiating outward from the center point. (See Fig. 1.10, p. 26, for an example.)

2.   Begin by painting the center shape one of the primary colors.

3.   Proceed by painting the next set of shapes, outward from the center, in the next color of the color wheel, an intermediate color. NOTE: No two shapes sharing a common side should be painted the same color.

4.   Paint the next set of shapes in the appropriate secondary color.

5.   Paint the next set of shapes in the appropriate intermediate color.

6.   Repeat steps 2–5, moving outward from the center and adding colors following the order of the color wheel, until all 12 of the colors have been used (e.g., begin with the primary red, paint the next set red-orange, the next set orange, the next set yellow-orange, the next set the primary yellow, etc.). If all 12 colors have been used and shapes still remain unpainted, repeat the order of colors until all shapes are painted.

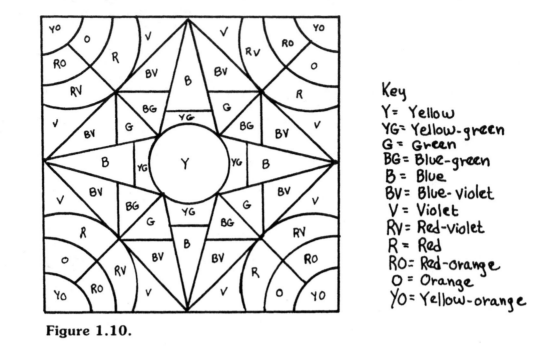

Key
Y = Yellow
YG = Yellow-green
G = Green
BG = Blue-green
B = Blue
BV = Blue-violet
V = Violet
RV = Red-violet
R = Red
RO = Red-orange
O = Orange
YO = Yellow-orange

Figure 1.10.

The Warm and Cool of Color

The colors of the color wheel can be divided into two groups: Red-violet, red, red-orange, orange, yellow-orange, and yellow are called warm colors; yellow-green, green, blue-green, blue, blue-violet, and violet are called cool colors. Warm and cool colors are used by artists to create a mood or atmosphere in their artwork. Warm colors create a feeling of joy and happiness and have a festive atmosphere about them. Cool colors are restful, cold, subdued, and quiet.

 ## 1.10
Warm and Cool Colors

Objectives

1. Students will understand how warm or cool colors aid in portraying a specific subject (all levels).

2. Students will apply the creative process and principles of good composition to an original work of art (levels two and three).

Level One:
Warm and Cool Colors I

Materials

Magazines and scissors.

Time

50 minutes

Procedure

1. Have students look through magazines and cut out examples of pictures in warm colors and pictures in cool colors.

2. Have students discuss how the pictures make them feel.

Level Two:
Warm and Cool Colors II

Materials

Magazines, glue, scissors, paper on which to glue the compositions.

Time

150 minutes

Procedure

1. Have students choose a descriptive theme (e.g., descriptive words such as *excitement*, *peaceful*, *busy*, and *sad* are possible themes). Each student should choose a different theme.

2. Have students find a variety of pictures in magazines to express their theme, cut them out, and arrange them into a composition, making effective use of warm and cool colors and the elements of design to best describe the theme.

Level Three:
Warm and Cool Colors III

Materials

Poster paints, paintbrushes, colored markers or colored pencils, 12-x-18-inch paper suitable for the chosen medium, a list of descriptive words.

Time

200 minutes

Procedure

1. Have students choose a word from the list made in Activity 1.1 and create a composition on 12-x-18-inch paper interpreting the word in either warm or cool colors, using the elements of design. The picture can be realistic or non-objective.

THE THREE PROPERTIES
OF COLOR

Hue. Hue refers to the quality of a color that we indicate by its name, such as red, orange, green, and blue. To change the hue of a color, it must be mixed with another hue (e.g., to change yellow to yellow-green some blue must be added).

Value. Value refers to the lightness or darkness of a color. This lightness or darkness depends on the amount of white or black added to the hue. To make a hue lighter, white is added. To make a hue darker, black is added. Adding black or white to a hue does not change the hue to a different hue; this only lightens or darkens it.

Intensity (or Chroma). Intensity, or chroma, refers to the color strength or saturation of a hue. A pure color as it appears on the color wheel is the strongest or most intense. The intensity of a color can be lessened by the addition of gray to the color, which dulls the color. A second way to lessen the intensity of a color is to add the hue that appears directly opposite on the color wheel. This opposite color is referred to as its complement.

The following is a list of significant modern artists and the properties of color represented in each artist's work:

Piet Mondrian	Primary colors, full intensity, neutrals
Stuart Davis	Primary and secondary colors, full intensity
Georges Braque	Primary and secondary colors, full intensity
Pablo Picasso	Low intensity, neutrals
Juan Gris	Low intensity, neutrals
James Abbott McNeill Whistler	Low intensity, neutrals
Hans Hoffman	Full intensity
Roy Lichtenstein	Full intensity, neutrals
Auguste Renoir	Light and dark values
Vincent van Gogh	Full intensity
Mark Rothko	Full and low intensity
Victor Vasarely	Light and dark values
Ellsworth Kelly	Full intensity

1.11

Solution Preparation and Pigment Primary Hues

Objectives

1. Students will explain the mole concept and use this concept to prepare chemical solutions of particular molarities.

2. Students will use colored chemical solutions to determine the outcome of mixing particular colors of pigments.

Materials

$CuSO_4$ (copper sulfate); K_2CrO_4 (potassium chromate); distilled water; periodic table; three small test tubes for each pair of students; red food color; three small flashlights; red, green, and blue transparency paper or filters; white paper; centigram balance.

Time

30 minutes

Procedure—All Levels

1. Prepare three flashlights by covering the lens of one flashlight with red transparency paper, the lens of another with green transparency paper, and the lens of the third with blue transparency paper. Red, green, and blue filters may be used instead of transparency paper.

2. Have students help prepare 0.1 M $CuSO_4$ and 0.1 M K_2CrO_4 solutions using the following combinations: 15.9 g $CuSO_4$/liter H_2O; 19.4 g K_2CrO_4/liter H_2O. (Note: Students should save these solutions for Activity 1.13.)

   During this procedure, introduce the mole concept: Have students use a periodic table to find the relative weights of all the elements in the molecules $CuSO_4$ and K_2CrO_4, respectively: Cu (copper), S (sulfur), O (oxygen); and K (potassium), Cr (chromium), O. Explain to students that the relative mass in grams for any element contains the same number of atoms. This number of atoms, 6.02×10^{23}, is called a mole. For each of the solutions, 0.1 mole of molecules is needed. A 0.1 M solution contains 0.1 mole of a substance dissolved in 1.0 liter of a solvent.

   To find the mass of one mole of molecules, add the relative masses of the elements contained in the molecule.

Table of Relative Masses (AMU)

Cu	63.5	S	32.1	O	16.0	K	39.1	Cr	52.0

   Note that the subscripts in a molecular formula represent the number of atoms in a molecule. Since a molecule of $CuSO_4$ has four oxygen atoms, the relative mass of oxygen must be multiplied by four and added to the relative mass of one copper atom and one sulfur atom to find the relative mass of a mole of $CuSO_4$, copper sulfate molecules. Two atoms of potassium, four atoms of oxygen, and one atom of chromium must be accounted for in potassium chromate, K_2CrO_4. Students should calculate the mass of one mole of each of the molecules needed, convert each to 0.1 mole (multiply by 0.1), and check their answers, which should be 15.9 g for $CuSO_4$ and 19.4 g for K_2CrO_4.

3. The $CuSO_4$ solution will be blue and the K_2CrO_4 solution will be yellow. Have students place a sample of each solution into a small test tube. In addition, students should fill a small test tube half full of distilled water and add red food color to attain a bright red solution. Next, have students place a sheet of white paper behind each test tube, then focus a beam of light through each solution, as follows: Red light through the blue solution ($CuSO_4$), blue light through the yellow solution (K_2CrO_4), and green light through the red solution.

4. Students should observe the white paper. In all three cases, students will see no transmission of color through the solutions because blue $CuSO_4$ solution absorbs red light waves, yellow K_2CrO_4 solution absorbs blue light waves, and the red solution absorbs green light waves.

Questions and Conclusions

Level One

1. List the primary colors of pigments (red, yellow, and blue), the color of light wave each absorbs (respectively: Green, blue, and red), and the colors of light waves each reflects (respectively: Red-orange and violet; red-orange and green; and green and violet).

2. Explain what a mole is in terms of the number involved and in terms of the relative weight of an element. How many atoms are present in one mole of any element; in one relative weight of any element? How do these two numbers compare? (Answer: They are the same.)

Level Two

1. Explain why some pigments are black and some pigments are white. Include absorption and reflection of colored light waves in your explanation.

2. Calculate the number of moles in 100.00 grams of sulfur, carbon, and iron. The relative masses of sulfur, carbon, and iron are 32.07, 12.01, and 55.85, respectively. (Answer: Sulfur, 3.118 moles; carbon, 8.33 moles; and iron, 1.790 moles.)

3. Explain why a chemist needs to use a mole as a unit when dealing with chemical change. (Answer: When atoms combine to form molecules, they bond in a definite number ratio. For example, when potassium sulfide, K_2S, is formed, two atoms of potassium bond to one atom of sulfur to form one potassium sulfide molecule. Knowing the mole concept, a chemist can use the relative mass of sulfur and the relative mass of potassium to combine the exact amounts needed to form a desired mass of potassium sulfide. Two relative masses of potassium, 78.2g, combine with one relative mass of sulfur, 32.1g, to form 110.2g of potassium sulfide. The mass ratio of 78.2 to 32.1 will provide a two to one ratio of the atoms. The mole concept tells the chemist how many atoms are in a certain mass of a substance.)

Activity 1.11 shows the relationship between pigment hue and the wave absorption and reflection properties of the pigment molecule. We will use this activity as a basis for learning about molecules, compounds, and ions, some of the particles that determine the colors of substances.

The Periodic Table:
Elements, Molecules, Compounds, and Ions

Elements are substances that are made of the same kind of atoms, except for isotopes of an element, which have a different number of neutrons. Molecules are made of two or more atoms bonded together. Compounds are made of two or more different atoms bonded together. Ions are charged particles, mainly atoms or groups of atoms. All of these particles can transmit, absorb, and reflect light and appear colored. If we intend to work with colored pigments, we should understand the language that the chemist uses to describe the particles contained in these pigments. Also, we need a method of organizing these particles. The periodic table is used to organize the elements. For the non-nuclear chemist, the atoms that come from the elements are the fundamental building blocks of all the other particles, including molecules, compounds, and ions. The periodic table organizes the elements into a meaningful pattern.

1.12

Elements and the Periodic Table

Objectives

1. Students will identify the families found on the periodic table.

2. Students will examine the color of various elements and look for regularities in the placement of these elements on the periodic table.

3. Students will relate the physical and chemical properties of the elements to their placement on the periodic table.

Materials

Periodic table, 0.1M $CuSO_4$, copper sulfate (from Activity 1.11), 0.1M K_2CrO_4, potassium chromate (from Activity 1.11), 5ml 0.2M $Fe(SCN)^{2+}$, $Fe(NO_3)_3$ (iron III nitrate), 5.0ml 0.002M KSCN (potassium thiocyanate), three large test tubes.

Time

30 minutes

Procedure

1. Show students samples of solutions of copper sulfate, $CuSO_4$, potassium chromate, K_2CrO_4, and iron thiocyanate complex, $Fe(SCN)^{2+}$ (prepared by combining 5.0ml, 0.20M $Fe(NO_3)_3$ with 5.0ml 0.002M KSCN).

2. Have students refer to the periodic table and make a list of the elements that appear in the following colored molecules:

Molecule	Color	Elements
$CuSO_4$ (copper sulfate)	Blue	Cu (copper), S (sulfur), O (oxygen)
K_2CrO_4 (potassium chromate)	Yellow	K (potassium), Cr (chromium), O
$Fe(SCN)^{2+}$ (iron thiocyanate)	Red	Fe (iron), S (sulfur), C (carbon), N (nitrogen)

Students should note the names and positions of these elements in the periodic table. Are they alkali metals, alkaline earth metals, transition metals, metalloids, or nonmetals?

3. Have students research the color of each of these elements:

C	black	K	silver-gray
Cr	gray	N	colorless
Cu	brown	O	colorless
Fe	gray	S	yellow

4. Have students look for a regularity or pattern in the element's color and the element's position on the periodic table. Point out that metals are gray, and nonmetals are a variety of colors. However, using the eight elements listed above, there is no definite pattern. Also, the colors of the individual elements seem to have little relationship to the colors of the solutions, so there must be another reason for the colors of the solutions. Have students consider the particles, ions, present in the solutions.

5. Have students examine the formulas for the colored pigments. Explain that a chemist uses element symbols to represent atoms in a molecule, and that the subscripts represent the number of atoms of each kind in the molecule. To explain the color-producing particles, a new concept and new symbols are needed.

Questions and Conclusions

Level One

1. Find the common physical and chemical properties for each family (a vertical column) in the periodic table. The families to consider are alkali metals, alkaline earth metals, inert gases, halogens, and transition metals.

2. Why do you think the table is called a *periodic* table?

3. Make a list of all the elements in the periodic table that are colored, recording the colors. Do elements in the same family tend to have the same color?

Level Two

1. Explain the arrangement of the periodic table, including why repeating rows of eight elements and eighteen elements appear on the table.

2. Relate the electron configuration of elements to the arrangement of the elements in the periodic table. Examine the outermost electrons for members of each Group A family and see if a pattern develops in the outermost electron configuration for members of the same family.

Ions

When particular substances are dissolved in water to make a solution, the solution is colored. This is apparent from Activity 1.11. The particles imparting the color are called ions, which are charged particles, mainly charged atoms or charged groups of atoms. We have considered neutral atoms, which have no overall charge because the number of protons, positively charged particles in the atomic nucleus, is equal to the number of electrons, negatively charged particles outside the atomic nucleus. (*Note:* Neutrons, uncharged particles, are also in the atomic nucleus.) When some compounds are placed in water, the compounds break apart, electrons are transferred from one atom to another, and ions are formed. *Voila!* Charged particles are floating around in the solution. If atoms lose electrons, the ions formed are positively charged (the atoms have more protons than electrons); if the atoms gain electrons, the ions formed are negatively charged. Ions are symbolized with the element symbol and the ion charge. The compounds used in the previous activities are ionized in the following way: $CuSO_4 \rightarrow Cu^{2+} + SO_4^{2-}$; $K_2CrO_4 \rightarrow 2K^{1+} + CrO_4^{2-}$; $Fe(SCN)^{2+} \rightarrow Fe^{3+} + SCN^{1-}$.

■   *Note:*
A chemical equation is a shorthand way for a chemist to show a chemical change. On the previous page, to show ion formation, chemical equations are used. In the equations, reactants are on the left and products are on the right. The arrow separating reactants and products ($\rightarrow$) means "yields." A chemical equation is balanced so that reactant atoms and product atoms are the same and equal in number, conforming to the law of conservation of matter. In an ionic equation, charge is also balanced.

Now we can identify the source of color in the solutions. Experiments show that copper ions (Cu^{2+}) are blue, chromate ions (CrO_4^{2-}) are yellow, and thiocyanate ions (SCN^{1-}) are red. Students should note that the elements in the ions producing the colors in the above solutions are either transition metals or nonmetals. Upon further examination, students would find that most of the colored ions in solutions contain transition metal elements or are transition metal ions.

Understanding ions can lead us to a new theory to explain why the sky is blue: Perhaps the sun provides the correct wavelength of energy to ionize atmospheric particles producing blue ions. However, there is no evidence that oxygen (O_2) and nitrogen (N_2) molecules in our atmosphere are ionized by the sun.

Value

An artist changes the value of a hue of pigment by adding black or white pigment, so that the hue becomes darker or lighter. Black pigment absorbs all wavelengths of visible light; when added to a hue of pigment, it reduces the number of light waves of the hue that reach the retina, thus making the hue appear darker. White pigment reflects all wavelengths of visible light waves; it increases the concentration of all wavelengths that reach the retina, which the brain interprets as white light, and makes a hue appear lighter.

Another way to change the value of a hue of pigment is to change the concentration of the hue particles in a particular pigment solution. In chemistry, solutions are prepared so that a specific concentration of particles, the solute, is added to a specific volume of solvent. When a uniform mixture of solute and solvent results, a solution is formed. The concentration of a solution is expressed as the ratio of solute to solution, solution being solute plus solvent. In the next demonstration, we will examine a change in value through dilution using mass percent as a means of expressing concentration of the solution. In mass percent, the ratio of grams of solute to grams of solution, multiplied by 100, is used to calculate the mass percent of the solution.

1.3

Copper Sulfate Dilution, Mass Percent, and Color Value

Objectives

1. Students will define *solution* and explain how to express the concentration of a solution using mass percent.

2. Students will describe the concept of color value change.

Materials

10.0 g $CuSO_4$ (copper sulfate), distilled water, 100 ml graduated cylinder, 10 ml graduated cylinder, 0.1 gram balance, eight 250 ml beakers.

■ *Note:*
Each specific mass-percent solution prepared in this demonstration should be saved for Activity 1.13.

Time

45 minutes

Procedure

1. The teacher should dissolve 10.0 g of $CuSO_4$ in 90.0 g of distilled water, H_2O (1.0 ml H_2O = 1.0 g). This results in a 10% solution of $CuSO_4$. Students should calculate the mass percent of this solution (mass of solute in grams, 10.0, divided by mass of solution in grams, 10.0 + 90.0 = 100.0, multiplied by 100 to find percent) to verify that it is a 10% solution. Have students observe the color.

■ *Note:*
For the purposes of this demonstration, assume that 1.0 ml of solution also equals 1.0 g.

2. The teacher should add 10.0 g (10.0 ml) of the 10% solution of $CuSO_4$ to 90.0 g (90.0 ml) of distilled water. This is a 1% solution. Have students observe the change in color.

3. The teacher should add 10.0 g (10.0 ml) of the 1% solution of $CuSO_4$ to 90.0 g (90.0 ml) of distilled water. This is a 0.1% solution. Have students observe the change in color.

4. The teacher should repeat this process until a colorless solution is achieved. (A total of eight solutions will be prepared. All of the solutions prepared should be saved for Activity 1.13.)

5. Have students calculate the mass percent of the colorless solution.

Questions and Conclusions

Level One

1. Define *solution* and name the parts of a solution. Where do solutions appear in a classification of matter? (Answer: A solution is a homogeneous mixture of a solute and solvent.)

2. Define *mass percent*. If 20.0 g of sodium chloride (NaCl) are added to 180.0 g of H_2O, what is the mass percent of the solution? (Answer: Mass percent expresses the concentration of a solution in grams of solute per grams of solvent. The mass percent would be 10%.)

Level Two

1. In this demonstration, color value was changed by dilution. How else can color value be changed?

2. Use the concept of light wave reflection to explain why color value changes when a solution is diluted.

3. Are any blue solute particles present when the solution appears colorless? (Answer: Yes, but these particles are not concentrated enough to see.)

> ■ *Note:*
> The value of a hue changes as a solution is diluted because, in a constant volume, the number of colored particles [ions] is reduced. There are fewer ions to reflect colored light waves. In this demonstration, the number of blue-green copper ions [Cu^{2+}] is reduced.

1.13
Color Value

Objectives

1. Students will create changes in value by adding white or black to a specific hue (all levels).

2. Students will observe the changes that occur when various amounts of black and white are added to a specific hue (all levels).

3. Students will apply the creative process and the principles of good composition to an original work of art (levels two and three).

4. Students will assemble a value cube, creating a design that continues from one surface of the cube to another (level three).

Level One:
A Chart for One Hue

Materials

Solutions from Demonstration 1.3; pencil; ruler; turquoise, black, and white poster paints; paintbrushes; white paper suitable for painting; mixing trays; water containers.

Time

50 minutes

Procedure—All Levels

> ■ *Note:*
> Use the solutions from Demonstration 1.3 as a guide to representing values of one hue using pigment.

1. Have students mix paints to achieve hues close to the hues of the eight solutions of $CuSO_4$, copper sulfate, Demonstration 1.3. They will use this hue to prepare a value chart.

2. Have students draw a series of seven 2-x-2-inch squares, arranged vertically on a sheet of white paper.

3. Have students paint the full-strength hue in the center square, then add a small amount of white paint to the original hue (until the color resembles the next lightest hue of solution) and paint the mixture in the square above the original hue.

4. Continue to add white paint and paint the squares above the previous square with the new, lighter mixtures.

5. Repeat steps 3–4, with the following exceptions:

    a. Substitute black paint for white paint.

    b. Paint the squares below the full-strength hue.

6. Have students compare the hue values on their chart with the hue values of the solutions. Explain that, for the solutions, the hue changed as the number of color-producing ions (Cu^{2+}) in a specific volume decreased. In preparing hue values in this activity, as black or white was added, the number of Cu^{2+} ions in the paint also decreased in a specific volume. However, the added white particles reflect all wavelengths to the eye, along with reflected blue wavelengths from the Cu^{2+} ions. We see blue with white: The value is lighter. When the black paint is added, all wavelengths striking the black particles are absorbed, but the Cu^{2+} ions still reflect blue-green wavelengths, which appear to be more highly concentrated—darker—in the absence of other interfering wavelengths.

Level Two:
A Picture of Great Value

Materials

Pencil, ruler, a full-strength color of poster paint (from the color wheel), black and white poster paints, paintbrushes, 9-x-12-inch white paper suitable for painting, mixing trays, water containers.

Time

100 minutes

Procedure

1. Have students print their first name in block letters diagonally across a 9-x-12-inch sheet of paper (see Fig. 1.11).

Figure 1.11.

2. Have students outline their name in pencil with consecutive lines about ½ inch apart, outward from the name to the edge of the page.

3. Have students paint all the letters of the name in one full-strength hue of the color wheel.

4. Continue by painting consecutive bands with increasingly lighter values of the original hue, by adding white paint, until the edge of the paper is reached. Or, in the case of a naturally light hue, such as yellow, follow the same procedure, except use increasingly darker values of the original hue, by adding black paint.

Level Three:
Three-Dimensional Value Cube

Materials

Handouts 1.2 and 1.3 (pp. 38–39), pencil, ruler, white posterboard 20 x 22 inches, scissors, glue or rubber cement, full-strength color of poster paint (from the color wheel), black and white poster paints, small paintbrushes, mixing trays, water containers, black markers.

Time

250 minutes

Procedure

1. Distribute Handouts 1.2 and 1.3.

2. Have students draw a cube on white posterboard according to the directions provided.

3. Have students paint their cubes showing a variety of light and dark values according to the instructions provided.

Intensity (or Chroma)

Intensity, or chroma, refers to the saturation of a color. A color is saturated when it reaches its maximum intensity. An artist lessens the intensity of a color by adding gray to dull it or by adding the complementary color on the color wheel. The artist is changing the concentration of colored particles in a solution. A chemist knows that a solution is saturated when no more solute can dissolve in a particular volume of a solvent. The chemist expresses solution concentration in a quantitative way. One way for a chemist to express the concentration of a saturated solution is grams of solute per 100 milliliters of solution. Another way to express the concentration is in moles of solute per liter of solution. In a colored saturated solution, the color is at maximum intensity. If the solution is not saturated, the color is less intense because there are fewer colored particles to bring to the eye the wavelengths that are colored.

Handout 1.2

Three-Dimensional Value Cube

Name: _____

1. Construct a cube by following the pattern provided (Handout 1.3). Use a piece of white posterboard. Pattern does not appear actual size. With pencil, draw the sections and flaps as shown.

2. Using scissors, cut out the cube and score all lines with the blade of the scissors. Score the cube on the outside surface.

3. Using a pencil, create a continuous design that moves from one surface of the cube to another (see Fig. 1.12 below). The design may be objective (pictures of objects) or non-objective (interesting, imaginative lines and shapes). It is important that the design extend over the edges of the cube, from one surface to another.

4. When the design is complete, test it to make sure it is a continuous design by folding the cube into its three-dimensional shape. **Do not glue:** It is easier to paint flat and glue last.

5. Choose one of the 12 colors of the color wheel and paint the entire surface of the cube using the full-strength hue and a variety of lighter and darker values of the hue.

6. When the cube is painted, enhance the design, if desired, by outlining it using a black marker.

7. Use glue or rubber cement to construct the cube.

Figure 1.12. Value Cube.

Handout 1.3

Pattern for a Three-Dimensional Value Cube

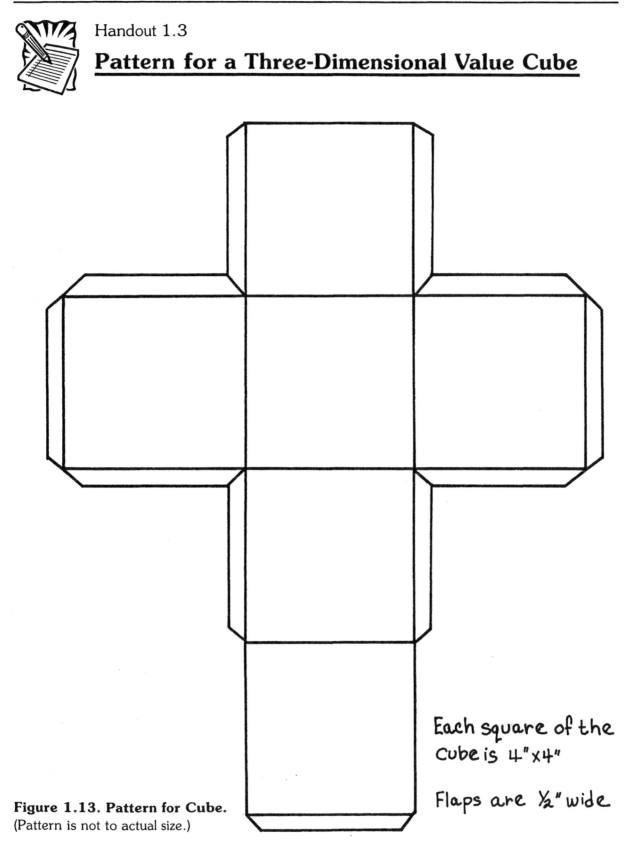

Figure 1.13. Pattern for Cube.
(Pattern is not to actual size.)

Each square of the cube is 4"x4"

Flaps are ½" wide

2. Have students choose two complementary (opposite) colors from the color wheel, such as red and green. Paint one color in the top square and the other color in the bottom square.

3. Show a decrease in intensity by mixing a bit of the color for the bottom square into a larger amount of the color for the top square and painting this mixture in the square below the top square.

4. Continue decreasing the intensity for the remaining squares, each time adding more of the color for the bottom square.

Level Two:
Intensity Chart II

Materials

Same as level one, but using 6-x-18-inch paper suitable for painting.

Time

75 minutes

Procedure

1. Have students create a series of seven shapes in a line lengthwise across a sheet of 6-x-18-inch paper. The same shape should be repeated, but its size should be increased from left to right.

2. Have students choose two complementary colors from the color wheel. Paint the smallest shape with one color and the largest shape with the other color.

3. Decrease the intensity from left to right: Add a small amount of the color for the largest shape to the color for the smallest shape and paint the next largest shape. Continue with this procedure until all the shapes are painted.

4. Describe the change in intensity from the smallest shape to the largest shape.

Level Three:
Making a Pyramid Intensity Critter

Materials

Handouts 1.4 and 1.5 (pp. 43–44), pencil, ruler, white posterboard, poster paints (complementary colors from the color wheel), paintbrushes, mixing trays, water containers, heavy scrap paper and small pieces of cardboard or posterboard, scissors, glue or rubber cement.

Time

250 minutes

Procedure

1. Distribute Handouts 1.4 and 1.5.

2. Have students construct a pyramid intensity critter by following the directions (Handout 1.4) and pattern (Handout 1.5) provided.

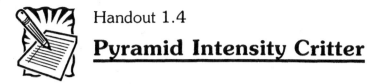

Handout 1.4

Pyramid Intensity Critter

Name: _____

1. Following the pattern provided (Handout 1.5, p. 44), draw the pattern onto a piece of white posterboard. Pattern does not appear actual size. Using pencil, draw the sections and flaps.

2. Cut out the pyramid and score all lines with the blade of the scissors. Score the pyramid on the outside surface.

3. Assemble the pyramid using glue or rubber cement.

4. Design an imaginary creature or animal. Use the pyramid as the body of the creature, attaching arms, legs, wings, horns, teeth, and so on, made from small pieces of cardboard or posterboard. The creature need not stand on its own; it might be made for hanging.

5. When the design is complete, choose two complementary (opposite) colors from the color wheel, such as red and green. Limit the colors used in painting the creature to different intensities of these colors. Dull each of the two original colors by mixing in a little to a lot of the second color. The two original colors may also be used in full strength. If using only two colors is too limiting, include the use of the neutrals—black, white, and gray—for more variety. Remember, this is not a realistic creature, so the colors may be a little weird!

**Figure 1.14.
Pyramid Intensity
Critter.**

Handout 1.5

Pattern for the Body
of a Pyramid Intensity Critter

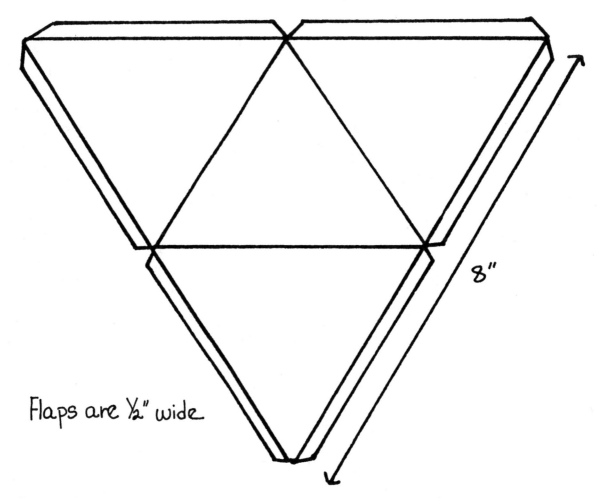

8"

Flaps are ½" wide

Figure. 1.15.
(Pattern is not to actual size.)

Intensity in Art;
Intensity in Chemistry

An artist changes the intensity of a hue by adding various amounts of the complementary color. When the complementary color is added, some of the wavelengths of light reflected by the original hue are absorbed by the complementary color particles. Less light of the original hue reaches the eye, so the color is less intense. A chemist looks at the intensity of color in a solution to determine whether the solution is concentrated or diluted. The ratio of solute particles to solvent particles determines the concentration of a solution. In a concentrated solution, in which the color is intense, the ratio of solute to solvent is high; in a dilute solution, the ratio of solute to solvent is low. In other words, the intensity of the color in a solution is determined by the number of color-producing solute particles in a given volume. The more color-producing particles, the more intense the color.

COLOR RELATIVITY:
ALL THINGS ARE RELATIVE

Since the time of Albert Einstein, we have been aware of the relative nature of time and matter. Now, we will consider the relative nature of color. Colors can best be discussed in relationship to one another. A particular color may appear one way against a black background and another way against a yellow background. The following activities and demonstration give students an opportunity to experiment with various color relationships to see the effects of a particular color against various backgrounds, or fields.

1.15
Color Relativity

Objectives

1. Students will become familiar with the works of professional artists who use color relativity in their work.
2. Students will create examples of color relativity.
3. Students will observe the relationship of one color to another and how color relationships affect a chosen color.

Materials

A variety of colors of paper (all 12 colors of the color wheel, plus white, black, and gray), pencil, ruler, scissors, glue or rubber cement, typing paper or other paper suitable for mounting samples.

Time

150 minutes

Procedure

1. Review the following definitions with students:

   Hue. The name given to a specific color, such as red, blue, blue-green, and yellow.

   Value. The lightness or darkness of a specific color. To lighten a color, white is added. To darken a color, black is added.

   Chroma. The intensity (brightness or dullness) of a specific color.

   Complements (or Complementary Colors). Colors that are direct opposites of each other on the color wheel, such as green and red.

   Warm and Cool Colors. Warm colors are red-violet, red, red-orange, orange, yellow-orange, and yellow. Cool colors are yellow-green, green, blue-green, blue, and blue-violet.

2. Show to students reproductions of works of contemporary non-objective artists who work with color relationships, such as: Josef Albers, Mark Rothko, Ad Reinhardt, Barnett Newman, Kenneth Noland, and Ellsworth Kelly.

3. Have students choose a specific hue and cut a sheet of paper of that hue into seven 2-x-2-inch squares.

4. Have students experiment with relationships between the hue chosen and other colors. In the following steps, they should try to change the appearance of the hue by placing it against backgrounds of various other colors available. Each sample should be compared to the sample on the white background.

   a. Place a square of the chosen hue on a 4-x-4-inch white background (all backgrounds should be of this size).

   b. Place a square of the chosen hue on a black background. Does the square of the chosen hue appear larger or smaller than it does against a white background? Does it appear lighter or darker than it does against the white background?

   c. Place a square of the chosen hue against a gray background. How does the gray background affect it? Does it look larger or smaller, lighter or darker?

   d. Place a square of the chosen hue against a background that affects its value (i.e., makes it look lighter or darker).

   e. Place a square of the chosen color against a background that affects its intensity, or chroma (i.e., makes it look brighter, gives it a vibrating effect, or makes it duller). What relationship on the color wheel exists between the subject color and the background color chosen?

   f. Place a square of the chosen hue against a background that makes it look warmer.

   g. Place a square of the chosen color against a background that makes it appear cooler.

5. Have students use glue or rubber cement to attach the squares of the chosen hue to the background squares and then attach each sample to a sheet of typing paper. Have students label each sample, indicating which properties and relationships of color the sample illustrates.

6. Have students compare their results and discuss them with the class.

1.16

Color Relativity: Physical Property and Physical Change

Objectives

1. Students will define and distinguish the difference between physical change and physical property.
2. Students will interpret how color relativity affects perception of an individual color.

Materials

Carbon powder; sulfur powder; K_2CrO_4 (potassium chromate); $CuSO_4$ (copper sulfate); spatula; red, yellow, blue, black, and white poster paints; paint brushes; paper for poster paints; small evaporating dish; paper.

Time

50 minutes

Procedure

■   *Note:*
Matter is something that takes up space and has mass. Physical properties are used to describe matter. Some physical properties of matter are shape, size, amount, density, distribution, and color. A physical change is a change in a physical property without a change in the actual substance.

1. Have students make a list of the physical properties of carbon and sulfur powder.
2. The teacher should mix a spatula of carbon powder with a spatula of sulfur powder. A physical change will occur. There is a change in the sulfur and carbon distribution and an apparent color change, but the sulfur and carbon remain. No new substance is formed.
3. Repeat steps 1–2 using K_2CrO_4 and $CuSO_4$.

Questions and Conclusions

Level One

1. How does the yellow sulfur affect the brightness of the black carbon? Why are some letters on road signs black on a yellow background?
2. How does the yellow K_2CrO_4 affect the brightness of the blue $CuSO_4$? Is it a good idea for a road sign to use blue-green letters on a yellow background? Why?

Level Two

1. Experiment with various color combinations by painting signs in two colors. What combinations make the sign letters look brighter? What combinations make the sign letters look duller?
2. List some physical properties of your signs.
3. Make a list of your physical properties (e.g., hair color, height, eye color, etc.).
4. State an example of how you could make a physical change in your appearance.

1.5
Color Relativity—Chemical Properties and Chemical Change

Objectives

1. Students will define and distinguish the difference between chemical property and chemical change.

2. Students will illustrate color relativity by producing a chemical change.

3. Students will write a balanced chemical equation and explain the meaning of the equation symbols.

Materials

1-inch magnesium strip, tongs, Bunsen burner, matches, black paper, white paper.

Time

15 minutes

Procedure

■   *Note:*
A chemical property of matter describes how a substance behaves during a chemical change. A chemical change occurs when a substance changes into a new substance or substances.

1. The teacher should hold the magnesium strip with tongs in the hottest part of the flame of a Bunsen burner (directly above the inner cone) until the magnesium burns. (Warning: Do not look directly at burning magnesium for more than a few seconds.)

2. Place a sheet of white paper behind the burning magnesium and have students observe the brightness of the magnesium flame.

3. Place a sheet of black paper behind the burning magnesium and have students observe the brightness of the magnesium flame.

Questions and Conclusions

Level One

1. Define *chemical property.*

2. Define *chemical change.*

3. Describe one common chemical change that occurs in the home and one common chemical change that occurs outside the home.

4. State a chemical property of magnesium.

5. Write a word equation for the burning of magnesium. Do most metals burn?

6. Which background enhanced the brightness of the burning magnesium? Propose a theory to explain this result.

Level Two

1. Did a chemical change occur when magnesium burns in this demonstration? Examine the product: Are its properties different than those of the reactants? (Magnesium and oxygen are reactants; magnesium oxide is the product.)

2. A chemical equation has reactants on the left side and products on the right side. The reactants and products are separated by a "yields" sign ($\rightarrow$). Numbers called coefficients are placed in front of the reactant and product symbols; these numbers balance the equation. What is being balanced in a chemical equation? Incorporate the law of conservation of matter into your answer.

3. Help students write a balanced symbol equation to show the chemical change observed. (Answer: $2Mg_{(s)} + O_{2(g)} \rightarrow 2MgO_{(s)}$.)

4. Explain to students some additional information that can be conveyed in a balanced chemical equation: $_{(s)}$ = solid, $_{(g)}$ = gas, $_{(aq)}$ = aqueous, and $_{(l)}$ = liquid. The following equation shows the proper use of these symbols: $S_{(s)} + 6\,HNO_{3\,(aq)} \rightarrow H_2SO_{4\,(aq)} + 6NO_{2\,(g)} + 2H_2O_{(l)}$. It should be noted that [aq] means aqueous solution and [l] means in the liquid phase. Students should use phase-indicating symbols in their balanced equation in no. 3 above.

COLOR FATIGUE

Our eyes adapt themselves to a change of color. The adaptation takes several steps, but we are usually not aware of them. We can observe the change if we stare at a colored area for about 30 seconds and then stare at a white surface. The color we see will be roughly the complementary color (the opposite color on the color wheel) of the color stared at. The size of the afterimage depends on the distance from the eye to the white surface: If closer to the white surface than to the original color, the afterimage will be smaller; if farther from the original color, the afterimage will be larger. It should be understood that color fatigue is a function of color relativity.

1.17
Color Fatigue

Objectives

1. Students will understand the principles of color fatigue by viewing examples (all levels).
2. Students will create an example of color fatigue using complementary colors (level two).

Level One: The Flag

Materials

Picture of the American flag colored in green, black, and orange (the complements of red, white, and blue); white paper.

Time

10 minutes

Procedure

1. Show the students a picture of the American flag colored in green, black, and orange. Have the students stare at the image and then look away to a blank sheet of white paper (or close their eyes) to see the afterimage in complementary colors.

Level Two:
Do It Yourself Fatigue

Materials

Bits of colored construction paper, white paper, glue, scissors.

Time

30 minutes

Procedure

1. Have students create an example of color fatigue by substituting complementary colors for the actual colors of objects they choose. (Example: A green strawberry with a red stem.)
2. Cut out the shapes and glue them to the white paper.
3. Stare at the image and then look away to a blank sheet of white paper or close their eyes to see the after image in the true colors.

WHY IS THE SKY BLUE?
FINALLY: AN ANSWER

Can we expect the sky to appear blue because of color relativity? It is not likely: Color relativity requires that two hues are superimposed. In a cloudless sky, we are looking at one hue: Blue. Do we see a blue sky because of color fatigue? If so, we would see the blue sky only after staring at an orange object. This does not happen. Previously, we ruled out excited atoms and ion formation as sources of blue in the sky.

To answer the question, we must reexamine color and light. We know that all wavelengths of electromagnetic radiation in the visible range are transmitted from the sun and enter the earth's atmosphere, where they encounter oxygen (O_2) and nitrogen (N_2) molecules. Almost all the wavelengths, except those seen as blue, travel straight through the atmospheric molecules and atoms and proceed to the earth's surface. However, the blue wavelengths become sidetracked. They are of such wavelengths that they bounce off the earth's atmospheric molecules, primarily oxygen (O_2) and nitrogen (N_2) molecules, and scatter across the entire sky. Everywhere we look, blue waves are present. They enter our eyes and strike the cones in our retinas, which relay a message to the brain: The sky is blue!

REFERENCES

Arnason, H. H. *History of Modern Art: Painting, Sculpture, Architecture.* 3d ed. New York: Harry N. Abrams, 1986.

Birren, Faber. *Color.* Secaucus, NJ: Citadel Press, 1963.

Busselle, Michael. *The Complete 35 mm Source Book.* New York: Watson-Guptill, 1993.

Dickinson, Terence. *Exploring the Sky by Day.* Camden East, Ontario, Canada: Camden House, 1988.

Hope, Augustine, and Margaret Walch. *The Color Compendium.* New York: Van Nostrand Reinhold, 1990.

Kent, Sarah. *Composition.* London; New York: Dorling Kindersley, 1995.

Lowry, Lois. *The Giver.* Boston: Houghton Mifflin, 1993.

McQuarrie, Donald A., and Peter A. Rock. *General Chemistry.* New York: W. H. Freeman, 1984.

Parramon, Jose M. *The Book of Color.* New York: Watson-Guptill, 1993.

Poore, Henry Rankin. *Composition.* New York: Sterling, 1969.

Sargent, Walter. *The Enjoyment and Use of Color.* New York: Dover, 1964.

Walker, John. *National Gallery of Art, Washington.* New York: Abradale Press; Harry N. Abrams, 1995.

Williamson, Samuel J., and Herman Z. Cummins. *Light and Color in Nature and Art.* New York: John Wiley, 1983.

2

Paint Does Matter

What Is Paint?

INTRODUCTION

A wagon without paint is like a day without sunshine. The plot of the musical play *Paint Your Wagon* involves gold prospectors hoping to make a fortune in the days of the California gold rush. They invite other prospectors to join them: "Paint your wagon and come along!" On a more mundane note, can you remember the little red wagon of your youth, during that time of joy and innocence? Would that little red wagon conjure up the same memories had it been unpainted? What is the function and significance of paint as applied to objects?

Objects are painted for many reasons: To prevent rusting and deterioration, to make them attractive, to evoke emotions, and to brighten our lives. Wagons are painted with these goals in mind. An artist has the same goals: Permanence, attractiveness, and emotional effect; in addition, an artist paints a work of art to preserve the past.

A BRIEF BUT COLORFUL HISTORY OF PAINT

The use of paint dates to prehistoric art, mainly about 35,000 years ago when the long-skull Cro-Magnon people of the Paleolithic period made cave paintings. They were restricted to only a few pigments of local colors—earth tones of yellow, red, black, brown, and white—derived from plants, animals, and minerals and mixed with animal fat to make the first paints. These paints required a binder to adhere them to cave walls: Chemists think that Cro-Magnon artists used saliva! Today, artists are attempting to duplicate the paints used in these cave paintings.

The ancient Egyptians were adept at creating water paints, which were used to decorate the interiors of their pyramids, temples, and palaces. Much like the cave painters' paints, their colors were earth tones—yellow ochre, sienna, red, black, and white—but two new colors were added: Blue and green. Later, between A.D. 117–161, the early Christians in Egypt made paints of pigment particles suspended in hot beeswax. Their works, called encaustic paintings, are still well preserved and brilliant in color. In the eighth century, the Phoenicians obtained a vibrant purple dye from a particular kind of oyster.

Throughout the Middle Ages, in wall paintings known as frescoes and in manuscripts and paintings on wood panels, water-based paints known as egg tempera were used to paint pictures bearing religious themes. Egg tempera paint consisted of colored natural pigments and the yolk of an egg mixed with water. More colors began to appear, including a deep blue called ultramarine, bright yellow, intense red, and a brilliant green, adding to an already rich medieval palette. Artists and their apprentices mixed their paints in the master artist's studio. They were constantly experimenting with various formulas and recipes, trying to produce better paint. At the same time, the prechemists, the alchemists, were trying to change lead into gold. Modern scientific method, in which theories are proposed and confirmed by controlled experiments, was not accepted until the eighteenth century.

Oil paint and watercolor can be traced to the fifteenth century. Oil paint, especially, became the new medium of choice, and egg tempura slowly dwindled from general use. Oil paint, pigments combined with oil, are thought to have been invented by the Flemish painter Jan van Eyck. Watercolor, pigments suspended in gum arabic, can be traced to traditional Japanese paintings, and to the German master Albrecht Dürer, whose watercolor enhanced his pen drawings of natural history.

By the eighteenth century, thousands of paint colors and many paint formulas were being used by artists. Paint was still mixed by the artist in the studio. During the eighteenth and nineteenth centuries, the medium of watercolor was used extensively by English artists and brought to a high degree of perfection in atmospheric painting of landscapes.

It was not until the nineteenth century that artists began to purchase ready-made commercial paints. Today, paint colors have standardized specifications. Regardless of type, paint still consists of pigment and binder, as it has for centuries. Many colors originally produced from natural pigments are now made synthetically. In 1841, the metal paint tube was developed. Paints that for centuries had been mixed and stored by the artist in various ways in the studio were suddenly available in an easily portable container. Artists who had found it difficult to paint on location were able to create many masterpieces outdoors, on location, as a result of tube paint.

Five centuries after the invention of oil paint, in the late 1930s, acrylic paint entered the art scene. David Alfara Sequeiros, a Mexican artist, was one of the first artists to adapt acrylic paint to a work of art. Acrylic paint consists of colored thermoplastic resins suspended in water. In the 1930s, chemists were experimenting with long-chain organic molecules. When a colored molecule appeared, it was logical to consider the use of the molecule as a pigment in a synthetic paint. Contemporary artists worldwide rapidly embraced acrylic paint for art expression. Acrylic paint dries quickly and is durable, brightly colored, and easily controlled by the artist.

THE COMPOSITION OF PAINT

It can be seen that, historically, a paint is anything that contains pigment, a colored, powdered substance, and a binder, a material that evenly disperses the pigment and adheres to a surface when the paint is applied and then dries. A pigment combined with a binder makes a paint. A medium is used to dilute a paint. The composition of watercolor, egg tempera, oil, and acrylic paints is discussed in this chapter.

A paint can be made from two main ingredients, a pigment and a binder, but other additives are often present. Transparent watercolor, for instance, usually purchased in tubes, contains many more ingredients. In addition to the pigment and binder (gum arabic) is the sap of the acacia tree. Glycerin is added for brushability, ox gall for absorbency, and a preservative for extending the paint's shelf life. An odorant, such as oil of cloves, gives the paint a pleasant smell.

When chemists think of paint, they wonder how paint fits into a scheme of classification of all matter. If paint can be classified as a particular form of matter, then generalizations pertaining to that class will apply to paint. These generalizations enable chemists to predict ways of making more unique and more useful paints. Chemists classify matter, anything that takes up space and has mass, as illustrated in Figure 2.1.

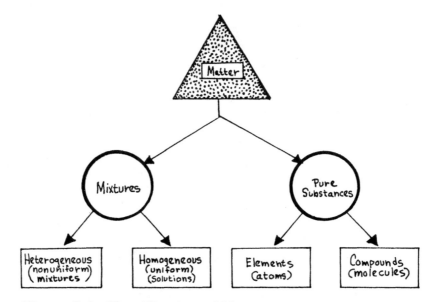

Figure 2.1. Classification of Matter.

All matter is placed into two main classes: Mixtures and pure substances. Mixtures consist of two or more different particles; pure substances consist of the same kind of particles. Mixtures are divided into heterogeneous mixtures, which are non-uniform throughout, and homogeneous mixtures, solutions, which are uniform throughout. Pure substances are divided into elements, which are made of atoms, and compounds, which are made of molecules. Paints are mixtures because they are made of at least two different particles: Pigment particles and binder particles. Most paints are uniform mixtures throughout, so they are solutions. If we can make some generalizations about solutions, we can better understand paints. The best way to make generalizations is to perform experiments in which a theory is tested and conclusions are drawn from the test results. Before experimenting with solutions, a basic understanding of this category of matter is required.

Types of Solutions

The two parts of a solution are the solute and solvent. The solvent does the dissolving; the solute is the part that is dissolved. A solution may be unsaturated, saturated, or supersaturated. In an unsaturated solution, additional solute can dissolve in the solvent. In a saturated solution, no more solute will dissolve. In a supersaturated solution, more solute is dissolved than would normally be the case at a particular temperature. Temperature affects the solubility of a solute in a solvent; usually, the higher the temperature of the solvent, the greater the solubility of the solute.

Activity 2.1 is an experiment to see the effects of solution saturation and temperature change on solution color intensity. From this experiment, we can predict how paint color intensity might be changed.

2.1

Unsaturated, Saturated, and Supersaturated Solutions and Temperature Change—Their Effects on Solution Color Intensity

Objectives

1. Students will compare and contrast the physical properties of unsaturated, saturated, and supersaturated solutions.

2. Students will evaluate paint color intensity in the context of each type of solution.

3. Students will discover the effects of temperature change on solute solubility and color intensity.

Materials

For each student group: 14.65 g $NaC_2H_3O_2$ (sodium acetate), three large test tubes, test tube holder, Bunsen burner or alcohol lamp, matches, Celsius thermometer, distilled water, tubes of red and blue watercolor paint pigment, stirring rod, test tube rack, 10.0 ml graduated cylinder, centigram balance, paintbrushes, 5-x-7-inch water-color paper.

Time

80 minutes

Procedure

A. Have students prepare unsaturated, saturated, and supersaturated solutions of sodium acetate:

1. Prepare a saturated solution of sodium acetate: In a large test tube, dissolve 4.65 g $NaC_2H_3O_2$ in 10.0 ml distilled water at 20°C.

2. Preparing an unsaturated solution of sodium acetate: In a large test tube, dissolve 3.0 g $NaC_2H_3O_2$ in 10.0 ml distilled water at 20°C.

3. Preparing a supersaturated solution of sodium acetate: In a large test tube, add 7.0 g $NaC_2H_3O_2$ to 10.0 ml distilled water and gradually heat the test tube contents over a Bunsen burner or alcohol lamp until all the sodium acetate is dissolved. Carefully place the test tube into a test tube rack and let it cool without being disturbed. All the sodium acetate will remain in solution.

4. Observe the appearance of all three solutions, recording observations. Add a small crystal of sodium acetate to each test tube, observe, and record observations.

B. Have students experiment with temperature change and color intensity:

1. Fill each of two test tubes with 1.0 ml distilled water.

2. Heat the water in one test tube to about 50°C.

3. Add watercolor pigment to each test tube until no more pigment will dissolve.

4. Observe the appearance of each solution and record observations.

5. Paint two small pictures having chemistry themes such as solute and solvent particles in saturated, unsaturated, and supersaturated solutions. For one, use the room-temperature paint; for the other, use the paint at 50°C. Make a list of differences between the two paintings. Compare the two paintings, noting differences in color intensity and the effect of the color intensity differences on the general appearance and the message contained in the paintings.

Questions and Conclusions

1. What was the appearance of each sodium acetate solution and each sucrose solution before a crystal of each compound was added?

2. How did the solutions change when the crystals were added? In some cases, did the solutions become heterogeneous (non-uniform) mixtures?

3. In a paint, the pigment is the solute and the binder is the solvent. Should a paint solution be unsaturated, saturated, or supersaturated? Why?

4. Imagine paint solutions that are unsaturated, saturated, and supersaturated. How would color intensity appear in each solution?

5. How does an increase in temperature affect the solubility of a solute in a solvent?

6. Was the color more intense in the room-temperature watercolor solution or in the 50°C watercolor solution?

A Summary of the Physical Properties of Solutions

A saturated solution contains more solute in a given volume of solvent than an unsaturated solution. A supersaturated solution contains more solute in a given volume than would normally be present at a particular temperature. A supersaturated solution is unstable: When a crystal of solute is added to a supersaturated solution, excess solute crystallizes out of solution; the remaining solution is saturated as it normally would be at that particular temperature. When a crystal of solute is added to an unsaturated solution, the crystal will dissolve. When a crystal of solute is added to a saturated solution, the added crystal will not dissolve. Most of the time, when the temperature of a solvent increases, the solubility of the solute increases in a given amount of solvent. The more colored solute dissolved in a given amount of solvent, the more intense the color of the solution. Most paints are solutions of pigments (the solute) and binders (the solvent).

Extension for Activity 2.1

1. Ionic solids are soluble in water. When an ionic solid such as sodium chloride (NaCl), or salt, is dissolved in water, the sodium chloride, NaCl, breaks apart into charged particles, called ions, which bond to polar water, H_2O, molecules. Sodium chloride forms sodium ions, Na^+, and chlorine ions, Cl^-, in water.

2. Polar molecular substances are also soluble in polar water molecules. When a molecular substance such as ethyl alcohol (C_2H_5OH) dissolves in water, H_2O, polar ethyl alcohol molecules bond with polar water molecules. In general, likes dissolve likes. Polar solutes will dissolve in polar solvents. In addition, nonpolar solutes dissolve in nonpolar solvents. Nonpolar octane, C_8H_{18}, dissolves in nonpolar carbon tetrachloride, CCl_4. It follows that solutes and solvents of opposite polarity do not form solutions. Nonpolar oil does not dissolve in polar water. (Polar means bearing a charge.)

3. In a saturated solution, an equilibrium exists between the rate of precipitation of solute particles and the rate of dissolution of solute particles. The rate of precipitation equals the rate of dissolution. A shape of a crystal of solute added to a saturated solution will change after a period of time at a constant temperature and pressure, but its mass will remain the same. The equilibrium between dissolving and precipitation is dynamic, a continuous process.

After a discussion of the above information, have students explain how their paintings illustrate solute and solvent particles in solution. Students can distinguish between unsaturated, saturated, and supersaturated solutions by differences in the ratio of solute particles to solvent particle. The lowest ratio would appear in unsaturated solutions and the highest ratio would be in supersaturated solutions. In addition, if the solute particles and solvent particles are polar, they would be bonded to each other. Nonpolar solvent and solute particles would not be bonded and could be separated from each other. If a saturated solution is depicted, a crystal in the solution should show the same number of particles leaving the crystal as bonding to the crystal. After considering this information, students may want to make changes to their paintings.

RESOURCES FOR STUDENT VIEWING

Are the students ready to paint their wagons? Now, they should understand the composition of various paints—watercolor, oil, egg tempera, and acrylic—and how paints are related to solutions. They should also be able to categorize paint in the vast world of matter as homogeneous solutions. However, are they ready to apply paint to a wagon or a work of art?

Following are a list of videos that will help students understand, through demonstration, how paints are applied to surfaces using particular media, and a list of artists proficient in particular media. After viewing videos and seeing specific works of the artists listed, ask students to decide which paint medium they prefer and explain its advantages and disadvantages. Finally, following the lists of videos and works of art is a list of book references useful for showing students examples of various painting techniques.

Videos

Introduction to Watercolor Technique. 60 min. New York: DEMOvision, 1983. Videocassette.

Learn to Paint Oils. 58 min. Midland Park, NJ: Teaching Art, 1990; distributed by Ramapo. Videocassette.

Of Course You Can Paint with Acrylics. 60 min. Paducah, KY: Lawter Studios; S & W, 1994. Videocassette.

Survey of Acrylic Techniques, with Russell Woody. 47 min. Easton, PA: Binney Smith, 1987. Videocassette.

Watercolor. 14 min. Van Nuys, CA: ACI Media, 1967; distributed by AIMS Media. Videocassette.

Artists

Acrylic Painting

Barnett Newman (1905–1970)
Victor Vasarely (1908–)
Robert Motherwell (1915–)
Helen Frankenthaler (1928–)

Oil Painting

Rembrandt van Rijn (1606–1669)
Paul Cézanne (1839–1906)
Claude Monet (1840–1926)
Vincent van Gogh (1853–1890)
Pablo Picasso (1881–1973)
Salvador Dali (1904–1989)
Jackson Pollock (1912–1956)

Watercolor Painting

Albrecht Dürer (1471–1528)
Thomas Eakins (1844–1916)
Winslow Homer (1836–1910)
John Marin (1870–1953)
Edward Hopper (1882–1967)
Norman Rockwell (1894–1978)
Andrew Wyeth (1917–)

Egg Tempera Painting

Italian fourteenth- and fifteenth-century artists (Giotto di Bondone 1267–1337, Fra Angelico 1387–1455, Paolo Uccello 1397–1475, Fra Filippo Lippi 1406–1469, Piero Della Francesca 1420?–1492, Giovanni Bellini 1430–1516, Sandro Botticelli 1445–1510).
Ben Shahn (1898–1969)
Andrew Wyeth (1917–)

PROS AND CONS—
WHICH MEDIUM IS BEST?

Each artist has a favorite medium that best fits their needs. Following is a short description of various paint media—watercolor, egg tempera paint, oil paint, and acrylic paint—and its advantages and disadvantages. A discussion of poster paint (or tempera paint), suitable for school use, is also included.

After sharing these advantages and disadvantages with the class, have students compare their list of advantages and disadvantages for their preferred paint medium (created in "Resources for Student Viewing") with the advantages and disadvantages that follow. If their list differs, they should provide reasons for their choice, basing their reasons on examples of professional works they have observed. Finally, have students experiment with various paint media by conducting Activity 2.2.

Transparent Watercolor

Watercolor is considered by many to be more like a stain on the paper than a paint that lies on the surface of the paper. Colors are applied in thin washes and can be built up, color on top of color. The white of the paper shining through beneath the paint adds a crisp effect to this medium. White paint is not used to lighten colors; this would create an opaque rather than a transparent effect. Colors are lightened by the addition of water.

The advantages of watercolor outweigh the disadvantages, as is evident from the following lists:

Advantages
1. Dries quickly
2. Easy cleanup
3. Lends itself well to atmospheric effects
4. Sold in a variety of forms: dry cakes, semi-moist pans, and tubes
5. Can be wetted and reworked
6. Color can be lifted off to lighten an area
7. Very portable; easy to use outdoors

Disadvantages
1. Actual texture cannot be produced
2. Difficult to control for beginners (can look muddy if not used properly)
3. Some colors may fade from exposure to sunlight

Egg Tempera Paint

Egg tempera was used as a paint medium at least as early as the fourteenth century. It was the dominant medium in Europe until the development of oil paint. In egg tempera, powdered pigment is bound with egg and water. Paint is applied layer upon layer, imparting a luminous quality unlike any other paint medium.

The advantages and disadvantages of egg tempera are about equal:

Advantages
1. Water-soluble when wet
2. Relatively easy cleanup
3. Unique appearance
4. Excellent for detail work

Disadvantages
1. Artists must prepare their paints from powdered pigments
2. Not sold commercially
3. Difficult to master
4. Can be used on only a small area at one time
5. Once the raw egg yolk has been mixed with pigment, the paint has a brief shelf life

Oil Paint

Oil paint has been a popular medium since the fifteenth century. An oil painting has depth and a unique, luminous quality. Oil paint is the favored medium of many artists today.

Advantages
1. Dries slowly, so it can be reworked easily
2. Versatile: Can be applied as a thick or thin coat
3. Can be applied with a brush or knife
4. Good shelf life lasting many years

Disadvantages
1. Cleanup not easy
2. Messy
3. Requires a non-water-based solvent
4. Strong odor
5. May crack and darken with age
6. Expensive

Acrylic Paint

Acrylic paint is the first new paint to be developed in hundreds of years. It is popular with older students and many professional artists.

For general use, the advantages of acrylic paint outweigh the disadvantages:

Advantages
1. Can be applied to a variety of surfaces successfully
2. Does not peel or crack
3. Does not fade
4. Easy to paint over when dry
5. Waterproof when dry
6. Versatile: Can be applied as a thick or thin coat
7. Good shelf life, lasting many years
8. Can be used with a variety of media to vary effect

Disadvantages
1. Dries very quickly
2. Dry areas cannot be reworked
3. Difficult to blend

Poster Paint (or Tempera Paint)

Tempera paint, often called poster paint, is a student-grade, water-based paint suitable for school use, especially in the lower grades.

The advantages of poster paint outweigh the disadvantages:

Advantages
1. Inexpensive
2. Water-soluble
3. Easy cleanup
4. Dries quickly

Disadvantages
1. Limited colors
2. Can have a chalky appearance when dry

2.2

Experimenting with Paint— Similarities and Differences

Objectives

1. Students will experience the characteristics of watercolor, poster paint, and acrylic paint through hands-on application (all levels).

2. Students will use various tools and methods for applying paint and observe their effects on the paint (level one).

3. Students will compare and contrast the results of the three paint media used (all levels).

Level One:
Comparison of Media I

Materials

Ruler; pencil; poster paints, watercolors, and acrylic paints in various colors; mixing trays; water container; paper towels; medium (#5) paintbrushes; 12-x-18-inch paper suitable for painting; small sponges.

Time

50 minutes

Procedure

1. Have students divide a sheet of 12-x-18-inch paper into 18 3-x-4-inch rectangles (three rectangles along the 12-inch side by six rectangles along the 18-inch side). Have students orient the sheet of paper so the 18-inch side is horizontal, then label the rectangles in each row with the numbers 1 through 6.

2. Using one of the three paint media provided, have students paint one six-rectangle row as follows:

   a. Rectangle 1: With the paintbrush, apply the paint in full strength, or with very little water, using long strokes.

   b. Rectangle 2: With the paintbrush, apply the paint in overlapping strokes, using at least two colors in this rectangle.

   c. Rectangle 3: With the paintbrush, apply the paint in watered-down strength.

   d. Rectangle 4: With the sponge, apply the paint using very little water.

   e. Rectangle 5: With the sponge, apply the paint using more water than was used in rectangle 4.

   f. Rectangle 6: Wet the rectangle and apply the paint full strength.

3. Repeat step 2 for the second row, using a second paint medium.

4. Repeat step 2 for the third row, using the third paint medium.

Questions and Conclusions

1. How are the three paint media alike?
2. How are the three paint media different?
3. Which paint medium do you prefer? Why?

Level Two:
Comparison of Media II

Materials

Same as level one, with the addition of chemistry books and books about insects, fish, and birds.

Time

150–200 minutes

Procedure

1. From the books provided, have students choose an interesting picture of a fish, bird, or insect, or a picture of an object such as a crystal or a molecule. Students should choose fish, birds, or insects with unusual or interesting silhouettes and interesting markings, or a crystal or molecule (for example) that has interesting parts and shapes and a variety of colors.

2. Have students draw their subject on a sheet of 12-x-18-inch paper. Students should try to fill the entire page, keeping interior shapes simple and avoiding tiny details.

3. Have students divide the drawing into three parts, as shown in Figure 2.2. The parts do not need to be equal in size.

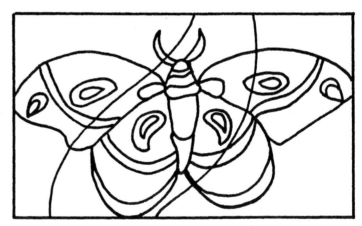

4. Have students paint the first area using various colors of one paint medium.

5. Paint the second area using various colors of a second paint medium.

6. Paint the third area using various colors of the third paint medium.

Figure 2.2.

Questions and Conclusions

1. Which area do you like most? Why?
2. Which area do you like least? Why?
3. Do you think the picture is a successful, unified composition? Why?

MAKING PAINTS

We have discussed the composition of paint, the attributes of various types of paint, and the place of paint in a classification of matter. Now, students will produce paint by preparing paint pigments and combining these pigments with binders. In addition to preparing paints, students will examine the physical properties of the substances produced in their activities.

Preparation of Colored Pigments

Artists' pigments may be prepared in many ways. The nature of the original materials and the treatment of these materials determine the type of color pigment that will be the final product. Pigments can be prepared by grinding naturally occurring minerals such as cinnabar, a bright-red mineral having the chemical formula HgS, or azurite, a brilliant-blue mineral having the chemical formula $2CuCO_3 \cdot Cu(OH)_2$. The finer the mineral is ground, the greater the chance of producing a smooth, even homogeneous paint solution rather than a coarse, uneven heterogeneous paint mixture.

Colored pigments can also be prepared by the precipitation of aqueous ions in solution. Precipitation occurs when ions, charged particles, combine in a water solution to form a solid substance. This solid substance, called a precipitate, can be used as a paint pigment. To separate the precipitate from the surrounding liquid, the precipitate and the liquid are poured through a conical filter paper in a funnel. The precipitate remains in the filter paper and the liquid flows through the filter paper into a receiving container. The liquid that flows into the container is called the filtrate.

In addition, pigments can be prepared by chemical changes, such as the combining of oxygen with metals to form metal oxides or the incomplete combustion of hydrocarbons, carbon hydrogen compounds, to produce carbon.

In Activity 2.3, students will prepare paint pigments by powdering a mineral, precipitating ions in solution, and burning a hydrocarbon. The students will save their pigments for preparing paints in Activity 2.5.

2.3

Preparation of Colored Pigments

Objectives

1. Students will prepare paint pigments from a variety of materials.
2. Students will write balanced chemical equations for the preparation of selected paint pigments.

Materials

Mortar, pestle, 100 ml beaker, evaporating dish, funnel, filter paper, tongs, three small test tubes, Bunsen burner or candle, matches, pea-size amount HgS (cinnabar) or $2CuCO_3 \cdot Cu(OH)_2$ (azurite), 3.0 g $Pb(NO_3)_2$ (lead nitrate), 1.5 g Na_2CrO_4 (sodium chromate), 25.0 ml graduated cylinder, distilled water, centigram balance, four small test tubes, small spatula, wash bottle, two 100 ml beakers.

Time

50 minutes

Procedure—All Levels

Paint pigments, colored powdered substances, come from a large variety of starting materials. We will prepare paint pigments in three different ways from three different resources.

A. Have students prepare color pigments from two minerals:

1. Place a pea-size portion of HgS in a mortar. Repeat with $2CuCO_3 \cdot Cu(OH)_2$.

2. Using a pestle, grind the mineral to a fine powder.

3. Save the powder in a small test tube.

B. Have students prepare a color pigment from combustion of a hydrocarbon:

1. Light the Bunsen burner or candle. The flame should be yellow. If using a Bunsen burner, adjust the air inlets. If using a candle, removal of oxygen (air) will create a yellow flame. (Most candles will burn with a yellow flame.)

2. Using tongs, hold the bottom of an evaporating dish about 4 inches above the flame until a black deposit appears on the bottom of the dish.

3. Using a spatula, scrape the black deposit into a small test tube.

4. Save the deposit (use the test tube as a container).

C. Have students prepare a color pigment from aqueous ion precipitation:

1. Dissolve 3.0 g $Pb(NO_3)_2$ and 1.5 g Na_2CrO_4 separately in 25.0 ml distilled water each (use a 50 ml graduated cylinder for measuring the water).

2. Combine both solutions in a 100 ml beaker.

3. Fold the filter paper to fit the funnel, set up the funnel for filtering, and pour the combination of the solutions into the filter paper. Use a 100 ml beaker to collect the filtrate.

4. Using a water bottle, squirt distilled water into the residue allowing this wash water to seep through the filter paper and become part of the filtrate.

5. Discard the filtrate into a container for safe disposal.

6. Unfold the filter paper and allow the residue to dry.

7. Save the residue.

Questions and Conclusions

Level One

1. Referring to the procedure in this activity, define paint pigment.
2. What is the color of each pigment prepared?
3. The pigment prepared by combustion is carbon. Write a word equation for the chemical change that produced the carbon.
4. The pigment prepared by precipitation is lead chromate. Write a word equation for the chemical change that produced the lead chromate.
5. Make a list of plants and animals that could be used to obtain paint pigments. How could pigment be extracted from each of these plants and animals?

Level Two

1. Write a chemical equation for the change that produced the carbon. (Answer: $CH_{4\ (g)} \rightarrow C_{(s)} + 2H_{2\ (g)}$.)

2. Write a chemical equation for the change that produced the lead chromate. (Answer: $K_2CrO_{4\ (aq)} + Pb(NO_3)_{2\ (aq)} \rightarrow PbCrO_{4\ (s)} + 2KNO_{3\ (aq)}$.)

3. Choose a plant or animal and research and write, in detail, the steps for extracting pigment (e.g., describe the chemical process for extracting the red pigment from a rose).

Preparation of Binders

To paint our wagon, we need complete paints. Pigments alone will not make a paint. It is necessary to combine binders with the pigments. Binders are substances that hold the pigments in solution so they can be spread evenly over a surface. Depending on the binder used, the resulting paint may be transparent or opaque. Binders must adhere to a surface and dry in a reasonable amount of time. In Activity 2.4, students will prepare binders.

2.4
Preparation of Binders

Objectives

1. Students will prepare a variety of binders and describe their physical properties.
2. Students will explain the requirements for a binder in a paint.

Materials

Linseed oil, turpentine, beeswax, 3.0 g $(NH_4)_2CO_3$ (ammonium carbonate), egg yolk, soluble starch, distilled water, 10 ml graduated cylinder, four 250 ml beakers, small test tube, Bunsen burner, stirring rod, four watch glasses, paint brush, centigram balance.

Time

50 minutes

Procedure

A. Have students prepare a binder for oil paint:
   1. Using a 10 ml graduated cylinder for measuring, combine 2 ml linseed oil and 4 ml turpentine in a 250 ml beaker and stir.
   2. Save the binder (use the beaker as a container). Cover the beaker with a watch glass.

B. Have students prepare a binder for water-soluble paint, using wax for permanence:
   1. Place a 1-inch cube of beeswax and 30 ml distilled water into a 250 ml beaker.

2. Heat gently over the colorless flame of a Bunsen burner until beeswax melts.

3. Add 3.0 g $(NH_4)_2CO_3$, a little at a time, while gentle heating is continued. Decrease the heat if the solution threatens to foam over the top of the beaker.

4. Save the binder (use the beaker as a container). Cover the beaker with a watch glass.

C. Have students prepare a binder for egg tempera paint:

1. Separate an egg yolk from the albumen. Discard the albumen.

2. Carefully place the egg yolk in hand and pass it from one hand to the other, without puncturing it, until it is fairly dry.

3. Place the egg yolk in a 250 ml beaker and puncture it.

4. Transfer the egg yolk to a 10 ml graduated cylinder and measure the volume.

6. Add to the egg yolk an equal volume of distilled water and stir the mixture until it is homogenous (has a uniform consistency). The mixture should have a thick consistency.

7. Save the binder (use the beaker as a container). It will keep for a day or two in the refrigerator but has a very brief shelf life.

D. Have students prepare a binder that covers well for temporary purposes, then make the binder more permanent:

1. In a 250 ml beaker, add 2.0 g starch to 4.0 ml cold distilled water and stir to make a paste.

2. Boil 4.0 ml distilled water in a test tube over the flame of a Bunsen burner. Add this to the starch paste, stirring well. This solution is a temporary binder.

3. To the starch solution, add 2.0 ml linseed oil, a little at a time, while stirring. This solution is a permanent binder.

4. Save the binder (use the beaker as a container).

Questions and Conclusions

Level One

1. Make a table that lists the four prepared binders in a column on the left and the following binder physical properties across the top: Viscosity, texture, adhesion (ability to adhere to a painting surface), and color. Paint a sample of each binder under the binder name. Then evaluate each binder for the physical properties listed in the table squares.

2. Make a list of physical properties that a good binder should have and explain why these properties are important.

Level Two

1. Explain the use of the turpentine in the binder for oil paint.

2. Explain the uses of the ammonium carbonate and beeswax in the binder for water-soluble paint.

3. What property of egg yolk makes it a good binder?

4. How does oil make a starch binder permanent?

Preparation of Paint
from Pigments and Binders

Now comes the moment of truth! Will the pigments prepared in Activity 2.3 combine with the binders prepared in Activity 2.4? If the pigments remain suspended in the binders, irregular heterogeneous mixtures will result. The pigment particles will separate from the binders and settle out of the mixtures. This kind of unstable system is called a suspension. Solute particles, in this case pigment particles, that are larger than 1,000 nanometers will separate from the solvent (a nanometer is 1×10^{-9} m). If such a mixture is applied to a surface, the paint will not uniformly cover it. Good paints are uniform throughout—homogeneous solutions. In a true solution, the solute particles (those particles dissolving in and combining with the solvent) are no larger than 1 nanometer, about the size of a small molecule. Our pigment particles would need to be no larger than 1 nanometer to form a true solution.

However, a usable paint may be formed. When a pigment is combined with a binder, a colloid can be formed—a solution in which the solute particles are between 1 and 1,000 nanometers in size. Like all solutions, colloids are uniform throughout. Many paints are colloids, so there is a good chance that our pigments will form usable paints when combined with our binders. We shall see!

2.5

Preparation of Paint from Pigments and Binders

Objectives

1. Students will prepare paints from the pigments and binders prepared previously.
2. Students will explain why many paints are colloid solutions.

Materials

Pigments prepared in Activity 2.3, commercial pigments, binders prepared in Activity 2.4, paintbrushes, 16 small test tubes, stoppers, stirring rods, eye droppers.

Time

30 minutes

Procedure—All Levels

1. Have students place a portion of each of the three pigments prepared in Activity 2.3 along with a commercial pigment into four separate test tubes. Each student or group should pick a different commercial pigment.
2. Have students use an eye dropper to add, drop by drop, enough of each of the four binders prepared in Activity 2.4 to each pigment, mixing thoroughly, in order to make a colloidal suspension.
3. Have students paint a sample of each prepared paint on a table prepared in the following manner: List the four pigments in a column on the left side of a sheet of paper and the four binders across the top.

4. Have students place stoppers in test tubes to save their remaining paints to use in Activity 3.4.

Questions and Conclusions

Level One

1. Using your table, determine:

    a. What combination makes the best paint? Why?

    b. What combination makes the worst paint? Why?

2. Do your paints appear to be solutions, suspensions, or colloids? Decide for each paint and explain your decision.

3. If you were to create a paint for your personal use, what qualities would you want it to have? What would you use the paint for, and how would each quality enhance that use?

Level Two

1. Consider the solute particles and solvent particles involved in the process of making paint. In what ways can solute particles, pigment, combine with solvent particles, binder, to form a solution or colloid? When these particles combine, we say that they "bond."

At last, we have some paints! Are they good enough to paint our wagon and head for gold-mine territory? Probably not, but we have a basic understanding of paint: A chemical solution or colloid consisting of a pigment and a binder. Good paints will cover a surface uniformly and completely and dry in a reasonable amount of time. In Activities 3.3–3.5, students will use their paints creatively. Meanwhile, we will need to use commercial paints to paint our wagon and seek our fortune.

REFERENCES

Albenda, Pauline. *Creative Painting with Tempera.* New York: Van Nostrand Reinhold, 1970.

Bettelheim, Frederick A., and Jerry March. *Introduction to General, Organic & Biochemistry.* New York: Saunders, 1988.

Blake, Wendon. *Acrylic Watercolor Painting.* New York: Watson-Guptill, 1972.

Daniels, Alfred. *Introduction to Painting with Acrylics.* Secaucus, NJ: Chartwell Books, 1988.

Gilbert, Rita. *Living with Art.* New York: McGraw-Hill, 1992.

Mayer, Ralph. *The Artist's Handbook of Materials and Technique.* New York: Viking Press, 1966.

Parramon, Jose M. *The Book of Color.* New York: Watson-Guptill, 1993.

CHAPTER

3

Supports and Grounds

Down Under—What Is Underneath?

INTRODUCTION

Most of us try to keep our feet on the ground, so to speak. Fortunately, the force of gravity helps us to remain attached to the earth and keep us from floating off into space on an endless journey through the universe and beyond. Attachment to a surface is basic to life on earth. It is also important to an artist creating a two-dimensional work of art. The support and surface on which the artist applies materials has a major effect on the final work.

A painting usually has more than one layer. First, there is the support, which is the foundation for the painting. Support materials may be manufactured, such as paper and canvas, or naturally occurring, such as wood and stone. The next layer, the ground, can be defined as the surface on which an artist draws or applies pigment. It is the background in a two-dimensional work of art, or the substance applied to a painting or drawing support in preparation for the pigmented material. Next, of course, comes the paint or pigmented material. Finally, a protective coating, such as varnish or fixative, may be added.

A BRIEF HISTORY OF SUPPORTS AND GROUNDS

Ancient Times

In ancient times, the support for a work of art was a cave wall. As caves were replaced by housing, the walls of dwellings served as supports for artwork. In the city of Pompeii, in southern Italy, fresco paintings on building walls dating back to 50 B.C. are well preserved to this day. In the fourteenth and fifteenth centuries in Italy, painting on specially prepared wood panels with egg tempera paint was one method used by artists of the day. By 1450, the printing press had been invented and was in prevalent use; this enhanced the availability of paper for books and for artwork. Throughout the ages, cloth, such as canvas, has been used as a painting support.

Modern Times

In modern times, artists continue to use a variety of supports. Henri de Toulouse-Lautrec, in the 1800s, painted on brown paper. His dull, brown backgrounds helped to emphasize his lively, colorful figures. Today, in America, artists commonly use canvas or paper for their artwork. However, if we travel to Olido, Nigeria, in western African, body painting is common. These body paintings often coexist with wall paintings; both show the same motifs, despite the contrasting painting surfaces. Continuing our travel to England, we will see sidewalk artists creating their fragile, temporary works of art on the concrete for passersby to admire, and, in the case of Mary Poppins, for fantasy seekers to enter and become a part of the drama portrayed. Even today, the list of materials for painting supports, what is down under, is seemingly limitless.

Fresco Painting

For one type of fresco painting, buon fresco painting, the ground is freshly spread plaster. Paint pigment is applied to the wet plaster, which absorbs the pigment as it dries. The painting and wall are one. Buon frescos are very durable, but the artist must prepare only a small area of fresh plaster at a time, then work quickly before the plaster dries. Among the most well-known frescos is Michelangelo's work on the ceiling of the Sistine Chapel at the Vatican in Italy. This fresco was completed in the sixteenth century, and has undergone extensive renovation from 1980 to 1989. Years of soot, salt stains, and coats of glue build-up were removed, revealing the original brilliant color. In modern times, artists still use fresco technique to paint murals depicting objects on a grand scale. As recently as the 1900s, fresco painting was embraced by Mexican artists to express events and feelings engendered by Mexican social and political upheaval.

Gesso painting is a version of fresco technique in which the painting support is not associated with a building. While buon fresco painting technique employs a ground of freshly prepared plaster on a building wall support, a gesso ground is prepared by applying layers of plaster-like paste, or gesso, to a masonite board. As each layer dries, a new layer is added. The final ground has a brilliant white, dry, hard surface. With a gesso ground, the paint remains on the surface instead of being absorbed into the ground, as with buon fresco painting.

Gesso is also used when preparing a canvas for oil or acrylic painting. Canvas stretched on a frame is the support. The gesso ground is applied with a brush to the support, a procedure called *priming*. The gesso acts to seal the canvas fabric so that the paint applied will not soak into the canvas.

PREPARING GROUNDS— CHEMICAL CHANGES

In Activity 3.1, the students will prepare whiting compounds, substances that impart a brilliant white to a ground, which will be combined with other chemicals to produce a gesso paste. In Activity 3.2, the gesso paste will be applied to masonite board to prepare a ground, which will be used in a subsequent activity as a painting surface for pictures that students will create using the paints they made in Chapter 2 (Activities 2.3–2.5, pp. 63–68). In the preparation of the whiting compounds, students will observe two types of chemical reactions: A composition reaction and a double displacement reaction. Students will review chemical change and examine four basic types of chemical changes: Composition, decomposition, single displacement, and double displacement; and examine two classes of compounds: Acids and bases.

3.1

The Preparation of Grounds—
Preparing Whiting Compounds

Objectives

1. Students will prepare two whiting compounds and observe the chemical changes involved.

2. Students will write balanced chemical equations for the chemical changes observed and explain that an equation is balanced to reflect the conservation of atoms in a chemical change as required in the law of conservation of matter.

3. Students will classify their equations according to a simple equation-classification system.

4. Students will identify the whiting compounds prepared as acidic or basic and research the chemical and physical properties of acids and bases.

Materials

Large funnel, filter paper, two 1-liter beakers, five 250 ml beakers, 1-liter graduated cylinder, distilled water, red and blue litmus paper, 21.2 g Na_2CO_3 (sodium carbonate), 22.2 g $CaCl_2$ (calcium chloride), 10.0 g CaO (calcium oxide), stirring rod, two watch glasses, distilled water, wash bottle.

Time

40 minutes

Procedure—All Levels

A. Have students prepare $CaCO_3$ (calcium carbonate):

1. In a 1-liter beaker, dissolve 21.2 g Na_2CO_3 in 1-liter distilled water to prepare a 0.2 M (molar) solution of Na_2CO_3.

2. In a 1-liter beaker, dissolve 22.2 g $CaCl_2$ in 1-liter distilled water to prepare a 0.2 M solution of $CaCl_2$.

3. In a 250 ml beaker, combine 100 ml 0.2 M Na_2CO_3 with 100 ml 0.2 M $CaCl_2$ and observe the chemical change.

4. Filter the product. Collect the filtrate into a 250 ml beaker. (Note: The filtrate can be discarded down a sink drain.) Save the residue and discard the filtrate (liquid).

5. Using a wash bottle, wash the residue several times with distilled water. Discard the additional filtrate in a sink drain.

6. Test the residue with red litmus paper and blue litmus paper and record the results.

7. Scrape the residue on the filter paper into a 250 ml beaker. Cover with a watch glass to prevent drying and save for Activity 3.2.

B. Have students prepare Ca(OH)$_2$ (calcium hydroxide):

1. Place 10.0 g CaO in a 250 ml beaker.

2. Add enough distilled water to make a thick paste. Stir with a stirring rod.

3. Test the paste with red litmus paper and blue litmus paper and record the results.

4. Scrape the residue on the filter paper into a 250 ml beaker. Cover with a watch glass to prevent drying and save for Activity 3.2 (p. 74).

Questions and Conclusions

Level One

1. Write a word equation for the chemical changes that produced the two whiting compounds: CaCO$_3$ (calcium carbonate), sometimes called precipitated chalk, and Ca(OH)$_2$ (calcium hydroxide), sometimes called slaked lime. After writing the equations, find for each equation the correct classification: Composition, decomposition, single displacement, or double displacement (see "An Artist's Materials and Chemical Change," following this activity).

2. Compare the whiting compounds, CaCO$_3$ and Ca(OH)$_2$, regarding brightness, texture, and consistency. Which compound would be a better whitener for a gesso ground? Why? (Answer: The whiting compound with the smoothest texture.)

3. An acid turns blue litmus paper red and a base turns red litmus paper blue. Are the whiting compounds acidic or basic?

Level Two

1. Write balanced chemical equations for the formation of the two whiting compounds (see "An Artist's Materials and Chemical Change," following this activity). (Answers: CaO $_{(s)}$ + H$_2$O $_{(l)}$ $\Rightarrow$ Ca(OH)$_2$ $_{(s)}$; Na$_2$CO$_3$ $_{(aq)}$ + CaCl$_2$ $_{(aq)}$ $\Rightarrow$ 2NaCl $_{(aq)}$ + CaCO$_3$ $_{(s)}$.)

2. Research the physical and chemical properties of acids and bases and list these properties. Explain why the whiting compounds are bases.

3. After classifying the chemical changes that produced the whiting compounds, explain the reason for placing each chemical change into a particular class.

An Artist's Materials and Chemical Change

When an artist prepares art materials, such as grounds, to be used in artwork, the artist becomes immediately involved in chemical change. Chemical changes deal with changes in the structure of substances, the *reactants*. Bonds between atoms in reactants are broken and atoms are rearranged and bonded into new substances called *products*. In the process of chemical change, atoms are conserved. That is, all the atoms present in the reactants are present in the product, a requirement of the law of conservation of matter.

Four basic classes of chemical changes (reactions) are used to classify most simple chemical changes: Composition, decomposition, single displacement, and double displacement. In a composition reaction, reactant substances (e.g., elements, compounds, ions) combine to form one product, a *compound*. This reaction is symbolized as A + B→AB. In a decomposition reaction, one reactant (a compound) forms more than one product: AB→A + B. In a single displacement reaction, an element reacts with a compound to form another element and compound: AB + C→AC + B (nonmetal single displacement) or AB + C→CB + A (metallic single replacement). In a double displacement reaction, two compounds combine to form two different compounds: AB + CD→AD + CB. The following balanced chemical equations illustrate these four classes of chemical changes [$_{(s)}$ = solid, $_{(g)}$ = gas, $_{(aq)}$ = aqueous, $_{(l)}$ = liquid]:

1. **Composition.** $CaO_{(s)} + H_2O_{(l)} \rightarrow Ca(OH)_{2 (s)}$

    ■ *Note:*
    This equation shows the formation of a whiting compound in Activity 3.1.

2. **Decomposition.** $2KClO_{3 (s)} \rightarrow 2KCl_{(s)} + 3O_{2 (g)}$

3. **Single Displacement (nonmetal).** $2NaCl_{(s)} + F_{2 (g)} \rightarrow 2NaF_{(s)} + Cl_{2 (g)}$

    Single Displacement (metallic). $Zn_{(s)} + CuSO_{4 (aq)} \rightarrow ZnSO_{4 (aq)} + Cu_{(s)}$

4. **Double Displacement.** $Na_2CO_{3 (aq)} + CaCl_{2 (aq)} \rightarrow 2NaCl_{(aq)} + CaCO_{3 (s)}$

    ■ *Note:*
    This equation shows the formation of a whiting compound in Activity 3.1.

Notice that in all the above reactions, atoms are conserved. Equations are balanced by adding coefficients to the reactants and products.

Acids and Bases: Special Types of Substances

When a group of compounds have similar chemical and physical properties, they are given a special name and called a class of compounds. Acids and bases are such classes. Before defining these classes, we should consider their relationship to grounds. The whiting compounds prepared in Activity 3.1 are bases. They make the gesso white and are fairly nonreactive when dry. Therefore, an artist can paint on the gesso ground without concern that the gesso will react with the paints and cause changes in color. Also, if the gesso is left unpainted in certain areas, these areas will remain white. Some papers used as supports for watercolor paint are advertised as being non-acidic. Similarly, these papers are desirable because they will not cause changes in the color of the paint, and areas left unpainted will remain white. This is not to say that bases are not reactive substances, but they remain more stable than acids in the presence of particular paints.

The words *acid* and *base* are commonly used and can be defined by their properties. The physical properties of these substances are simple: Acids taste sour (consider the taste of a lemon), and they can burn your skin. Bases taste bitter and feel slippery. Soaps and most cleaning solutions are bases. Many chemical reactions can be used to identify acids and bases: Acids turn blue litmus paper red and phenolphthalein (another commonly used indicator) clear. Bases turn red litmus paper blue and phenolphthalein red. Acids react with some metals, such as magnesium and zinc, to produce hydrogen gas. Acids and bases react with each other, in a process called neutralization, to form salts and water.

3.2

The Preparation of Grounds— Using Whiting Compounds to Prepare Gesso Solutions

Objectives

1. Students will construct gesso grounds.

2. Students will compare and contrast the properties of various types of gesso grounds.

3. Students will debate the pros and cons of using a gesso ground for a painting.

Materials

Dry-curd cottage cheese, rabbit-skin glue, 2-x-3-inch masonite boards, cheese cloth, 1-inch-width paintbrushes, fine-grit sandpaper, 100 ml graduated cylinder, two 250 ml beakers, two 100 ml beakers, utility knife, TiO_2 (titanium dioxide), ZnO (zinc oxide), plaster of Paris, $CaSO_4 \cdot H_2O$ (hydrated calcium sulfate), hot plate, distilled water, $CaCO_3$ (calcium carbonate) prepared in Activity 3.1, $Ca(OH)_2$ (calcium hydroxide) prepared in Activity 3.1, centigram balance, stirring rods, 20 g TiO_2, 20 g ZnO, 20 g $CaSO_4 \cdot H_2O$, watch glass, Bunsen burner or alcohol lamp, weighing paper, hot plate.

Time

100 minutes (extra time will be needed for applied gesso layers to dry)

Procedure

A. Have students prepare a glue-based gesso:

1. Place 7.0 g of rabbit-skin glue in a 250 ml beaker.

2. Using a Bunsen burner or alcohol lamp, warm 100 ml of distilled water. Do not boil.

3. Add the warm water to the glue and stir.

4. Find the mass of each of the whiting compounds prepared in Activity 3.1: $CaCO_3$ and $CaSO_4 \cdot H_2O$. Select the compound of greater mass. Combine it with an equal mass of $CaSO_4 \cdot H_2O$.

5. Add the combination prepared in step 4 to the glue mixture prepared in step 3 and stir until a thick, creamy consistency is achieved.

6. Apply the gesso to a masonite board (see part C). Cover the beaker with a watch glass. Store the gesso in a refrigerator between applications (it will gel between applications and should be warmed on a hot plate until it is just melted and then used).

7. Repeat the above preparation, but use a commercially prepared whiting compound such as about 20 g TiO_2 or about 20 g ZnO in step 4. Continue with steps 5 and 6.

B. Have students prepare a casein-based gesso:
1. Place 6.0 g dry-curd cottage cheese in a 100 ml beaker.
2. Place 1.0 g $Ca(OH)_2$ on weighing paper.
3. In a 100 ml beaker, combine 7.0 g ZnO with 7.0 g TiO_2.
4. Mix together the solids prepared in steps 1–3 and add enough distilled water (about 7.0 ml) to form a thick paste.
5. Strain the mixture through cheese cloth and apply the gesso to a masonite board (see part C). Store the gesso in a covered 250 ml beaker in a refrigerator between applications.

C. Have students create a gesso ground by applying the gesso to a masonite board:
1. Using a utility knife, score one side of a 5-x-7-inch masonite board.
2. Using a 1-inch-width paintbrush, apply a thin layer of gesso to the scored side of the board.
3. After the layer dries (about four hours), apply a new layer, making brush strokes at a right angle to the strokes made for the first layer.
4. Continue applying layers of gesso (alternating the direction of brush strokes) until the gesso surface is about 3 millimeters thick.
5. When the final layer is dry, sand the gesso surface using fine-grit sandpaper.
6. Save all gesso grounds for use in Activity 3.3.

Questions and Conclusions

Level One

1. Compare the gesso grounds prepared with regard to color and texture.
2. In a class discussion, have students decide which gesso ground is the best ground for a two-dimensional work of art.

Level Two

1. Research the names of artists who painted on gesso grounds. Find reproductions of their paintings. Using one of these reproductions, explain how the gesso ground provided a unique background for the two-dimensional work of art.
2. For each chemical used in this activity, explain its role in creating the gesso product.

NON-OBJECTIVE ART: NO OBJECTS, BUT PLENTY OF FEELING

The ground for a work of art is the choice of the artist. Non-objective art is an art form that often makes the ground a significant part of the work. Non-objective art is not based on any observed subject matter. It frequently addresses aspects of life that cannot be seen, such as emotion and feeling, music, and sound. These aspects are expressed in visual form through the use of lines and shapes that are free-form or geometric. Color provides the non-objective artist with another visual tool for evoking emotion and arousing feelings.

The following artists are among those of the twentieth century who have worked in the non-objective style:

Jackson Pollock (1912–1956)   Piet Mondrian (1872–1944)
Hans Hoffman (1880–1966)   Vassily Kandinsky (1866–1944)
Franz Kline (1910–1962)

Activity 3.3 allows students to experiment with non-objective art using the gesso grounds prepared in Activity 3.2 and egg tempera paint prepared in Activity 2.5. Egg tempera was used by many artists in Europe during the fourteenth and fifteenth centuries. Today, it is still used by some artists, notably Andrew Wyeth. In this technique, egg yolk is mixed with distilled water to form a binder and a pigment is added to make egg tempera paint, which is applied to a gesso ground.

It would be appropriate to show students works by Andrew Wyeth and by the artists listed above. Also, appropriate parts of the following video about non-objective art might be shown:

Cubism and Non Objective Art and Surrealism. 53 min. Aspen, CO: Crystal Video, 1993.

3.3
Non-Objective Art—Egg Tempera Paint on a Gesso Ground

Objectives

1. Students will mix pigment with egg yolk and distilled water to prepare egg tempera paint (or use prepared egg tempera paint).

2. Students will apply paint to a prepared gesso ground.

3. Students will learn the meaning of the term *non-objective* by creating non-objective works of art.

4. Students will express movement and ideas through the use of non-objective shapes, lines, and colors in paintings.

Materials

Egg yolks, pigments (see below), powdered or liquid tempera (poster paint) in assorted colors, and distilled water, or egg tempera paint prepared in Activities 2.3–2.5; gesso grounds prepared in Activity 3.2; short-width paintbrushes with soft bristles; paper towels; mixing trays; water containers; pencils.

Time

30 minutes

Procedure

Preliminary

1. Have students follow Activity 2.5 to prepare egg tempera paints. In activity 2.5, students combined pigments with binders (vehicles for carrying the pigment and binding it to a surface) to make paints. If egg tempera paints remain from Activity

2.5, they should be used. These paints will be deep red (cinnabar pigment), deep blue (azurite pigment, $2CuCO_3 \cdot Cu(OH)_2$), yellow ($PbCrO_4$ pigment), and black (carbon pigment).

2. New and/or different color egg tempera paints can be prepared as follows:

   a. Follow steps in Activity 2.4, Procedure C.

   b. Add powdered or liquid tempera paints of various colors to portions of the prepared egg yolk binder to produce paints of desired colors. Powdered or liquid tempera may be added to the egg yolk solution to make egg tempera paint in additional colors.

Level One

1. Have students paint on the gesso ground, creating a feeling of movement—across, up, down, around, in, out, or any combination of these—using shapes and lines. Students should try to vary the size and type of shapes and lines, vary the colors, and use the entire gesso surface.

2. Have students display their work and try to identify the movement expressed in their classmates' pictures.

Level Two

1. Have students choose a descriptive, chemistry-related word, phrase, or term, such as *acid, base, energy, molecule, explosive chemical change, the solution process,* and *atoms bonding to form molecules* that could be expressed in a non-objective painting. Then students should paint their idea on a gesso ground using egg tempera paint. They should avoid painting a picture of an object, and should try to use only shape, line, and color to express their ideas.

Level Three

1. Have students listen to a brief excerpt of music that evokes a strong feeling of rhythm or strong emotion. Suggested musical selections include the following:
   La Mer by Claude Debussy
   Capriccio Espagnol by Rimsky Korsakov
   Moonlight Sonata by Ludwig van Beethoven
   The Elements by Tom Lehrer
   jazz, rock, or pop selections

2. Have students create a non-objective painting, varying the size and type of shapes and lines, and varying the colors, to express an interpretation of the music.

SUPPORT FOR THE ARTIST: PAPER

The Great Paper Chase:
A Brief History

Throughout history, there has been a need to write messages on a surface. Humanity has always been involved in a paper chase. However, paper, as we know it today, is different than the paperlike surfaces that came before it, the first of which was invented by the Egyptians around 2000 B.C. The Egyptians made a flat surface from the papyrus plant that grew in the marshes of their country. By flattening the inner fibers and attaching them side by side, a flat sheet was formed. A second layer was pasted crosswise on the first layer; this process was continued until the surface was strong. Our word *paper* comes from the Egyptian word *papyrus*.

In the second century B.C., parchment was developed in the city of Pergamum, in Asia Minor. It was made from the hides of animals and was a better surface than papyrus for writing. It could be rolled into a scroll or cut and made into pages for a book. Still, it was thick and irregular.

In China, around A.D. 105, the first true paper was made. The Chinese emperor of the day decreed that this discovery must be kept a secret—and for 500 years it was! Papermaking eventually spread to Korea and, in A.D. 610, a Korean monk named Dancho brought paper from Korea to Japan. Papermaking then traveled across Asia to Egypt in the tenth century, then to Spain in the twelfth century. From Spain, it spread through Europe. In 1690, papermaking came to America. In Europe and America, until the end of the eighteenth century, paper was made by hand from rags. When a machine was invented to manufacture such paper, the demand for rags increased until a new source of raw material was needed. Suddenly, it was discovered that paper could be made from cellulose fiber found in trees. This discovery dramatically increased the production of paper, as well as the varieties of paper.

Today, paper is still made in essentially the same way as it has been for decades. Wood chips are treated with solvents to clean and separate wood containing cellulose fiber. This fiber, known as pulp, is spread on a flat surface, where a machine shakes it for even distribution and to interlock individual fibers. This mixture is then rolled and pressed to squeeze out excess water and solvent. A flat piece of wet paper is the result. Finally, the paper is hung to dry.

Characteristics of Paper: Watercolor Paper

Artists use many different types of paper to create their artwork. Artists using watercolor, for example, paint on paper that is specially designed for this medium. Watercolor paper may be rough in texture, medium textured, or smooth. Rough- and medium-surfaced papers are called cold press (CP) paper because the textured surface is effected by rolling the newly formed sheet through a set of cold rollers. Smooth-surfaced paper is called hot press (HP) paper because the newly formed sheet is rolled through a set of hot rollers to effect a smooth surface.

In addition to the different textures of paper, watercolor paper is made in various weights. Watercolor paper, whether cold press or hot press, is available in weights from 72-pound to 400-pound; a typical weight is 140-pound. The greater the number, the thicker the sheet of paper. Pound-weight is determined by the weight of a stack of 500 22-x-30-inch sheets of the particular paper. Therefore, the designation of 140-pound means that 500 22-x-30-inch sheets of the paper weigh 140 pounds.

When purchasing watercolor paper, the pound-weight system helps identify the paper needed for a particular purpose. The heavier weights of papers can be painted upon without any support beneath them to keep them flat. Lighter weights of papers—72-pound, 90-pound, and 140-pound—must be supported or stretched. Stretching involves soaking the paper in a tray of cool water for several minutes, causing the fibers of the paper to relax, until the paper becomes limp. The paper is removed and all excess water is allowed to drip. Next, the paper is stapled or taped to a flat surface. For stapling, an ordinary office stapler will do the job. Care should be taken to place the staples about ½ inch in from the edge and about ¼ inch apart from one another. Gummed water-based tape may be used instead of staples. Strips of tape should be cut slightly longer than the four edges of the paper. Care should be taken to center the tape between the edge of the paper and the board so that the paper will be held securely. Wet the tape and press it firmly in place. When the paper is dry, the fibers have tightened and the paper will appear taut. If paint is applied to paper that has not been stretched, the paper will ripple and, when dry, remain uneven. Stretching the paper provides the artist with a flat working area and an even-surfaced painting.

Watercolor paper, in addition to having various finishes and weights, is also available in a variety of grades. The best and most expensive paper has 100% linen rag content, meaning only linen cloth fibers, have been used to make the paper. Less expensive grades contain cotton and wood, fibers, and synthetic substances. There are many suitable papers for painting in watercolor in addition to those already discussed. Interesting effects can be achieved using Japanese rice papers, fine art printing papers, and illustration boards. There are ground-wood papers with no chemical purification, such as manila drawing paper, and wood pulp papers chemically purified for better color strength and longevity. Each provides the artist with a unique result, and all help to create interesting effects.

3.1
Comparing Results of Paint Applied to Various Watercolor Papers

Objective

1. Students will observe differences in the appearance of watercolor paint when it is applied to a variety of watercolor papers.

Materials

Variety of watercolor papers, each piece cut to the same size (suggested papers: Cold press—one medium texture, one rough texture; Hot press—manila; white drawing; rice; and other available papers), watercolor paint, paintbrushes, mixing containers, water containers, water, masking tape.

Time

10 minutes

Procedure

1. The teacher should arrange the papers so that the edges touch. To hold them together, it may be necessary to tape them from the back. The papers need not be stretched for this demonstration.

2. Paint a wide line of watercolor across the sheets several times. Have students observe the various results as the paint moves from one surface to another.

3. Have students compare the results and determine which papers are suitable for watercolor paint. They should explain why one paper is more suitable than another paper.

3.4

Papermaking

Objectives

1. Students will make a fiber paper.
2. Students will evaluate the qualities of the fiber papers.
3. Students will calculate grams of solute and grams of solvent for a particular amount of a particular mass-percent solution.
4. Students will explain oxidation and how it relates to papermaking.

Materials

Lint from clothes dryers, kitchen blender, transparent or masking tape, animal hide glue, embroidery hoops, thinly woven fabric, trays slightly larger than embroidery hoop, NaClO (5% sodium hypochlorite solution: Bleach), about 100 ml 10% NaOH solution (sodium hydroxide), $KAl(SO_4)_2 \cdot 12H_2O$ (potassium aluminum sulfate: Alum), starch, 250 ml beaker, red and blue litmus paper, watercolor paint prepared in Activity 2.5, commercial watercolor paint, paintbrushes, mixing trays, water containers, centigram balance, hot plate, watch glass.

Time

First day 50 minutes, second day 200 minutes.

Procedure—All Levels

Have students make paper from lint:

1. In a 250 ml beaker, prepare a mixture of lint and water about the consistency of cream.
2. Place the mixture in a blender and blend at medium speed until smooth.
3. Add about 5.0 g of the blender mixture in 2 to 10.0 g of starch and blend. The mixture should resemble a very thick gravy.
4. Add 5.0 ml NaClO (bleach) to the mixture and blend.
5. Pour the mixture into a tray and test with litmus paper to determine whether it is acidic or basic. (An acid turns blue litmus red; a base turns red litmus blue.)
6. Stretch thinly woven fabric over an embroidery hoop and dip the hoop into the tray, spreading the mixture evenly over the cloth.
7. Lift the hoop out of the tray and let the lint mixture dry in the hoop.
8. Remove the paper from the hoop.

Questions and Conclusions

Level One

1. Describe the color, texture, and strength of the paper. Was the paper pulp acidic or basic?

2. Describe the function of bleach and of starch in the papermaking processes.

3. Use watercolor paint prepared in Activity 2.5, as well as commercial watercolor paint, to paint pictures on the prepared paper.

Level Two

1. Use watercolor paint prepared in Activity 2.5, as well as commercial watercolor paint, to paint a picture that incorporates the paper's shape and texture.

2. Research acid-free paper and explain the chemical process through which paper is made free of acid.

3. Solution concentrations are often presented as a percent concentration (mass percent). Ten percent NaOH solution is used to break down wood fibers often used to make paper. For this example, how many grams of solute are added to how many grams of solvent to prepare 100 grams of solution? (Answer: 10 g of NaOH added to 90 g H_2O.)

4. In making paper, bleach (NaClO) acts as an oxidizing agent for whitening the paper. An oxidizing agent reacts with another substance, removing atoms from colored molecules. Explain how the ClO^- ion in bleach acts as an oxidizing agent when it changes from the ClO^- ion to the Cl^- ion. Research oxidation numbers and use that concept in the explanation. (See "Oxidation-Reduction," following this activity.)

Oxidation-Reduction

Bleach is often used to whiten clothes. It can also be used to whiten paper pulp that will be converted into sheets of paper. Bleach (NaClO, or sodium hypochlorate) belongs to a class of compounds called oxidizing agents. Oxidizing agents whiten substances by removing oxygen atoms from colored molecules. The new molecule, said to have been "reduced," is usually colorless. The chemical change is called an oxidation-reduction, or redox, reaction. If the new, reduced molecule is exposed to the air, which contains 20% oxygen (O_2), it may recombine with oxygen atoms, become oxidized, and return to its colored state. This occurs when white newspaper yellows with age.

Many substances act as oxidizing agents and whitening materials. Even though many oxidizing agents contain oxygen atoms, oxidizing agents cannot always be identified by their molecular structure. We must examine redox reactions to identify the oxidizing agents involved in the chemical change. To find the oxidizing agent, an arbitrary system of numbers called oxidation numbers is used. This system helps a chemist keep track of the number of electrons gained or lost by an atom during the chemical change. When oxidation occurs, an oxidizing-agent atom gains electrons and a reducing-agent atom loses electrons.

Oxidation Numbers

The system of oxidation numbers is designed as follows:

1. The oxidation number of an atom in a pure element is 0 (e.g., the oxidation number of chlorine [Cl] in Cl_2 is 0). The oxidation number of iron (Fe) in metallic

iron is 0. For 4, 5, and 6 below, we can look to the periodic table to find generalizations about oxidation numbers.

2. In most compounds, oxygen (O) atoms have an oxidation number of -2 and hydrogen (H) atoms have an oxidation number of +1.

3. Finally, the sum of the oxidation numbers in a neutral compound is 0; the sum of the oxidation numbers in a polyatomic ion (an ion with at least two atoms) is equal to its ionic charge.

4. Looking at the periodic table of elements, the oxidation number of a group IA atom in a compound is +1; the oxidation number of a group IIA atom in a compound is +2.

5. For group VIIA atoms, the oxidation numbers of chlorine (Cl), bromine (Br), and iodine (I) are -1 except when they combine with oxygen (O) or Fluorine (F).

6. Oxidation numbers for the transition metals, the group B atoms, in compounds are equal to their ionic charges.

Oxidation-Reduction in Papermaking

The active ingredient in bleach is NaClO (sodium hypochlorite). In water, the NaClO ionizes into Na^+ and ClO^-. The ClO^- ion is the oxidizing agent. In a basic solution, this ion removes color by oxidizing pigments and, in so doing, changes to the Cl^- ion. The oxidation number of the chlorine atom changes from +1 in the ClO^- ion to -1 in the Cl^- ion. For the ClO^- ion to oxidize pigments, it must gain electrons (negative charge) from atoms in the pigment molecule. Therefore, when an oxidizing agent oxidizes another species, such as an element, compound, or ion, and gains electrons, its oxidation number must decrease. The substance in an oxidation-reduction reaction that shows a decrease in oxidizing number is the oxidizing agent.

Oxidizing agents are good bleaches. ClO_2, a reddish yellow gas, is also used to bleach paper pulp. However, ClO_2 is such a strong oxidizing agent that it is explosive in high concentrations; therefore, it is only used in low concentrations.

In Activity 3.4, paper is made in a basic solution. For paper where wood fibers are used, NaOH (sodium hydroxide) can make the pulp mixture basic by providing an excess of OH^- ions. The NaOH breaks down cellulose fibers in the wood and other plant materials that form the primary paper structure. It is a suspension of these fibers that can be placed on fabric on an embroidery hoop. Also, ClO^- ions can act as oxidizing agents in the basic solution. Finally, $KAl(SO_4)_2 \cdot 12H_2O$ (potassium aluminum sulfate: Alum) is added to the cellulose fibers to coagulate the pulp (clay is added when it is not naturally present). The aluminum ion (Al^{3+}) helps the clay loosely bond to the cellulose fibers so that the resulting paper is dense and smooth.

Video Resources for Papermaking

Practical Papermaking by Vicki Lever, 60 minutes. Colfax, CA: Victorian Video Productions, 1990.

Western Papermaking I, 30 minutes. Iowa City, IA: University of Iowa, 1994.

COLLAGE

Collage involves the combining of various media in one picture. In a collage, both two- and three-dimensional materials may be combined in the picture. Materials such as paint, newspaper, pieces of cloth, magazine pictures, and thread might be used. Written words might also be added.

It would be helpful to show students collage works by the following artists:

Pablo Picasso (1881–1973) Jean Arp (1888–1966)
Juan Gris (1887–1927) Kurt Schwitters (1887–1948)
Georges Braque (1881–1963)

3.5
Handmade Paper and Collage

Objectives

1. Students will make a collage using paint and handmade paper.

2. Students will apply the principles of good composition and the creative process to an original work of art.

Level One: Collage I

Materials

Handmade paper; tempera paint (poster paint); oil or egg tempera paint prepared in Activity 2.5; paintbrushes; mixing trays; water containers; water; construction paper, newspaper, magazine pages, and other available paper; bits of cloth, thread, and other materials; scissors; glue; 12-x-18-inch collage ground, such as cardboard.

Time

50 minutes

Procedure

1. Have students use paint prepared in Activity 2.5, as well as tempera paints, to paint an image on a piece of handmade paper. The shape or contour of the handmade paper may suggest an animal or object. Students should try to create an interesting unit of painted paper.

2. Glue the painted paper in some position on the collage ground. The painted paper should be the center of interest in the collage, though it need not be at the center of the collage.

3. Have students choose a theme suggested by the painting.

4. Arrange and glue other pieces on the collage ground to complement the painting and reinforce the theme of the collage.

5. If desired, paint some areas in the collage.

Level Two: Collage II

Materials

Handmade paper; paint prepared in Activiy 2.5; short-width soft paintbrushes; various watercolor papers; drawing paper, paper towels, brown paper bags, tissue paper, tracing paper, notebook paper, and other available papers torn or cut into various sizes and shapes; 12-x-18-inch collage ground, such as cardboard or illustration board.

Time

100 minutes

Procedure

1. Have students create a collage made of various sizes and types of unpainted paper glued to a collage ground. The pieces of paper should overlap and cover all or most of the ground, and all corners should be secured so that the paper is as flat as possible. Students should include their handmade paper in the collage.

2. Have students select one of the following themes for their collage:
   Down Under—Elements, Compounds, and Minerals Found Inside the Earth
   Above and Beyond—Hydrogen and Helium: Atoms of Our Universe
   Inside Out—Chemical Change: From Inside Matter, Out Comes Energy
   Here and There—Atoms, Atoms Everywhere
   Upside Down—Relative Terms

3. Have students paint a picture, based on their theme, using the collage of various papers as a ground. It is not necessary to paint all areas of the collage. The picture can be realistic, a fantasy, or non-objective, and paint prepared in Activity 2.5 should be used in at least one area of the picture.

THE FUTURE OF PAINTING SUPPORTS AND GROUNDS

In this chapter, we have examined painting supports and grounds for two-dimensional works of art. Just as humanity is anchored to the earth by the force of gravity, a two-dimensional work of art is affixed to a support and ground by the artist. However, humanity constantly seeks to defy gravity by creating a means for escaping its pull. Will future artists find a means to create two-dimensional works of art without the need for painting supports and grounds? In this era of digital imaging, nothing is impossible.

REFERENCES

Arnason, H. H. *History of Modern Art: Painting, Sculpture, Architecture.* 3d ed. New York: Harry N. Abrams, 1986.

Brommer, Gerald F. *The Art of Collage.* Worcester, MA: Davis, 1978.

Buehr, Walter. *The Magic of Paper.* New York: William Morrow, 1966.

Herberts, Dr. Kurt. *The Complete Book of Artists' Techniques.* New York: Frederick A. Praeger, 1958.

Meilach, Dona Z. *Collage and Found Art.* New York: Van Nostrand Reinhold, 1964.

O'Reilly, Sue. *Paper Making.* New York: Thomson Learning, 1993.

Smith, Elizabeth Simpson. *Inventions That Changed Our Lives: Paper.* New York: Walker, 1984.

Smith, Stan, and H. F. Tenholt. *The Artist's Manual: Equipment, Materials, Techniques.* London: QED, 1980.

Sorgman, Mayo. *Brush and Palette: Painting Techniques for Young Adults.* New York: Van Nostrand Reinhold, 1965.

4

Three-Dimensional Works of Art

Playing with Clay

INTRODUCTION

If we examine the past or the present, or look into the future, somewhere we will observe someone playing with clay. Playing with clay is very satisfying. Clay is plastic and pliable. It is cooperative. It responds to pushing, pulling, pounding, and pinching. There is no wonder that playing with clay has survived through the history of humanity.

Clay has many moods, and many small children are especially intrigued with the feel and easy versatility of clay. They like to squeeze, roll, punch, flatten, and shape it. They can impress it with designs, scratch it, hollow it out, and cut it. In liquid form, it can be poured into a mold. Many children make their first three-dimensional work of art while they are playing with clay. Often, they use clay three-dimensional works of art to express emotions that they cannot express in words.

A BRIEF HISTORY OF CLAY, POTTERY, AND CERAMICS

Clay is an old material used by many ancient peoples. Around 10,000 B.C., Neolithic peoples used clay to make shaped vessels for holding food and water. Centuries later, as early as the pre-dynastic period of 4000–3500 B.C., the Egyptians used clay to make vessels with linear and geometric designs, as well as animals and human figures.[1] Some of the oldest manuscripts, the Dead Sea Scrolls, written more than 2,000 years ago, were found preserved in clay jars. Clay has been a key factor in the preservation of our past.

As early as 1100 B.C., the Greeks were producing pots decorated with geometric designs. Later, the pot decorations were changed to plants and animals, and in the 6th century B.C., warriors and processional figures adorned some of the finest examples of clay and ceramic pieces ever to be made.

The clay work of China can be traced to prehistoric times. In the thirteenth century, Marco Polo probably brought the first Chinese clay or ceramic pieces to Europe from the East.[2] These pieces were made of a special clay heated to a high temperature to produce a strong, durable ceramic that we refer to by the name of its place of origin, China. Around 1300, the art of ceramics took on a new life during the Renaissance in Italy in the form of majolica, a style using bright colors and designs learned by the Italians from the Arabs. European ceramic work of Italy, Holland, and Spain, as well as many other parts of Europe, continued to develop in the centuries following, reflecting the individual characteristics of each area in Italy during the fifteenth and sixteenth centuries; beautiful terra cotta pieces were made by the Della Robbia family. Throughout the eighteenth century, many technical advances were made in the field of ceramics, leading to a great variety of forms and finishing techniques. Names such as Delft, Meissen, and Wedgwood, to mention only a few, are still famous today in the field of ceramics.

Mention must also be made of the clay work of the Native Americans of North and South America. Made primarily for everyday use, their pieces have a beauty of form and decoration unique to their cultures.

Examples of Pottery Types

It would be helpful to show students examples of the types of works discussed above. Following is a chronological list of significant examples, pictures of which can be found in pottery and art books:

Neolithic pottery
Egyptian pottery
Egyptian hieroglyphic tablet
Greek black-face or red-face vase,
    fifth century B.C.
Chinese vase, Sung dynasty
Della Robbia Italian ceramic work,
    sixteenth century

Dutch Delft, seventeenth century
English Wedgwood, eighteenth century
German Meissen, eighteenth century
Mayan Native American pottery
Pueblo Native American pottery

THE THIRD DIMENSION: ADDITIVE AND SUBTRACTIVE CONSTRUCTION METHODS

When we look at a painting or read a book, the surface we are looking at is flat. If we look out the window or view a sculpture or a piece of pottery, we are looking at something in three dimensions (or 3-D). Three-dimensional artwork might be solid and massive, or it might be linear, or it might be a combination of both massive and linear parts.

To create a work of art in three dimensions, the artist has a choice of materials and construction methods. Three-dimensional pieces can be constructed by adding material to create a form, or by removing material to reveal a form. These two methods represent the additive and subtractive methods of construction. A material such as clay is appropriate for the additive method: Pieces of clay can be pressed onto an existing form. The form can be built up by adding piece after piece of clay. Clay can be very easily added and pushed into shape, making it an ideal medium for the beginning three-dimensional artist.

Figure 4.1. Example of the Additive Method.

The subtractive method involves removing portions of the material. A sculptor working in stone, for instance, chisels away areas of marble or granite to create the three-dimensional image. A wood carver removes areas of the material to reveal a shape. Generally, in the subtractive method, once pieces of the material are removed, they cannot be replaced (clay is an exception).

Figure 4.2. Example of the Subtractive Method.

A third construction method involves creating a form in three dimensions by casting. Casting is a technique that requires a mold, into which a material such as plastic, metal, or clay in liquid form is poured or injected.

Of all the materials used for three-dimensional construction, clay can be used in the greatest variety of ways, making it the most versatile of materials. We can push, pull, bend, and twist it. It never complains. Why is clay so versatile? What is this thing called clay?

CLAY

Natural Clay

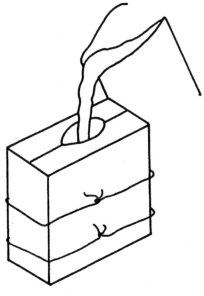

Figure 4.3. Example of the Casting Method.

There are many types of clay. Natural clay is earth or soil generally found beneath topsoil. Found almost everywhere, natural clay is formed when rocks—mostly feldspar, which is a mixture of potassium oxide (K_2O), aluminum oxide (Al_2O_3), and silicon dioxide having the empirical formula $K_2O \cdot Al_2O_3 \cdot 6SiO_2$—breaks down under the action of weather and through chemical reactions. Variations in this empirical formula, and the addition of other substances such as Na_2O (sodium oxide), change the clay color and texture. Natural clay becomes plastic and cohesive when moist because it consists of platelets made of silicon (Si), oxygen (O), hydrogen (H), and aluminum (Al) atoms, bonded into an arrangement having the empirical formula $Al_2Si_2O_5(OH)_4$, that slide over one another when water is present. Natural clay becomes hard when exposed to heat, either from the sun or when baked or fired in a kiln. Ordinary baked clay pottery has a rough, porous surface. To make it more attractive, waterproof, and useful, it is given a smooth, shiny surface by a process called glazing.

Plasticene, Low Fire, and Self Hardening Clays

Plasticene clay includes synthetic polymers (see Chapter 5) so that it does not harden. It can be modeled repeatedly, and it has many of the qualities of elasticity that natural clay has, but it cannot be fired and glazed to make it permanent.

Low-fire clay is available in a variety of colors and can be used successfully for making small decorative items. It will harden when baked in a regular kitchen oven at a low temperature, but it cannot be glazed. A variety of brands of self-hardening clay is available. It will harden in air, drying with a permanent finish, and it is available in a variety of colors suitable for small decorative objects such as beads and jewelry.

Keramikos, Keramos, Ceramics

What Is It?

Ceramics is the art of molding and firing or heating clay to a high temperature, resulting in hard, permanent objects. The Greeks, who played an important role in the development of ceramics, called their works by the word *keramos*, from Keramikos, a section of Athens, Greece, where most of the ceramic artists worked and sold their art. Our word *ceramics* comes from this Greek word.[3] Today, the word *ceramics* indicates something much broader than just the art of pottery. It includes the making of such products as bricks, kitchen sinks, bathtubs, floor tiles, and walls. Ceramics are used in many industries to make components that resist high temperatures. Ceramics are a part of our everyday lives.

The Life Cycle of a Natural-Clay Ceramic Piece

The Baby Is Born

A ceramic piece, like a human being, has a life cycle that begins at birth and ends at death. At birth, a ball of wet natural clay emerges as the new baby. The new baby must be properly prepared for the harsh world it has entered. First, the ball of wet natural clay must be wedged to remove any air trapped inside. In other words, the baby is burped. This is necessary because a clay piece containing pockets of air will explode or shatter when heated in an oven or kiln. To wedge clay, it is slammed or thrown onto a hard, nonporous surface until it is free of air pockets. The baby is spanked, and what a spanking it is! If the clay is too soft, it is wedged on a plaster slab, which absorbs excess water from the clay. To check for air pockets, the lump of clay is cut into two pieces with a wire (harsh treatment for this baby clay, but necessary). If free of air pockets, the clay is ready to be formed into a ceramic piece.

Childhood, the Teenage Years, Adulthood, and Death

A natural-clay baby can be formed into a multitude of desired shapes, unlike a human baby. After a desired shape is achieved, the clay piece is allowed to dry. As it dries, it becomes lighter and shrinks about 10% as water evaporates. The baby gets smaller as it grows older. This process of evaporation may take several days.

When the piece is partly dry, it is known as leather-hard clay. At this point, it is stiff and will hold its shape, but it can still be smoothed to remove imperfections, and it can be scratched to add designs. It is a teenager experiencing the pains of growing up, which can be minimized with love and affection, and wearing the designs of its teen culture. When the piece is completely dry, it is known as greenware. It is a green teen. At this point, its shape can no longer be changed, but if it is placed in water, it will dissolve into its original state. A few tears will dissolve a teenager into a babylike state.

When greenware is placed in an oven or kiln and heated to a high temperature, it becomes hard and permanent. It is now a young adult. At this stage, it is known as bisque ware. If placed in water after firing, it will absorb water but will not lose its shape. A permanent change has taken place with heating to make the piece permanent. A liquid sealer or glaze is applied to the surface and the piece is fired once more.

This final firing results in the stage known as glazed ware. The clay piece is an adult. It can live for hundreds of years with proper care. Death occurs only when someone is careless and mishandles the clay piece. Dropping a piece is a common cause of death.

THE GLAZE MAZE

In glazing, a thin layer of a liquid mixture called a glaze is applied to a clay object. Glazes can be applied with a paintbrush, sprayed on, or the object can be dipped into the glaze. The glaze should be applied after the object has been baked in a kiln one time.

When glazing, it is necessary to observe the following rules:

1. The bottom of a piece should not be coated with glaze. Coated bottoms, when heated, will melt and stick to the shelf of the kiln. (Kiln firing is discussed later in the chapter.)

2. More than one coat of glaze must be applied, usually two or three coats.

3. When applying the glaze, coat the object evenly to avoid thick and thin spots in the glaze finish.

Usually, glazes are tested on small samples of bisque-fired clay called test tiles or clay slabs (see Activity 4.3). It is advisable to test glaze colors first to determine if the color is suitable before using it on a ceramic piece.

Glazes are made of a variety of ingredients. Each glaze ingredient has a role in producing an attractive, waterproof, and useful product. Some ingredients determine the glaze color; others produce particular textures. A glaze finish may appear shiny or dull. A dull finish is called a matte finish. A shiny finish is called a glass finish. A glaze must contain ingredients that integrate the glaze into the object's surface, so that the glaze and clay become a single substance (we will be examining the chemical makeup of glazes to understand how they work). Glazes have preserved works of clay for centuries. They allow us to admire an object made 2,000 years ago, as well as recently created works of art.

GLAZE OR GLASS: WHAT IS IT?

A glaze is a glass, which is a solid that sometimes behaves as a liquid at a temperature when it should normally be solid. It cannot make up its mind! A glass has this identity problem because of its molecular structure. Glass ionic structure (see Fig. 4.4) is based mainly on tetrahedral-shaped silicate ions (SiO_4^{4-}). These negative ions, or anions, are connected to one another not in an orderly fashion as in a crystalline solid but with a large degree of disorder. Glass usually appears to be a solid. It has a definite shape and volume. However, on occasion, when a glass sheet remains in one place over a long period of time, glass will

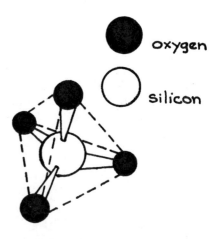

Figure 4.4. A Silicate Anion.

flow. Evidence of this is the appearance of old glass windows that have become uneven, having waves with thick and thin portions. The glass in the window has slowly flowed like a viscous liquid to make the window uneven. Glass has a constant identity problem: It appears to be a solid, but it has an atomic structure different than that of a typical solid.

Note that a crystalline solid is not a glass. A crystalline solid is made of particles arranged in a very definite order (see Fig. 4.5). In emeralds, silicate tetrahedral anions, negative ions, crystallize in a hexagonal pattern while in asbestos, the crystalline structure consists of an extended chain of double tetrahedral silicate anions. A crystalline solid has a regular shape. The particles in a glass, however, are in disarray (see Fig. 4.5 below). A glass is an amorphous solid. A glass has an irregular shape.

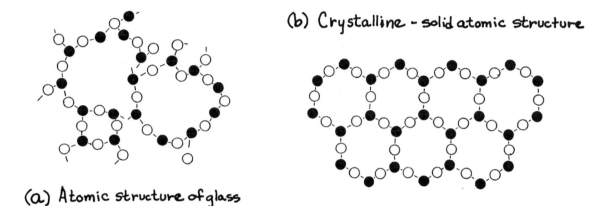

(b) Crystalline - solid atomic structure

(a) Atomic structure of glass

Figure 4.5. Atomic Structure of Glass vs. Crystalline-Solid Atomic Structure.

Crystalline Solids: Three-Dimensional Works of Art

At one time or another, many children will attempt to make sugar candy: Crystals of sugar, or sucrose ($C_{12}H_{22}O_{11}$), that form on a string placed in a saturated sucrose solution. This saturated solution becomes supersaturated when some of the water evaporates. In nature, crystals are formed in a similar manner. A rock surface may harden, leaving mineral-filled liquid inside the rock. Slowly, water evaporates from the rock interior and crystals form. Anyone who has cracked open a geode has observed such crystals.

There are three main types of crystalline solids: Atomic, ionic, and molecular solids. Phosphorus (P), sulfur (S), and carbon (C) form atomic crystalline solids. All three of these elements exist in allotropic forms: Different forms of the same element at the same temperature and physical state. Phosphorus has two allotropic forms, red and white phosphorus. Red phosphorus has P_4 units bonded in a chain and white phosphorus is made of tetrahedral-shaped P_4 molecules. Sulfur has three allotropic forms. Rhombic sulfur, the most stable form, has eight sulfur atoms (S_8) bonded in a puckered ring. Monoclinic sulfur has eight sulfur atom rings packed to form a monoclinic crystal and "plastic" sulfur has sulfur atom chains tangled together so that the atomic structure more closely resembles a glass than a crystal. Carbon has two allotropic forms, graphite and diamond. In graphite, six atoms are bonded to form a planar hexagon, which bonds to other planar hexagons. In diamond, four carbon atoms bond to form a tetrahedral, which is bonded to other tetrahedrals, making a strong, three-dimensional network of atoms.

Sodium chloride (NaCl) is an ionic crystalline solid. In sodium chloride, there is an extended regular array of sodium ions (Na$^+$) and chlorine ions (Cl$^-$); each ion is surrounded by six ions of the opposite charge to form a cubic crystal.

Ice (H$_2$O) is a molecular crystalline solid. Six water molecules bond to each other to form a hexagonal pattern. This pattern is reflected in the hexagonal geometry exhibited in snowflakes. Activity 4.1 allows students to construct models of basic crystalline solids and to "grow" molecular-solid crystals. The students will consider the basic structures of crystalline solids and look upon these structures as three-dimensional works of art.

4.1

Atomic, Ionic, and Molecular Crystalline Structures—Three-Dimensional Works of Art

Objectives

1. Students will construct models of four basic crystalline structures, noting the different possibilities for crystalline-solid particle arrangement.

2. Students will compare and contrast the atomic, ionic, and molecular structures modeled with the atomic structure of a glass.

3. Students will describe their crystalline-solid models as three-dimensional works of art and determine if they are solid works, linear works, or a combination of both.

Materials

Styrofoam balls (13 ½-inch-diameter balls and 54 two-inch-diameter balls per student or group), toothpicks, C$_{12}$H$_{22}$O$_{11}$ (sucrose; use about 50 g), NaCl (sodium chloride), hand magnifying lens, 250 ml beaker, about 15 g KAl(SO$_4$)$_2$·12H$_2$O (potassium aluminum sulfate: Alum), paper and pencil, distilled water, spatula.

Time

50 minutes, several days for evaporation, then 30 minutes

Procedure—All Levels

In the four models prepared below, the three layers (top, middle, and bottom) should not be secured to each other.

A. Have students prepare models of four basic crystalline solids using Styrofoam balls:

1. The alkali metals barium (Ba) and uranium (U) are atomic crystalline solids. Their atoms pack in a body-centered cubic arrangement. Use nine 2-inch-diameter balls and eight toothpicks to form three layers of a body-centered cubic crystal, as illustrated in Figure 4.6 (the top layer is the same as the bottom layer). Put the layers together like a sandwich. Draw a picture of this atomic crystalline solid.

2. Copper (Cu), silver (Ag), and gold (Au) are also atomic crystalline solids. Their atoms pack in a face-centered cubic arrangement. Use 14 2-inch-diameter balls and 12 toothpicks to form three layers of a face-centered cubic crystal, as illustrated in Figure 4.7 (the top layer is the same as the bottom layer). Put the layers together like a sandwich. Draw a picture of this atomic crystalline solid.

3. Magnesium (Mg) and zinc (Zn) are atomic crystalline solids that pack in a hexagonal-closest packing arrangement. Use 17 2-inch-diameter balls and 15 toothpicks to form three layers of a hexagonal-closest packing crystal, as illustrated in Figure 4.8 (the top layer is the same as the bottom layer). Put the layers together like a sandwich. Draw a picture of this atomic crystalline solid.

4. To prepare a model of an ionic crystalline solid, such as sodium chloride (NaCl), use 14 2-inch-diameter balls, 13 ½-inch-diameter balls, and 28 toothpicks to form three layers of an ionic crystal, as illustrated in Figure 4.9 (the top layer is the same as the bottom layer). Put the layers together like a sandwich. Draw a picture of this ionic crystalline solid.

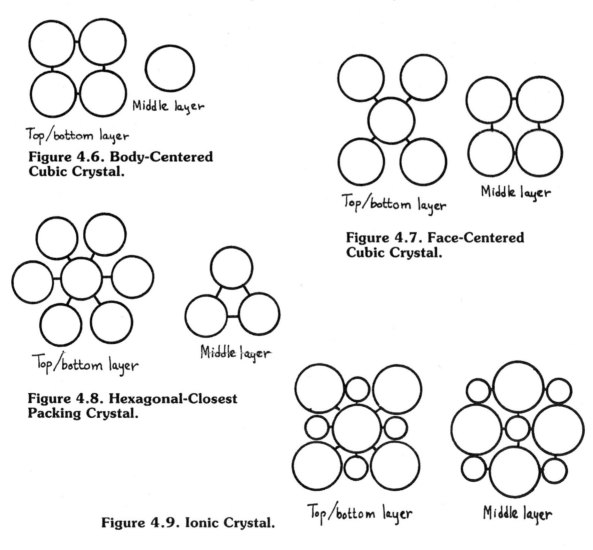

Top/bottom layer   Middle layer

Figure 4.6. Body-Centered Cubic Crystal.

Top/bottom layer   Middle layer

Figure 4.7. Face-Centered Cubic Crystal.

Top/bottom layer   Middle layer

Figure 4.8. Hexagonal-Closest Packing Crystal.

Figure 4.9. Ionic Crystal.   Top/bottom layer   Middle layer

B. Have students prepare a molecular crystalline solid:

1. Pour 100 ml distilled water into a 50 ml beaker.

2. Add $KAl(SO_4)_2 \cdot 12H_2O$ and stir. Using a spatula, keep adding about two gram increments until no more will dissolve.

3. Let the beaker stand uncovered in a cool place where it will not be disturbed. Observe daily.

4. When the water has evaporated, observe the crystals with a hand magnifying lens.

5. Draw the crystals, showing their shape.

C. Have students use a hand magnifying lens to examine crystals of the molecular solids $NaCl$ and $C_{12}H_{22}O_{11}$, then draw these crystals, showing their shape.

Questions and Conclusions

Level One

1. This activity includes models of atomic, ionic, and molecular crystalline solids. List the names of the solids represented by each of these models (magnesium and zinc, among others, were modeled as atomic solids). Make a generalization concerning the shape of the solid crystal and the type of solid.

2. Describe the crystalline-solid models prepared in this activity as three-dimensional works of art that are solid (massive), linear (made mostly of thin, line-like parts), or both, explaining why they are solid or linear works of art.

3. A glass is an amorphous solid. How would the atomic structure of a glass differ from the particle structure of a crystalline solid?

Level Two

1. From this activity, it would appear that metals form atomic crystalline solids. However, different metals have adopted different atomic packing arrangements. Offer an explanation for this occurrence.

2. Research three-dimensional works of art that resemble the atomic packing arrangements of crystalline solids and explain the artwork in terms of the structures of crystalline solids.

3. Consider your models of three atomic solids and one ionic solid. Are atomic solids more dense or less dense than ionic solids? Explain your answer.

4. When a glass cracks, it shatters. When a crystal cracks, it cleaves along a flat plane. Explain why.

From Activity 4.1, it can be seen that crystalline solids are made of atoms, ions, or molecules that line up in an orderly fashion and form a predictable crystalline shape. It is not known why different metals choose different atomic packing arrangements such as body-centered cubic, face-centered cubic, or hexagonal-closest packing. Differences in atomic size and electron configuration might be determining factors. Certainly, the difference in size between the sodium ion (Na^+) and the chlorine ion (Cl^-) account for cubic ion packing in a sodium chloride crystal, which is not a closest packing arrangement. Here ions are not touching one another. There is unfilled space when small ions and large ions are arranged alternately in a three-dimensional array. However, face-centered cubic packing and hexagonal-closest packing result in solids in which the atoms are actually touching one another. Because of this touching, a calculation of atomic radii is possible. In a glass, the disorderly particle arrangement does not allow any such calculation. Atomic or ionic radii calculated from crystalline solid measurements of touching atoms or ions can be used to predict crystalline solid structures for a large variety of crystalline solids containing these atoms or ions. Also, we can use atomic radii to make correct molecular models.

The models prepared in Activity 4.1 have the properties of a solid and linear three-dimensional work of art. The toothpicks give the work a linear look and the Styrofoam balls provide mass. The closer the atoms, ions, or molecules are packed, the more the artwork appears to be solid and massive, not linear.

Many works of art, two-dimensional as well as three-dimensional, depict subject matter resembling (or resemble, in the case of sculpture) structures of crystalline solids, such as the following:

> *Cube* (sculpture), Sol Lewitt, 1967
> *Twelve Cadillacs* (silk-screen on canvas), Andy Warhol, 1962
> *Green Coca-Cola Bottles* (oil on canvas), Andy Warhol, 1962
> *Untitled* (nine steel units), Robert Morris, 1967
> *White Cascade* (mobile metal), Alexander Calder, 1972–73
> *Study of the Regular Division of the Plane with Horsemen*
>   (India ink and watercolor), M. C. Esher, 1946

All these works of art include an orderly arrangement of a particular object, similar to the arrangement of structural units in a crystalline solid: Atoms, ions, or molecules.

Crystalline-Solid Formation vs. Glass Formation

It is necessary to consider the method of formation of a crystalline solid as compared to the formation of a glass to understand why a crystalline solid is made of particles distributed in a uniform manner whereas a glass has a disordered particle structure. Demonstration 4.1 compares glass formation to crystal formation. Because the preparation of a glass requires temperatures above 1600°C, prepared glass is melted in this demonstration (requiring a much lower temperature) to show glass formation.

4.1
The Difference Between Crystalline-Solid Formation and Glass Formation

Objectives

1. Students will state observed differences between crystalline-solid formation and glass formation.

2. Students will explain why glasses have disordered particle arrangements and crystals have orderly particle arrangements.

3. Students will write a word equation and a chemical equation for the preparation of silver (Ag) crystals.

Materials

Large test tube, distilled water, 30 cm 12- to 14-gauge copper (Cu) wire, pencil, 15 ml 0.1M $AgNO_3$ (silver nitrate), two lengths of 20 cm soft glass tubing, paper and pencil, Bunsen burner, matches, wash bottle, 250 ml beaker.

Time

30 minutes

Procedure

1. Heat the tip of a 20 cm length glass tubing in the hottest part of a Bunsen burner's flame (directly above the inner cone) until the glass melts and a globule of molten glass is formed.

   ■ *Note:*
   Because it would be impractical to prepare glass from silicon dioxide (SiO_2), requiring temperatures above 1600°C, prepared glass is melted to represent the stage of glass making before the glass is cooled.

2. Remove the glass from the flame and let it cool. Have students record the length of time needed for cooling and draw a picture of the globule.

3. Repeat steps 1–2 with another piece of glass tubing.

4. Pour 15 ml 0.1 M $AgNO_3$ into a large test tube. (Caution: Silver nitrate will turn clothes and hands brown.)

5. Twist a piece of copper wire around the length of a pencil, leaving a portion of the wire straight to form a handle. Remove the pencil from the twisted copper wire and immerse the twisted portion of the wire in the $AgNO_3$ solution.

6. Have students observe the copper wire every five minutes until a large quantity of silver crystals are seen.

7. Remove the copper wire from the solution and gently wash the crystals with distilled water. Use a wash bottle filled with distilled water to remove the crystals from the wire washing them into a 250 ml beaker. Decant the wash water from the crystals into the sink.

8. Have students draw a picture of several of the crystals and observe the color of the remaining solution.

Questions and Conclusions

Level One

1. Do both glass globules have the same shape? If both glass globules do not have the same shape, what does this mean about the atomic structure of glass?

2. Do all the silver crystals have the same geometric shape? If all the silver crystals have the same geometric shape, what does this mean about the atomic structure of a metallic crystal?

3. Write a word equation for the chemical change that occurred in this demonstration. (Answer: Copper plus silver nitrate yields copper II nitrate and silver.)

4. Describe a physical change that occurred in this demonstration. (Answer: Glass melting and solidifying.)

Level Two

1. Using evidence presented in this demonstration, explain why crystalline solids have uniform atomic structures and glasses have disordered atomic structures.

2. Write a balanced chemical equation for the chemical reaction that occurred in this demonstration. Identify the class of chemical reactions to which this reaction belongs. (Answer: $2AgNO_{3(aq)} + Cu_{(s)} \rightarrow Cu(NO_3)_{2(aq)} + 2Ag_{(s)}$ Class: Metallic single replacement [see Chapter 3].)

3. What causes the blue color to appear in the solution as the reaction involving copper and silver nitrate proceeds?

Demonstration 4.1 shows that the formation rate makes the difference. Glass, as it cools, solidifies quickly from the molten state. There is no time for the atoms and ions to line up in an orderly structure. They are frozen in place like pebbles in ice. Silver crystals, however, form slowly as silver atoms line up in a face-centered cubic arrangement. The atoms are as uniform as soldiers waiting for inspection.

Glass Components Determine Glass Properties

Glasses contain a number of substances that impart particular physical properties to the glass. The main ingredient in a glass is silicon dioxide (SiO_2), which forms a tetrahedral crystalline structure with a silicon atom at the center surrounded by four oxygen atoms, having the formula SiO_4^{4-}. When sodium carbonate (Na_2CO_3) is added to the silicon dioxide, common glass results. Adding diboron trioxide (B_2O_3) to a glass composition and decreasing the amounts of calcium oxide (CaO) and sodium oxide (Na_2O) in the formulation will result in a glass that will not easily expand during heating or contract during cooling. The addition of potassium oxide (K_2O) to a glass composition will produce a very hard glass.[4] Colored glass is made by adding small amounts of certain transition-metal oxides, such as copper oxide (CuO), chromium oxide (Cr_2O_3), and cobalt oxide (CoO), which produce blue-green glass, orange glass, and cobalt-blue glass, respectively. The color possibilities for glasses, and therefore glazes, are endless. By using specific amounts of selected substances, glazes can be designed to please even the wildest and most exotic of tastes.

Preparing a Glaze

Not only must we include the above-mentioned components in a glaze composition to provide desired physical properties, but also we need ingredients that will make the glaze adhere to the surface of a clay object and make it waterproof. Therefore, a glaze composition will contain a large variety of chemical compounds equipped to fulfill a medley of glaze objectives. Not only is it important to have specific chemical compounds in a glaze composition, it is important to include the correct amount of each component in the glaze formula. In preparing a glaze, one way to formulate a glaze composition is to consider the number of molecules of each compound used rather than the mass of the compounds needed. How can we do this? Can we count the number of molecules in each compound used? If molecules were large enough for us to see and count, what a strange world this would be!

RELATIVE WEIGHTS: PERIODIC TABLE BASICS

Fortunately, there is a way to know how many molecules are in a particular mass of a compound. In Chapter 1, we investigated the periodic table to determine if it was arranged by element color. We discovered that there was no such arrangement. However, we noted that families, vertical columns on the table, had similar physical and chemical properties. The periodic table was originally arranged according to the relative weights of the elements, in order of increasing relative weight, where most elements of similar physical and chemical properties fell into place in vertical columns when rows of eight and eighteen elements are established. However, some elements such as argon and potassium and tellurium and iodine were not in the correct columns. It was discussed that the number of protons in each element provided a means for placing the elements in their correct columns. The elements on the periodic table are arranged according to increasing atomic number.

Relative Weights: Relative to What?

In 1808, John Dalton proposed his atomic theory, which included the statement that when atoms of two or more elements combine to form a compound, they combine in a definite ratio by number of atoms and by mass. This provided a means to determine the mass of one atom relative to another. It was necessary to assign a mass to one element to find the mass of another element in a compound. Today, we use the most common carbon isotope, assigned a mass of 12.00 atomic mass units (amu), as the basis for comparative weights of the atoms.

Relative Weights and the Mole

The relative weights of the elements represent the relative mass of one kind of atom to another kind of atom. For example, the relative weight of a carbon (C) atom is 12.0 amu; the relative weight of a magnesium (Mg) atom is 24.3 amu. This means that a carbon atom has about half the mass of a magnesium atom. If we add together the relative weights of the elements in a compound, we will find the relative weight of the compound. For sodium chloride (NaCl), the relative weight of sodium is 23.0 amu, and the relative weight of chlorine is 35.5 amu. Therefore, the relative weight of sodium chloride is 58.5 amu. The relative weight of lithium oxide (Li_2O) is 6.9 amu twice, 13.8 amu, plus 16.0 amu, which is 29.8 amu. In one relative weight of every compound, there is the same number of molecules. We can change amu to grams and prepare 58.5 grams of sodium chloride and 29.8 grams of lithium oxide. Both amounts contain the same number of molecules. You might be thinking, what is this number? A very large number: 6.02×10^{23} molecules. This number has a name: It is called a mole, abbreviated as mol (and not related to the small, burrowing animal of the same name). Because 6.02×10^{23} molecules are a mole of molecules, and because the relative weight of a substance contains this number of molecules, then the relative weight of a substance must be one mole of that substance.

Glazes can be prepared by combining a particular number of molecules of each ingredient. This can be accomplished using moles, which Activity 4.2 allows student to do.

4.2

Glazing Pottery—Calculations Needed to Prepare a Glaze

Objectives

1. Students will calculate the relative mass of each compound needed to prepare a pottery glaze that waterproofs and decorates a pottery piece for Activity 4.7.
2. Students will use the periodic table to determine the relative weights of elements and compounds.
3. Students will determine the mass of one mole of an element and the mass of one mole of a compound.
4. Students will learn that one mole of a substance represents the number of particles contained in that substance.
5. Students will learn that the relative weight in grams of a compound contains one mole of molecules.

Materials

Calculator, periodic table.

Time

30 minutes

Procedure

1. Have students use a calculator and a periodic table to calculate relative weights for the following compounds: PbO (lead oxide), CaO (calcium oxide), and SiO_2 (silicon dioxide).
2. Have students record the mass of one mole of each of these compounds. (The relative weight of a compound is the weight of one mole of the compound.)
3. Students will calculate the mass of 0.70 mole of lead oxide, PbO, 0.15 mole of calcium oxide, CaO, and of 1.75 mole of silicon dioxide, SiO_2.
4. Using the procedure above, have students calculate the mass of the following number of moles of each compound listed:
   0.05 mole ZnO (zinc oxide)
   0.10 mole K_2O (potassium oxide)
   0.12 mole Al_2O_3 (aluminum oxide)
5. For the masses calculated in steps 3 and 4, have students multiply each answer by 0.1 to find the number of grams of each compound that will be used to prepare a glaze in Activity 4.3.

Questions and Conclusions

Level One

1. In one mole of each of the compounds considered in the activity, how many molecules are present? (Hint: Is the number of eggs in a dozen eggs different than the number of oranges in a dozen oranges?)

2. One mole represents a very large number, 6.02×10^{23}. Find ways to explain just how large this number is. For example, if we were to make a stack of a mole of notebook papers, how high would the stack be?

Level Two

1. Explain why one mole of PbO has a larger mass than one mole of CaO.

2. Sometimes a small amount of clay is added to a glaze composition. What is the function of the clay?

3. If copper compounds are added to a glaze composition, after firing, what, most likely, will be the color of the glaze? Explain your answer.

■ *Note:*
Students will find the relative weights of PbO, CaO, and SiO_2 to be 223.2 amu, 56.1 amu, and 60.1 amu, respectively. Therefore, 0.70 mole PbO is 156 g, 0.15 mole CaO is 8.4 g, and 1.75 mole SiO_2 is 105 g. The masses of one mole of ZnO, K_2O, Al_2O_3 are 81.4 g, 94 g, and 102 g, respectively, so 0.05 mole ZnO is 4.1 g, 0.10 mole K_2O is 9.4 g, and 0.12 mole Al_2O_3 is 12.2 g.

GLAZE INGREDIENTS: THE KEY TO GLAZE PROPERTIES

There are unlimited combinations of compounds and elements that result in glaze formations. The elimination or addition of one substance can radically change the product. In Activity 4.3, a glaze and variations of the glaze will be prepared. Then the prepared glazes will be applied to bisque ware clay slabs, which will be fired. The results obtained from the different glazes will be compared.

THE KILN: CLAY IN THE OVEN

Hansel and Gretel's Worst Nightmare

A kiln is a specially designed oven for heating or firing clay. The word *kiln* comes from the Latin word *culina*, meaning "kitchen." A kiln is constructed to withstand the high temperatures necessary to change greenware into bisque ware and to melt the glazes applied to the surface of

Figure 4.10. Top-Loading Kiln.

clay pieces. Depending on the type of clay, different temperatures are needed to make these changes occur. Hansel and Gretel would never make it in this oven!

The first kilns were used around the sixth century B.C. It was quickly realized that the amount of oxygen in the kiln could determine the color of the glaze. Iron oxide (Fe_2O_4) will lend a red color to a glaze when much oxygen is available. If little oxygen is available, the Fe_2O_4 will donate oxygen to the kiln fire by releasing an oxygen atom and converting to black iron III oxide (Fe_2O_3). When little oxygen is available, the fire is referred to as a reduction fire (see Chapter 3 for a detailed discussion of oxidation-reduction, page 81).

Clay Glazes and Apple Pie Glazes: The Same Concept

A kiln works very much like a kitchen oven. When clay reaches a particular temperature, it changes into a hard, permanent material, and the glaze melts and adheres to the surface of the piece, much the way a brown-sugar glaze on an apple pie melts and sticks to the apples at a particular oven temperature. When firing the kiln, it is necessary to raise the temperature slowly over a period of several hours. At first, the lid of the kiln should be propped open to allow moisture trapped in the seemingly dry clay to escape. Then the lid is closed and the temperature increased to its final level. Most ceramic kilns have a temperature gauge that allows the user to know when to shut off the kiln (*ceramic* is used here as a general term for materials prepared from clay and made rigid by high-temperature treatment). Some kilns are equipped with an automatic shutoff, which shuts off the kiln when the appropriate temperature is reached. When firing, greenware can be stacked, one piece inside another, with surfaces touching. Bisque ware that has been glazed, however, must be set in the kiln carefully so that pieces do not touch one another. (For information on the hazards and dangers of kiln firing, see Chapter 10, pages 227–28.)

4.3
Preparing Glazes and Clay Slabs and Testing the Glazes on the Clay Slabs

Warning! Proper ventilation is necessary during glaze firing. See Chapter 10, Glazes, page 227, and Firing, pages 227–28.

Objectives

1. Students will prepare glazes and clay slabs, apply their glazes to bisque ware clay slabs, and compare the physical properties of the glazes after the slabs have been fired.

2. Students will research the glaze ingredients used to determine why each ingredient is used.

3. Students will design a glaze formula, predict the physical properties of the glaze, and test their predictions.

Materials

PbO (lead oxide), CaO (calcium oxide), SiO_2 (silicon dioxide), ZnO (zinc oxide), K_2O (potassium oxide), Al_2O_3 (aluminum oxide), $CaCO_3$ (calcium carbonate), CuO (copper oxide), Fe_2O_3 (iron III oxide), CoO (cobalt oxide), Cr_2O_3 (chromium oxide), and white clay (see below for amounts); distilled water; four small beakers; kiln; four watch glasses; rolling pin.

Time

50 minutes, one day firing time

Procedure

1. In a small beaker, have students combine the following amounts of the ingredients discussed in Activity 4.2: 15.60 g PbO; 0.84 g CaO; 10.50 g SiO_2; 0.41 g ZnO; 0.94 g K_2O; 1.22 g Al_2O_3.

2. Have students combine, with the ingredients listed above, the following: 0.50 g $CaCO_3$, 0.09 g clay, and an additional 1.86 g SiO_2.

3. Have students add distilled water to the combined ingredients to make a mixture with the consistency of cream.

4. Have students divide the mixture into four equal parts in the beakers and add the following: (The beakers should be labeled Glaze 1, Glaze 2, Glaze 3, and Glaze 4.) Glaze 1: 0.40 g CuO; Glaze 2: 0.80 g Fe_2O_3; Glaze 3: 0.50 g CoO; Glaze 4: 0.50 g Cr_2O_3.

5. Have students prepare bisque clay slabs by:

    a. Wedging a ball of clay;

    b. Rolling the clay to a uniform thickness (about ¼ inch);

    c. Cutting out rectangular slabs; and

    d. Firing the dried slabs at about 1841°F (1031°C).

6. Have students apply each of the four glazes prepared to a separate fired clay slab. (Some of each glaze should be saved for a natural-clay pinch pot in Activity 4.7. Cover beakers with watch glasses.)

7. Fire the slabs in a kiln at recommended temperature (usually about 1950°F).

8. Have students prepare a table as follows: Along the left side of a sheet of paper in a vertical column, list Glaze 1, Glaze 2, Glaze 3, Glaze 4; across the top, list color, opaque or transparent, texture. Record your observed properties for each glaze.

Questions and Conclusions

Level One

1. What is the purpose of adding the following ingredients to the glazes: SiO_2, CuO, and PbO?

2. What problems will be encountered if the glaze is too thick? Too thin?

3. How can you tell that the glaze is a glass?

Level Two

1. Research the physical property imparted by each glaze ingredient.

2. Propose the addition of a new ingredient to the glaze formula and predict the outcome in glaze appearance from this addition. Check the safety and availability of your proposed ingredient with your teacher. Test your prediction by preparing your proposed glaze, applying it to a bisque ware slab, and having it fired in a kiln.

THE PERIODIC TABLE

Relative Weights: An Historical Perspective Involving the Periodic Table

We used relative weights and the mole concept to prepare glaze formulas based on the number of glaze ingredient molecules needed for the glaze formula. Now, we will consider the relative weights of the elements and their importance in developing the modern periodic table. In 1808, Joseph Louis Proust, a French chemist, found that when pure compounds were prepared, they always required the same mass ratio of constituent elements. This was called the Law of Definite Proportions. John Dalton, an English scientist, introduced his atomic theory in 1803 and, using Proust's Law of Definite Proportions, subsequently determined experimentally the relative weights of a number of elements. In 1817, Johann Dobereiner found several groups of three elements that had similar properties. He grouped these together as triads. The average of the relative weights of the heaviest and lightest elements in a triad equaled the relative weight of the middle element. Chlorine (Cl), bromine (Br), and iodine (I) are such a triad. The average of the relative weight of chlorine, 35.5 amu, and the relative weight of iodine, 126.9 amu, is 81.2 amu. The relative weight of bromine is 79.9 amu.

Dobereiner's Triads Come Home

Dobereiner's triads found a home in Dmitri Mendeleev's periodic table, published in 1872. Mendeleev arranged the elements according to their relative weights, beginning with the lightest element, hydrogen (H). He placed elements with similar properties together vertically so that Dobereiner's triads appeared within Mendeleev's periodic table. About 52 elements had been discovered at the time of Mendeleev's periodic table. He used his table to accurately predict the discovery of additional elements, such a gallium (Ga), selenium (Se), and germanium (Ge). In 1914, Henry Moseley found that elements with similar chemical and physical properties fit more properly in columns when the elements were arranged according to atomic number, the number of protons in the atomic nucleus. The modern periodic table is arranged according to atomic number.

The Modern Periodic Table:
Order from Chaos

Metals, Nonmetals, and Metalloids

The modern periodic table provides us with volumes of information about the elements. Metals are on the left side of the table, nonmetals are on the right side, and metalloids divide these two groups. In general, metals are shiny, malleable, ductile, and conduct electricity. Nonmetals are dull, brittle, and do not conduct electricity (many nonmetals are gases at room temperature). Metalloids have properties of both metals and nonmetals.

Families: They Get Along Fairly Well

A column of the periodic table is called a family. Some families have special names. Group IA elements are called alkali metals, group IIA elements are called alkaline earth metals, group VIIA elements are called halogens, and group VIIIA elements are called the noble gases. The group B elements are called transition elements. Elements with atomic numbers from 58 to 71 are called lanthanides, and elements with atomic numbers from 90 to 103 are called actinides. Families have similar chemical and physical properties. For example, the alkali metals are soft metals at room temperature; they are shiny, conduct electricity, and react vigorously with water, producing hydrogen (H_2) that burns from the heat produced by the reaction.

Rows and Families: They Get Trendy

Looking across a row (from left to right), or period, of the periodic table, or looking down a column, or family, one will see trends in element properties develop. Generally, moving across a row, atomic radii decrease, ionization energy (the minimal energy needed to remove an outermost electron from a neutral atom in the gaseous state) increases, and metallic properties diminish. Moving down a column, atomic radii increase, ionization energy decreases, and metallic properties remain the same or, in groups IIIA, IVA, VA, and VIA, decrease.

The Periodic Table and Electron Configuration

We learned in Chapter 1 that electrons are outside the atomic nucleus. Though we do not know the exact location of these electrons, we can use equations to determine the most probable location of the electrons. This most probable location or region in atomic space is called an orbital. Electrons fill into orbitals around the atomic nucleus. As the electrons fill into orbitals, they move farther from the nucleus. Their distance from the nucleus is described as their energy level, or shell. The first shell is closest to the nucleus. The periodic table organizes the elements according to their electron configurations.

Eight Is Great!

Atoms are most stable when they have eight outermost electrons, called valence electrons. Considering the group A elements as we move across the periodic table, each kind of atom has one more valence electron than the previous kind of atom. The alkali metals have one valence electron. The noble gases have eight valence electrons. Almost all of the elements want to be like the noble gases: They want some stability in their lives. Hydrogen (H) and helium (He) are exceptions to the eight-electron stability rule. Helium is quite stable with two valence electrons, and hydrogen can achieve stability by losing, gaining, or sharing one electron. Upon gaining or sharing an electron, hydrogen achieves the electron configuration of helium and is quite stable and content.

There are two principal ways for atoms to acquire eight outermost electrons: They can share electrons or they can transfer electrons. The alkali metals have one valence electron, and the alkaline earth metals have two valence electrons. It is easy for them to transfer these loosely held valence electrons to atoms needing only one or two electrons to achieve eight valence electrons. Electron transfer gives stability to the atoms. The halogens have seven valence electrons, and the atoms from the oxygen (O) family have six valence electrons. Between these families, we see a great possibility for electron transfer. Sodium (Na) loses an electron and chlorine (Cl) gains it. Magnesium (Mg) loses two electrons and oxygen gains them. Sharing electrons is a very compatible arrangement. Sharing of electrons also works to achieve a stable, eight-electron arrangement. Two oxygen atoms can share two valence electrons so that both atoms have eight valence electrons and an oxygen molecule (O_2) is produced. In the same way, two chlorine atoms can share a valence electron to have the magic number, eight, and a chlorine molecule (Cl_2) results.

The Periodic Table: An Organization of Atomic Electron Configurations

The outermost electrons in atoms fall into a neat pattern in the periodic table. All the group IA elements, the alkali metals, have one outermost electron. The group IIA elements, the alkaline earth metals, have two outermost electrons. group IIIA elements have three outermost electrons, group IVA have four, group VA five, group VIA six, group VIIA seven, and group VIIIA eight. A pattern emerges. By looking at the periodic table, the viewer can predict how atoms bond and, thus, determine molecular formulas. Oxygen atoms need two valence electrons to have eight, and hydrogen atoms can share one electron, so two hydrogen atoms will provide an electron arrangement good for all. Accordingly, the formula for water is H_2O.

4.4

Construction of a Three-Dimensional Periodic Table

Objectives

1. Students will construct a work of art based on a three-dimensional periodic table and using the principles of good composition.

2. Students will show that their periodic table includes all the information presented in a two-dimensional periodic table.

3. Students will debate the advantages of using their periodic table rather than a traditional periodic table.

Materials

Periodic table, scissors, string, tape, colored markers.

Time

50 minutes

Procedure

1. Have students cut a periodic table into portions appropriate for constructing a three-dimensional table.

2. Have students use string or tape, or both, to reconnect the parts of the table into a three-dimensional table that is more useful than the traditional table.

   ■ *Note:*
   To decrease the length of the table, the inner transition metals of the traditional periodic table should be cut out of their positions according to increasing atomic number. Students should include the inner transition metals in the main body of their three-dimensional table.

   One approach to constructing a three-dimensional periodic table is to arrange the elements by increasing atomic number in a spiral where families remain in a vertical relationship. Inner transition metals will be included in the main body of this three-dimensional periodic table and consider a table where the inner transition metals are included in the main table.

3. Have students use markers to color the various parts of the three-dimensional table to show important divisions and sections.

4. Display the three-dimensional periodic table in a prominent location.

Questions and Conclusions

Level One

1. Point out the following on the three-dimensional table: Atomic number (number of protons), mass number (relative weight), alkali metals, alkaline earth metals, transition metals, metalloids, nonmetals, halogens, noble gases, and rare earths.

2. Where would elements numbered 110 to 118 appear on the table?

3. As a three-dimensional work of art, is the table mainly solid (massive) or linear (made of thin, line-like parts)? Describe a famous work of art that resembles this table (refer to an illustrated book about art history for examples).

Level Two

1. Explain the advantages and disadvantages of the three-dimensional periodic table compared to a traditional table.

2. Sometimes hydrogen (H), by itself, is called a family. Point out where hydrogen is placed on the three-dimensional table. Why would hydrogen, by itself, be called a family?

3. How can the three-dimensional table include new elements as they are created in the laboratory? How will the table grow?

4. Using the three-dimensional table, explain why it is called a *periodic* table.

5. Explain why the three-dimensional table is not only useful but also an attractive three-dimensional work of art.

BONDS IN MARRIAGE AND IN ATOMS

Sharing, Transferring, and Bonding

A chemical bond is a force between atoms in particular forms of matter. When a sodium (Na) atom loses an electron, it acquires a positive charge. We call it a sodium ion (Na^+), or, in general, a cation. A chlorine (Cl) atom that receives an electron from a sodium atom acquires a negative charge. We call it a chlorine ion (Cl^-), or, in general, an anion. In science, opposites attract. A positive sodium ion is attracted to a negative chlorine ion, so they form a bond, specifically, an ionic bond. This bond is the force that allows the formation of sodium chloride (NaCl) as a cubic crystalline solid. In general, ionic bonds result when electrons are transferred from one atom to another. When two oxygen atoms share a pair of outermost electrons, a covalent bond results. For example, one chlorine atom can share an outermost electron with another chlorine atom. These two atoms are not oppositely charged, as is the case with sodium ions and chlorine ions. Here, the two chlorine atoms are held together by a covalent bond.

Covalent Bond or Ionic Bond: Eight Is Still Great

As discussed previously, many atoms are most stable with eight outermost electrons. Notice that when a sodium atom loses an electron and forms a sodium ion, eight outermost electrons remain. When a chlorine atom gains an electron, it has eight outermost electrons. It is not surprising that two chlorine atoms share an outermost electron to attain the magic number of electrons, eight, in their outer energy level, or shell. The noble gases have eight outermost electrons and are perfectly happy to remain alone. They do not want to bond. They remain single.

Classifying Crystalline Solids by Their Bonds

In Activity 4.1, students described and modeled crystalline solids according to the way their atoms packed into a regular structure. We found that their atoms could pack into face-centered, body-centered, or hexagonal-closest arrangements. Another way to understand the structure of a crystalline solid is to consider the bonding forces between its structural units.

Ionic Solids

Solids such as sodium chloride (NaCl) and zinc chloride ($ZnCl_2$) are made of ions that are held together by the attractive force of these oppositely charged particles. If ionic solids are dissolved in water, their ions are separated and can conduct an electric current. This physical property of ionic solids can be used to decide if a solid is held together by ionic bonds.

Molecular Solids

Molecular solids are crystalline solids where molecules are held together by weak electrical forces between molecules. These bonds between molecules are usually weaker than bonds within molecules. Molecular solids dissolved in water are not good electrical conductors. Examples of molecular solids are sulfur (S_8); phosphorus (P_4); and water, or ice (H_2O).

Bonds between H_2O molecules in ice are stronger than bonds between S_8 molecules and P_4 molecules. This is because H_2O is a polar molecule. The shape of the H_2O molecule and the intramolecular bonds (within the H_2O molecule) give the molecule positive and negative ends. The negative end of one H_2O molecule bonds to the positive end of another H_2O molecule and ice is formed (see Fig. 4.11). This intermolecular bond (between H_2O molecules) is called a hydrogen bond. We will look more closely at the shape of the H_2O molecule in Chapter 5.

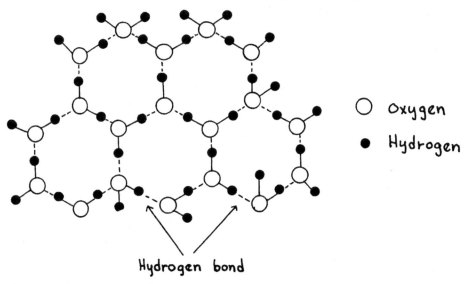

○ Oxygen

● Hydrogen

Hydrogen bond

Figure 4.11. Crystalline Structure of Ice.

Metallic Bonds

Metal atoms bond into solid structures because the positively charged metal ions attract free-flowing negative electrons. Metallic bonds have been described as uniformly arranged metallic cations surrounded by a sea of electrons. Needless to say, these mobile electrons provide good electrical conductivity.

Covalent Network Bonds

In covalent network solids, large numbers of atoms are held together by covalent bonds. The resulting particle structures are like large Tinkertoy constructions resembling spiders or centipedes in which the body is the central atom and the legs are bonds holding surrounding atoms in place. A common geometric shape for the atoms in a covalent network solid is the tetrahedron. The diamond form of carbon is a covalent network solid with tetrahedrally-

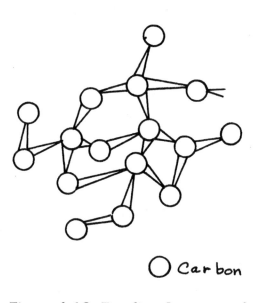

○ Carbon

Figure 4.12. Bonding Structure of Diamond.

bonded carbon atoms (see Fig. 4.12). More importantly, the molecule needed to make glass and glazes, silicon dioxide (SiO_2), found in sand and quartz, is covalently bonded in chains of SiO_4 molecules to make a network solid.

4.5

Solid Bonding and Clay Construction

Objectives

1. Students will model in clay a three-dimensional work of art that represents the bonding structure of a crystalline solid.

2. Students will discuss the differences and similarities in the four bonding structures of crystalline solids using the three-dimensional clay artwork.

Materials

Clay; toothpicks; descriptions of molecular, ionic, metallic, and covalent network bonding structures in solids (see "Classifying Crystalline Solids by Their Bonds," pp. 107–8). (Teachers should reproduce this section for student reference.)

Time

50 minutes

Procedure

1. Have students read descriptions of the four types of solid bonding structures and select one type to model in clay.

2. Have students make a model of the bonding structure using clay and toothpicks. The additive method of three-dimensional construction should be used (see "The Third Dimension: Additive and Subtractive Construction Methods," p. 87).

3. Have students label their model with the type of bonding structure represented.

Questions and Conclusions

Level One

1. For each type of bonding structure (molecular, ionic, metallic, and covalent network), describe the structural units in the solid and how they are bonded. How are the four types similar and different?

2. What are some examples of substances with these bonding structures?

Level Two

1. Explain the kind of attractive force, the bond, that holds the structural units together in each type of bonding structure.

2. Considering the types of bonds that each solid has, predict the following physical properties for each solid and explain your predictions:
   a. melting point
   b. electrical conductivity
   c. brittleness
   d. malleability and ductility
   e. hardness

3. Explain how the subtractive method of three-dimensional construction could be used to model the boding structure for a crystalline solid in clay.

Bond Types Determine Physical Properties

In marital bonds, the stronger the bond, the better the marriage. In chemical bonds, the stronger the bond, the higher the melting point. There is a similarity here. A strong bond results in a stable structure. Of the four types of bonding structures in a solid—covalent network, ionic, metallic, and molecular—covalent network solids have the highest melting points and molecular solids have the lowest. Most ionic solids have higher melting points than metallic solids. A high melting point means strong bonds. In the case of crystalline solids, the bonds are between the structural units.

The nature of the bonds between the structural units of crystalline solids impart other physical properties to these solids. Metals are good conductors of electricity because metallic bonds allow a free flow of electrons. Covalent network, molecular, and ionic solids do not conduct electricity because their bonds do not provide for mobile electrons. Remember, however, that ionic solids in a water solution have free electrons and are good conductors of electricity. Metallic solids are malleable and ductile; covalent network solids are brittle and hard. These differences in physical properties are caused by the chemical bonds between the units: It is all in the bonds!

THREE-DIMENSIONAL CONSTRUCTION: FORMING THE CLAY OBJECT

Many Ways with Clay

Just as crystalline solids are bonded in many ways, clay artwork may be constructed in a variety of ways. Many construction techniques are available, several of which are noted here. These methods may be used alone or combined, allowing the artist to create an endless variety of forms.

Pinch Pot: Press and Squeeze. This is the oldest and most basic method of producing a clay piece. A ball of clay is placed in the palm of the hand. With the other hand, the clay is pressed and squeezed between the fingers and thumb to produce a small vessel or container, usually with curved sides. The thickness of the walls of the piece is regulated and made uniform with the fingers. (See Fig. 4.13.)

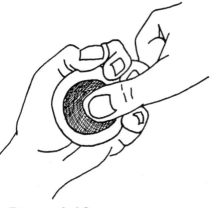

Figure 4.13.

Figure 4.14.

Coil Method: Roll, Press, and Smooth. In this construction technique, the clay is first rolled into a sausage-like string, which is then coiled and attached upon itself. The layers formed by the coiled clay are smoothed together, either inside or outside the piece, to hold the coil together. (See Fig. 4.14.)

Slab Method: Roll and Cut. In the slab method, the clay is rolled into a flat sheet using a rolling pin, the thickness being regulated with guide sticks. Pieces are cut from the sheet and assembled. (See Fig. 4.15.)

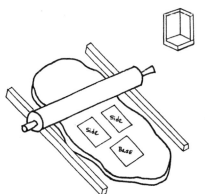

Forming in or on a Mold: Press and Form. In this method, wet clay is shaped over or pressed into a mold made of a material such as plaster. This is often done to duplicate a preexisting shape. (See Fig. 4.16.)

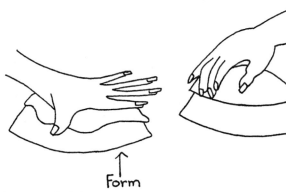

Figure 4.15.

1. roll out
2. cut out pieces
3. assemble

Figure 4.16.

Throwing or Forming on a Potter's Wheel: Pulling Up. A lump of clay can be formed or thrown on a potter's wheel. The wheel, whether manual or electric, consists of a flat, revolving, circular surface attached to a base. The revolution is controlled by a foot pedal or pump. Once the clay is centered on the wheel and the wheel is revolving, the clay can be pulled up with the hands and formed into a variety of shapes. This technique of forming clay, however, requires patience and practice and should not be attempted without first experiencing the other methods. (See Fig. 4.17.)

Figure 4.17. Electric Potter's Wheel.

Resources for Student Viewing

The following videos and films explain the many techniques of clay construction:

Ceramic Art: Handbuilding Methods. 18 min. Carlsbad, CA: CRM Films, 1968. 16mm film.

Craft of the Potter: Throwing. 25 min. New York: British Broadcasting (TV), 1983. Videocassette.

Daughters of the Anasazi. 28 min. Albuquerque, NM: (film project), 1990. Videocassette.

Introduction to Throwing on the Potter's Wheel. 53 min. Geneva, FL: Thoughtful, 1993. Videocassette.

Maria of the Pueblos. 15 min. Deerfield, IL: Centron Educational Films, 1971. 16mm film.

TEXTURE AS AN ELEMENT OF DESIGN IN CERAMICS

In this chapter, we have considered three-dimensional ceramic constructions and nature's three-dimensional crystalline structures and glasses. There are many similarities between the construction of a ceramic work of art and the construction of a crystalline solid or glass. In both cases, units are built into a structure. The units are bonded together in a variety of ways. Both can result in pleasing works for the viewer to enjoy. A quartz crystal, made of silicon dioxide (SiO_2), can be just as beautiful as a carefully crafted ceramic piece. Particular elements of design make these objects beautiful. When considering ceramic pieces and natural crystals, texture is an important element.

How Does It Feel and Look?

Texture can be seen all around us. Texture is the feel and the look of things. How does something feel? Soft, rough, and smooth are all examples of one type of texture called actual texture, or the actual surface of something. A second type of texture is visual texture, or the look of something. Dots, zigzag lines, stripes—these designs and many more can be arranged into patterns of visual texture.

Show students examples of visual and actual textures in two and three dimensions while discussing the following questions: Which examples have actual texture? Which examples have visual texture? What would be the result if visual textures were removed from the examples? How would you feel about the piece without its original texture? Which examples have both visual and actual textures? How do artists use visual and actual textures in their work? Can a sculpture have only visual texture? Why?

Examples of textures in two and three dimensions include the following artwork:

Lamp by Louis Comfort Tiffany, early twentieth century
Painting by Gustav Klimt, early twentieth century
Detail of cast-iron ornament from Carson Pirie Scott building
    (located on State Street, Chicago), Louis Sullivan, 1903–04
Architecture: Church of Sagrada Familia (Barcelona, Spain),
    Antoni Gaudi, 1883–1926
Painting by Henri Rousseau, early nineteenth century
Painting by Henri Matisse, early twentieth century
Sculpture by Constantin Brancusi, early twentieth century
Sculpture by Edgar Degas, early twentieth century
Wallpaper by William Morris, late nineteenth century
Architecture: Eiffel Tower, Gustave Eiffel, 1889
Acoma Native American Pottery
San Dominico Native American Pottery

4.6
Experimenting with Actual Textures

Objective

1. Students will create a variety of actual textures on clay using a variety of tools.

Materials

Water-based clay, rolling pin, variety of objects for pressing or scratching clay (paperclip, stick, pin, comb, burlap fabric, lace, string, Popsicle stick, pencil, etc.).

Time

30 minutes

Procedure

1. Have the students roll out the clay using a rolling pin or pat it flat with their hands.

2. Have students use the tools provided to scratch or press a variety of textures into the clay. They should try repeating patterns as well as overall textures.

4.7
Making Pinch Pots Using Actual Textures

Objectives

1. Students will create a three-dimensional clay form using the pinch pot method of construction.

2. Students will apply appropriate actual textures based on experimentation in Activity 4.6.

Level One:
Simple Pinch Pot

Materials

Water-based clay, sponge, various tools for making textures (see Activity 4.6), water, student prepared glaze (Activity 4.3), flat stick for smoothing clay, kiln.

Time

150 minutes construction, two to three days drying time, one day firing time, a second firing day after glazing

Procedure

1. Have students wedge a ball of clay to remove the air bubbles. The clay ball should be a size that can be easily held in one hand, no larger than a tennis ball.

2. Have students hold the ball of clay in one hand and press into it with the thumb of the other hand, gradually making the opening larger by pressing with the thumb and fingers until a desired size and shape are achieved. Students should try to keep the walls of the piece about ¼ inch thick.

3. Smooth the walls with a stick and a damp sponge.

4. Apply the texture, at this point if appropriate, or allow the piece to become leather-hard before applying the texture.

5. Allow the piece to dry thoroughly (to greenware state).

6. The teacher should fire the piece in a kiln.

7. Apply a glaze prepared in Activity 4.3 to the bisque ware.

8. The teacher should fire the piece in the kiln a second time.

Level Two:
Combination Pinch Pots

Materials

Same as level one.

Time

250 minutes construction, remainder of time same as level one

Procedure

1. Have students follow steps 1–3 from the procedure in level one, making two or three separate pinch pots. Students should try to vary the size of the pots.

2. Assemble the pinch pots to form a group (see Fig. 4.18). Wet all surfaces (both surfaces) that will touch and use a stick to score these areas with crosshatch marks. Press the pots together and add a small amount of wet clay to the outside of the joints for reinforcement.

3. Have students follow steps 4–8 from the procedure in level one.

Figure 4.18.

Clay is one of the most important building materials conceived by humanity. Without clay, little from our past would remain preserved. Without clay, we would have fewer beautiful works of art to enjoy; we would not have useful electrical insulators and other modern-day appliances. Recently, "high"-temperature, 90°K or -183°C, ceramic superconducting materials have been developed. Ceramic materials are used to make heat shields for space vehicles, such as the space shuttle. Clay is the material of the past and of the future. We will always be playing with clay.

REFERENCES

Arnason, H. H. *History of Modern Art: Painting, Sculpture, Architecture.* 3d ed. New York: Harry N. Abrams, 1986.

Camusso, Lorenzo, and Sandro Bortone. *Ceramics of the World.* New York: Harry N. Abrams, Inc., 1991.

Chavarria, Joaquim. *The Big Book of Ceramics.* New York: Watson-Guptill, 1994.

Hofsted, Joyon. *Step by Step Ceramics.* New York: Golden Press, 1967.

Horn, George F. *Elements of Design: Texture.* Worcester, MA: Davis, 1974.

Lee, Ruth. *Exploring the World of Pottery.* Chicago: Childrens Press, 1967.

Lundkvist, Husberg. *Making Ceramics.* New York: Van Nostrand Reinhold, 1967.

Nigrosh, Leon. *Claywork Form and Idea in Ceramic Design.* 2d ed. Worcester, MA: Davis, 1986.

Roussel, Mike. *Clay.* East Sussex, England: Wayland, 1989.

Weiss, Harvey. *Ceramics from Clay to Kiln.* New York: Young Scott Books, 1964.

NOTES

1. Lorenzo Camusso and Sandro Bortone, *Ceramics of the World* (New York: Harry N. Abrams, Inc., 1991), 18.

2. Ruth Lee, *Exploring the World of Pottery* (Chicago: Childrens Press, 1967), 34.

3. Ibid., 25.

4. Steven S. Zumdahl, *Chemistry*, 2d ed. (Lexington, MA: D. C. Heath, 1989), 438.

5

Sculpture and
Organic Chemistry

Macroscopic and Microscopic Sculpture

INTRODUCTION

Organic chemistry is the study of compounds that contain carbon (C). Carbon atoms have a strong affinity for each other. Like children playing "crack the whip," during which they hold hands to bond in an endless variety of kinetic shapes, carbon atoms bond together in long chains to form an endless variety of organic molecules. We would expect the other members of the carbon family, such as silicon (Si), to form long-chain molecules by bonding with each other. However, silicon atoms are larger than carbon atoms and fit better into a silicon-oxygen bond arrangement than a silicon-silicon bonded molecule. Silicon atoms bond with oxygen (O) atoms in a network arrangement to form silicates.

In Chapter 4, we learned how silicates give clay its plastic properties. In this chapter, we will see how carbon atoms bond in chain arrangements to produce organic compounds that can have the plastic properties of clay. We will study sculpture and describe molecular forms as sculptures. Finally, we will see how organic molecules, microscopic sculptures, have the same properties as macroscopic sculptures, which are visible to the naked eye.

MACROSCOPIC
SCULPTURE

Sculpture: Form in the Round

Everyone has seen sculpture. It is all around us: In the park or as part of the front of a building, in an art museum, on a table in a living room, in the lobby of an office building, or for sale in a department store and art gallery. Even if it is as small as a piece of jewelry or as large as Mt. Rushmore, we can see it. We are also surrounded by invisible sculpture. Organic compounds made of chains of carbon atoms form the unseen sculptures that are the molecules of living objects. These microscopic sculptures express the same elements of design as the macroscopic sculptures that we see all around us.

It's Sculpture: But What Is It?

Macroscopic sculpture, the sculpture we see around us, can be realistic or representational, like paintings and drawings, meaning it is similar to or resembles an observed subject. It may also be non-objective, a piece not based on any observed subject matter. It may be abstract, a term used to describe forms created by the artist based on actual subject matter, but altered or distorted in some way. Sometimes in an abstract work, there is little resemblance to the original subject, causing the viewer to ask, "What is it?" Microscopic sculptures, organic compounds, may be non-objective, representing only their atomic arrangement (determined by their atom types and their bonds types), or abstract, resembling actual subject matter. However, abstract microsculptures are not meant to resemble an observed subject. They represent a composition of matter. Finally, some macrosculptures are called kinetic because they have moving parts. All microsculptures are kinetic because molecules are always in motion, unless they are reduced to a temperature of absolute zero, a state at which, theoretically, all molecular motion stops.

Examples of Sculpture by Professional Artists

Any African sculpture (abstract)
Any work of Henry Moore (abstract), twentieth century
Any Native American totem pole (wood, abstract)
Any Italian Renaissance sculpture (realistic)
Greek Parthenon frieze (marble relief, realistic), fifth century
Statue of Liberty (copper sheet over steel frame, realistic), nineteenth century.
    (Steel frame—Gustave Eiffel, Artist—Frederic Bartholdi.)
Any nonobjective mobile by Alexander Calder (kinetic), twentieth century
Any sculpture by David Smith (non-objective), twentieth century
Life Death (neon, abstract, kinetic), Bruce Nauman, 1983
Any piece of jewelry by Salvador Dali (abstract), twentieth century

THE ELEMENTS OF SCULPTURE

The Shape of Things: Shape As an Element of Design

Most forms of sculpture have shape as a common element of their construction. Shapes appear in all forms of art. Paintings and drawings contain shape as an element of their composition. Shapes describe subject matter. Shapes, whether realistic, abstract, or non-objective, can be curvilinear, angular, organic-based, based on natural forms (free-form), or geometric. Shapes can express movement, direction, emotion, or mood. The following examples of art contain shape expressing movement, direction, emotion, or mood:

Two-Dimensional Shapes

The Red Horseman, Roy Lichtenstein, 1974
Composition in White, Black and Red, Piet Mondrian, 1936
Guernica, Pablo Picasso, 1937
The Harlequin Carnival, Joan Miro, 1924–25
Nude Descending the Staircase, Marcel Duchamp, 1912
The Starry Night, Vincent van Gogh, 1889

Three-Dimensional Shapes

The Bird, Constantin Brancusi, 1914
Black Beast, Alexander Calder, 1940

5.1

Exploration of Shape

Objectives

1. Students will identify organic and geometric shapes.

2. Students will compare and contrast the characteristics of various types of shapes.

Level One: Organic and Geometric Shapes

Materials

Reproductions of the example artwork listed above (or other reproductions with shapes expressing movement, direction, mood, and emotion).

Time

30 minutes

Procedure

1. Have students view the reproductions of example artwork and answer the following questions for each:

   a. Describe the shapes you see in the piece. What feelings or emotions do they suggest?

   b. Are the shapes organic (free-form) or geometric?

   c. If the organic shapes were changed to geometric and the geometric shapes were changed to organic, how would this affect the intent of the work?

   d. Do you think the artists are successful in expressing their ideas through the use of the shapes? Explain.

Level Two: Organic to Geometric

Materials

4-x-24-inch drawing paper, ruler, pencil, magazines or original drawings by students.

Time

50 minutes

Procedure

1. Have students choose a realistic image from a magazine or an original drawing. The image should be an organic shape (e.g., an animal or a plant).

2. Have students orient the paper so the long edge is horizontal and divide the sheet into six 4-x-4-inch squares.

3. Draw the realistic image in the leftmost rectangle (see Fig. 5.1).

4. Choose a geometric shape and draw it in the rightmost rectangle. This geometric shape should be very different from the shape in the leftmost rectangle.

5. Use the three remaining rectangles to transform the realistic, organic image in the leftmost rectangle into the geometric shape in the rightmost rectangle. Each drawing should gradually change the subject from a realistic, organic image to a geometric image.

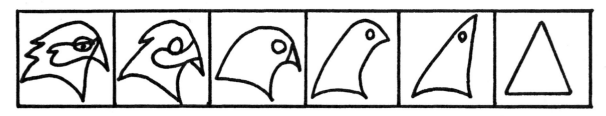

Figure 5.1.

MICROSCOPIC SCULPTURES: ORGANIC MOLECULES AND SCULPTURE ELEMENTS

Organic molecules are minute, non-objective sculptures, or are considered abstract when they resemble familiar, identifiable objects. They have shapes that are curvilinear, angular, or geometric (or a combination). Just as in macroscopic sculptures, these shapes can express movement and direction. If one considers organic molecules to be amazing tiny sculptures of the stuff of which matter is made, such a microsculpture can evoke an emotion or set a mood in the same way that a macrosculpture evokes emotions and sets moods.

THE NAMES AND SHAPES OF ORGANIC MOLECULES

Count the Carbon Atoms

The simplest class of organic compounds are hydrocarbons. As the name implies, these are carbon molecules that contain carbon (C) atoms and hydrogen (H) atoms. In Chapter 4, we learned that carbon atoms form covalent bonds with other carbon atoms. Carbon atoms have four outermost electrons and, therefore, four bonding sites. A carbon atom can share its four electrons with four other atoms. Remember, eight is great! Atoms are comfortable with eight outermost electrons. In hydrocarbons, carbon atoms will bond with each other to form chain and/or cyclic molecules. Then, hydrogen atoms step into the remaining, unoccupied bonding sites.

Carbon atoms can bond in an infinite number of arrangements. They can bond in straight chains. They can add branches to these straight chains. They can bond in cyclic arrangements. Hydrocarbons can have only single bonds; they can have double bonds in which two pairs of electrons are shared; and they can even have triple bonds—sharing of three pairs of electrons is possible. With all these possible arrangements, it is necessary to have a simple hydrocarbon naming system.

To discern how many carbon atoms are in a straight chain or branch of a carbon compound, prefixes are used. If all the carbon-carbon bonds are single bonds, the hydrocarbon name ends in -*ane*. These molecules are called alkanes. If there is a double carbon-carbon bond, the name ends in -*ene*. These molecules are called alkenes. If there is a triple carbon-carbon bond, the name ends in -*yne*. These molecules are called alkynes.

Table 5.1 lists the names and formulas of the first 10 unbranched, sometimes called normal, alkanes, alkenes, and alkynes. Photocopy and distribute this table to students. As students study this table, they should look for relationships between the number of carbon atoms and the number of hydrogen atoms in the various hydrocarbons. They will soon discover that the general formula for alkanes is C_nH_{2n+2}, the general formula for alkenes is C_nH_{2n}, and the general formula for the alkynes is C_nH_{2n-2}.

Table 5.1
Names and Formulas of Alkanes, Alkenes, and Alkynes

Alkanes		Alkenes		Alkynes	
Name	**Formula**	**Name**	**Formula**	**Name**	**Formula**
Methane	CH_4	None		None	
Ethane	C_2H_6	Ethene	C_2H_4	Ethyne	C_2H_2
Propane	C_3H_8	Propene	C_3H_6	Propyne	C_3H_4
Butane	C_4H_{10}	Butene	C_4H_8	Butyne	C_4H_6
Pentane	C_5H_{12}	Pentene	C_5H_{10}	Pentyne	C_5H_8
Hexane	C_6H_{14}	Hexene	C_6H_{12}	Hexyne	C_6H_{10}
Heptane	C_7H_{16}	Heptene	C_7H_{14}	Heptyne	C_7H_{12}
Octane	C_8H_{18}	Octene	C_8H_{16}	Octyne	C_8H_{14}
Nonane	C_9H_{20}	Nonene	C_9H_{18}	Nonyne	C_9H_{16}
Decane	$C_{10}H_{22}$	Decene	$C_{10}H_{20}$	Decyne	$C_{10}H_{18}$

Hydrocarbons Are Shapely Molecules

As discussed previously, each carbon atom in a hydrocarbon has four bonding sites. This is because the four outermost carbon atom electrons are seeking four additional electrons to have the comfortable arrangement of eight outermost electrons. Hydrogen atoms are the ideal companions for carbon atoms. Each hydrogen atom can offer one electron to a carbon atom. If one carbon atom bonds with four hydrogen atoms, methane (CH_4) is formed. The angle between each of the bonds in the carbon atom is 109.5°, which results in the formation of a tetrahedral-shaped molecule. When carbon atoms bond to each other, they form zigzag chains. If hydrogen atoms are bonded to the carbon atoms, they will project from the carbon atoms and form a molecule shaped like a caterpillar with projections. In alkenes, with one double bond, and alkynes, with one triple bond, the tetrahedral shape becomes distorted.

In Activity 5.2, students will build models of various alkanes, alkenes, and alkynes and view these molecules as sculptures that exist in nature on a microscopic level. They will consider these shapes as an element of sculpture design.

5.2

Modeling Hydrocarbon Molecules— Microscopic Sculptures

Objectives

1. Students will model hydrocarbon molecules and observe their shapes.

2. Students will describe how the molecular models represent chemical formulas.

3. Students will discuss the rules for naming simple (normal) hydrocarbons.

4. Students will view the molecular models as microscopic sculptures and explain why they are either abstract or non-objective.

Materials

Ball-and-stick molecular-model building kit, protractor, drawing paper, colored pencils.

Time

100 minutes

Procedure

1. Have students work in groups to research the chemical formulas for and build models of the following molecules: Methane, propyne, pentene, butane, ethyne (acetylene).

   Use a four-hole ball with the holes equally spaced to represent a carbon atom, and use a one-hole ball to represent a hydrogen atom. Use sticks for single bonds, and springs for double or triple bonds. Students should measure the bonding angle between the carbon and hydrogen atom in the methane molecule.

2. Label each model as either a non-objective or an abstract sculpture.

3. Using colored pencils, draw each model.

4. With colored pencils, make either a non-objective or an abstract drawing using at least one molecular model.

Questions and Conclusions

Level One

1. Explain how to write a chemical formula using a hydrocarbon name (see Table 5.1). In the explanation, describe the general formulas and rules for naming alkanes, alkenes, and alkynes.

2. Explain why a four-hole ball is used to represent a carbon atom, and why a one-hole ball is used to represent a hydrogen atom.

3. What is the bond angle between the carbon atom and a hydrogen atom in the methane molecule? Is this angle the same for all the carbon-hydrogen bonds in methane?

4. What is the shape of the methane molecule?

5. How does the shape of a chain of carbon atoms change when a molecule has one double bond and one single bond? Why are springs used to represent double and triple bonds?

6. For each of the molecular models, explain your choice for labeling it as a non-objective or abstract sculpture. For each of your drawings, explain why it is a non-objective or abstract work of art.

7. Explain how the shapes in your artwork show movement, direction, emotion, or mood.

Level Two

1. Write the chemical formulas for an alkane, an alkene, and an alkyne, each containing 25 carbon atoms, and explain how you derived the formulas.

2. Considering the tetrahedral shape of methane, construct a multiple-methane-molecule sculpture, or draw a picture of such an arrangement. Explain why the sculpture or drawing is abstract or non-objective. How do the shapes in the sculpture or drawing evoke a mood or emotion? How do the shapes show direction or movement?

3. Considering the length of a chain of carbon atoms in a hydrocarbon molecule, theorize how the length of a carbon chain might influence hydrocarbon physical properties such as boiling point, melting point, and density.

SHAPE IN MACROSCULPTURES AND IN MICROSCULPTURES

Shape Can Determine Properties

Just as shape is a common and essential element in the construction of a sculpture, the shape of a molecule is extremely important in determining the physical and chemical properties of a substance. For the alkanes, as the number of carbon atoms in the molecule increases, thereby increasing the molecular weight, the boiling point and the melting point of the substances increase. This would indicate that intermolecular forces, the attractive forces between molecules, increase as the number of carbon atoms and the molecular weight of the alkane molecules increase.

Weak Intermolecular Forces: London, Dipole-Dipole, and Van der Waals

Because unbranched alkanes are neutral, nonpolar molecules, it is difficult to explain the existing intermolecular force between such alkanes that increases as the alkane molecules become larger. We will see that this attractive force is weak and tenuous. These molecules do not become overly friendly with each other. In theory, as atoms within one alkane molecule approach the atoms of another alkane molecule, the electrons around these atoms, for an instant, arrange themselves asymmetrically around the atoms so that instant dipoles are formed—the positive side of one atom attracts the negative side of another atom. This weak intermolecular attractive force is called a London Force. When there is a weak intermolecular attractive force between polar molecules, the force is called a dipole-dipole force and together, London forces and dipole-dipole forces are called Van der Waals forces.

Another theory explaining an increase in boiling and melting points with increases in alkane molecular weight caused by the addition of carbon atoms is that the longer-chain molecules intertwine like strands of spaghetti. Additional energy is needed to untangle these long-chain alkane molecules and allow melting and boiling to take place.

Normal, Straight, or Unbranched Chains; Branched Chains or Cyclic Molecules: Microscopic Sculptures Have a Variety of Shapes

Our discussion has centered around hydrocarbon molecules that consist of carbon atoms bonded to each other in long chains. These chains are called normal, straight, or unbranched. The chains may have only single bonds (alkanes), double bonds (alkenes), or triple bonds (alkynes). Hydrocarbons with only single bonds are called saturated; hydrocarbons with double or triple bonds are called unsaturated. Not all hydrocarbons want to form straight chains. After all, who among us wants to be straight and serious all the time? Some of us will always be comedians. In the world of hydrocarbon molecules, the comedians are the branched and cyclic molecules.

Naming the Straight Hydrocarbons and Naming the Comedians

In a straight-chain hydrocarbon, the name of the hydrocarbon prefix indicates the number of carbon atoms in the chain; the suffix indicates the kind of bonds—single, double, or triple—in the chain. For a branched hydrocarbon molecule, the location of the branch is indicated by a number, then a word ending in -*yl* indicates how many carbon atoms are in the branch (the prefixes to indicate number of carbon atoms are, in order from one through ten: *meth-*, *eth-*, *prop-*, *but-*, *pent-*, *hex-*, *hept-*, *oct-*, *non-*, *dec-*), then the remaining straight chain is named as if it were a straight-chain molecule without a branch. Sounds simple, right? This is why we call branched molecules comedians. However, it is not as confusing as it sounds. Just one more rule: Carbon atoms in the straight chain, the longest unbranched chain of carbon atoms, are numbered to give the branch the lowest possible number.

The best way to learn to name branched hydrocarbon molecules is to apply the rules to an example molecule:

$$\underset{6}{\overset{1}{CH_3}} - \underset{5}{\overset{2}{CH_2}} - \underset{4}{\overset{3}{CH_2}} - \underset{3}{\overset{4}{CH_2}} - \underset{2}{\overset{5}{CH_2}} - \underset{1}{\overset{6}{CH_3}}$$

(correct numbering)

(incorrect numbering)

$$CH_3$$

The correct numbering shows us that the branch comes from the third carbon atom in the straight chain. Therefore, the hydrocarbon name begins with the number 3. There is one carbon atom in the branch, so the branch name begins with *meth-* and ends in -*yl*—methyl.

The straight chain has six carbon atoms (*hex-*) with only single bonds (*-ane*), so it is named hexane. Put it all together and we have 3-methylhexane.

When a hydrocarbon has more than one branch, the branches are named as indicated above, beginning with the branch of smallest number. For example:

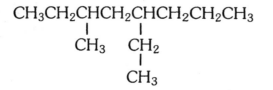

This hydrocarbon is named 3-methyl 5-ethyloctane. In this octane molecule, if both branches were methyl branches, the name would be 3,5 dimethyl octane.

Cyclic (or ringed) hydrocarbons are simply named with the prefix *cyclo-* followed by an ending that is determined by how many carbon atoms are in the molecule. For example, a ringed hydrocarbon molecule containing five carbon atoms and only single bonds would be named cyclopentane. If the same molecule had a double bond between two carbon atoms in the ring, the name would be cyclopentene.

Hydrocarbon Molecules: An Infinite Number of Microsculptures

An endless variety of hydrocarbon molecules can be constructed. Each molecule will have different physical and chemical properties. For example, gasoline is made of hydrocarbon molecules having from five to ten carbon atoms. When smaller-chain hydrocarbon molecules and branched hydrocarbon molecules are added to the gasoline, a car engine works more smoothly. Each hydrocarbon molecule has unique properties and a unique structure. We can consider a hydrocarbon molecule as a microsculpture having a unique shape. We will examine shape further and understand the relationship between shape and branched and cyclic hydrocarbon molecules.

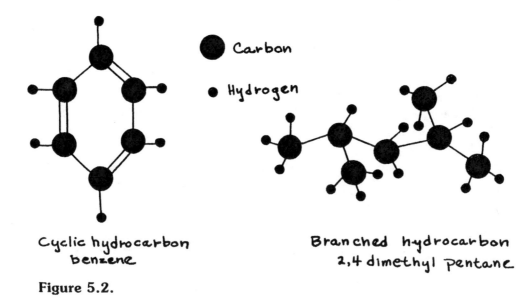

Cyclic hydrocarbon
benzene

Branched hydrocarbon
2,4 dimethyl pentane

Figure 5.2.

When Is Shape Not a Shape?
Positive and Negative Shapes

The shapes of objects in a work of art are considered positive shapes. These are the shapes drawn, painted, or sculpted by the artist as the subject of the work. However, works of art have other shapes that are of great importance to the success of a composition.

In Chapter 1, a discussion of composition included both positive and negative shapes. In a two-dimensional picture, the negative shapes are the spaces remaining around the subject. In a sculpture, the negative space is the space surrounded by the sculpture material. Negative space, as well as positive space, should be interesting in size and shape. The negative space, however, should not overpower the positive space.

The following artwork exhibits positive and negative space:

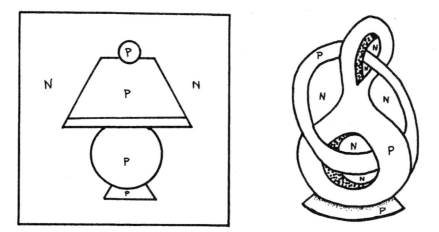

Figure 5.3. Negative (N) and Positive (P) Space.

Two-Dimensional Artwork

The Old Guitarist, Pablo Picasso, 1903
Eight Bells, Winslow Homer, 1886
Whaam, Roy Lichtenstein, 1963
Boy in Red Vest, Paul Cezanne, 1890–95
A Ballet Seen from an Opera Box, Edgar Degas, 1885
The Card Players, Paul Cezanne, 1892

Three-Dimensional Artwork

Walking, Alexander Archipenko, 1912
The Three Shades, Auguste Rodin, 1880
King and Queen, Henry Moore, 1952–53
Statuette: Dressed Ballerina, Edgar Degas, 1922

Activity 5.3 will acquaint students with positive and negative space in macrosculptures (two- and three-dimensional works of art) and in microsculptures (unbranched, branched, and cyclic hydrocarbon molecules).

5.3

Examination of Negative and Positive Shapes in Macrosculptures and in Microsculptures

Objectives

1. Students will identify positive and negative shapes in two- and three-dimensional works of art (macrosculptures) and in unbranched, branched, and cyclic hydrocarbon molecules (microsculptures).

2. Students will list ways in which negative space can enhance a two-dimensional work of art.

3. Students will construct models of hydrocarbon molecules (three-dimensional microsculptures) and describe the negative space that surrounds these sculptures in terms of size, shape, and relationship to positive space.

Materials

Pencil, tracing paper, magazines, reproductions of two-dimensional artwork using positive and negative space, ruler, ball-and-stick molecular-model building kit. (Comment: Don't use Styrofoam balls—correct bond angle holes are needed for tetrahedral shape.)

Time

60 minutes

Procedure

1. Have students point out positive and negative shapes in the examples and answer the following questions:

   a. Is the negative space interesting? Why?

   b. Is there too much or too little negative space? Explain your answer.

   c. Do the positive shapes fill the space successfully? Explain your answer.

2. Have students choose an example or a picture from a magazine and place a sheet of tracing paper over it.

3. Draw the perimeter of the picture on the tracing paper.

4. Trace the outline of positive shapes in the picture.

5. Using pencil, darken in the negative spaces, leaving the positive shapes white.

6. Have students observe the arrangement of the positive shapes and negative shapes.

7. Have students build ball-and-stick models of the following molecules: Unbranched—methane (CH_4), branched—2-methyl 4-ethylhexane (C_9H_{20}), and cyclic—cyclohexane (C_6H_{12}) and identify positive and negative space.

Questions and Conclusions

1. How can negative space enhance a picture? How can negative space overpower a picture?

2. Explain the qualities of the negative space in the molecular models constructed (in terms of size, shape, and relationship to positive space) and arrange the models as a microsculpture, making good use of the negative space.

PRINCIPLES OF GOOD COMPOSITION IN THREE-DIMENSIONAL SCULPTURE

What Makes It Work?

Regardless of the subject matter, a successful three-dimensional sculpture should have the following characteristics:

Variety. The sculpture should possess an interesting silhouette and interesting interior negative space.

Unity. As the negative space is viewed from various angles, there should be a continuity of design. The eye should move easily from view to view.

Interest. The sculpture should be interesting from all angles.

Truth in Materials. The piece should be appropriate in design for the material from which it is made. A piece designed for stone would not work well in wire. The material should fit the idea.

Catalysts and Negative Space

A catalyst is a special chemical substance that, when viewed as a microsculpture, has many of the characteristics of a successful three-dimensional sculpture; mainly variety, unity, and interest. A catalyst is a chemical substance that accelerates the rate of a chemical reaction but is not itself changed into a product. The catalyst is not consumed in the chemical change. If the catalyst is viewed as a microsculpture, it is the negative space of this microsculpture that is involved in the catalyst mechanism for changing the rate of a chemical reaction. This can be illustrated either with heterogeneous or homogeneous catalysts. Heterogeneous catalysts are catalysts present in a phase, solid, liquid, or gas, different from the phase of the reactants; and homogeneous catalysts are present in the same phase as the phase of the reactants. Both heterogeneous and homogeneous catalysts operate on the same principle; a reactant particle, a molecule atom or ion, bonds with a catalyst particle similar to a key fitting into a lock. When the door is open, the key is removed. (The bond breaks.) Some homogeneous catalyst systems involve large, complex, organic molecules. In the case of such homogeneous catalyst molecules, the catalysts are called enzymes and the reactants are called substrates. The enzymes bind with the substrates and form complexes. Referring to the lock key analogy, the key represents the positive space of the substrate and the lock (keyhole) representing the negative space of the enzyme. For most catalysts, how they affect the reaction rate of the reactants is dependent upon the geometry of the reactants. Most catalysts operate in a lock-and-key manner.

Locks and Keys:
Catalysts and Positive and Negative Space

When a heterogeneous catalyst is considered, platinum (Pt) often comes to mind. The platinum surface provides the right geometry for particular molecules to adhere to and easily react with other molecules. The platinum surface is a microsculpture in which the negative space is filled with reactant substances, and reaction rate is accelerated. The following examples show specifically how platinum works as a catalyst.

Sulfur dioxide (SO_2) is oxidized to sulfur trioxide (SO_3) when sulfuric acid (H_2SO_4) is prepared. This process would be very slow without the use of a platinum catalyst. When the platinum catalyst is used, oxygen molecules are adsorbed on the platinum surface, where they dissociate into very reactive oxygen (O) atoms. The oxygen atoms are situated on the platinum-surface negative space, from which an SO_2 molecule can pluck an oxygen atom and escape as an SO_3 molecule (see Fig. 5.4). The following chemical change has occurred [$_{(g)}$ denotes "gas"]: $2SO_2{}_{(g)} + O_2{}_{(g)} \rightarrow 2SO_3{}_{(g)}$. An intermediate step involves the oxygen (O_2) dissociating into separate oxygen atoms with the aid of the platinum surface. The reactants and product are in the gas phase and the catalyst is a solid, thus making the platinum a heterogeneous catalyst. If we consider the catalyst, the platinum, as being a microsculpture metal surface having an attractive shape and size, the shape and geometry of the microsculpture's negative space is essential to the catalyst in enhancing the reaction rate. Considering the lock-and-key principle of catalyst operation, the platinum is the lock (keyhole) and the reactant O_2 molecule is the key. The platinum catalyst's negative space is invaded by the O_2 reactant, providing a new, simple pathway to the formation of products. An uncatalyzed reaction pathway would be more complex and, thus, take longer.

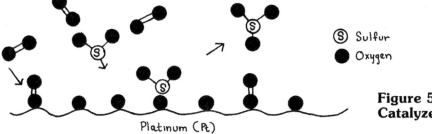

Platinum (Pt)

Ⓢ Sulfur
● Oxygen

Figure 5.4. Using Platinum to Catalyze the Formation of SO3.

WHAT IS MATERIAL TO THE SCULPTURE?

Truth in Materials

An important consideration for a three-dimensional macrosculpture is selecting the material from which the sculpture will be made. For example, the Statue of Liberty would not be effective as a wire sculpture. The function of the Statue of Liberty is to welcome travelers to the New York harbor as a gateway to the United States. In wire, the statue would be missed entirely by travelers. The materials used in a sculpture can determine its success or failure as a work of art. In Activity 5.4, students will be instructed about the use of plaster, sometimes called plaster of Paris, as a medium for three-dimensional macrosculpture. The preparation of plaster of Paris and the chemical changes that occur during preparation are discussed.

5.4
Plaster Three-Dimensional Macrosculpture

Objectives

1. Students will create three-dimensional macrosculptures appropriate for the plaster medium.

2. Students will use principles of good three-dimensional composition (variety, unity, interest, truth in materials).

3. Students will write chemical equations for the formation of plaster of Paris from gypsum from plaster.

4. Students will distinguish between exothermic and endothermic chemical reactions.

5. Students will work with non-objective volume and mass in planning and executing a macrosculpture.

Level One:
Simple Free-Form, Non-Objective Plaster Form

Materials

Plaster of Paris, heavy-duty aluminum foil, X-ACTO knife, plaster files, sandpaper, soft cloth or towel, spoon. Steps 1 through 4, three days drying time before step 5.

Time

90 minutes

Procedure

1. Have students use their hands to bend or crumple a segment of aluminum foil into a non-objective depression deep enough to hold plaster. The foil may be depressed with a spoon to create smoother areas. Place a soft cloth or towel beneath the foil to avoid breaking it.

2. Have students prepare the plaster and pour it into the depression.

3. Allow the plaster to become hard but still damp, then remove the foil from the plaster.

4. While the form is still damp, use an X-ACTO knife to gently refine the piece and define the shape. Some areas may need to be removed to create a more pleasing silhouette for the piece. Students should try to incorporate negative space into the piece.

5. When dry, use files and then sandpaper to create a smooth finish for desired areas.

Level Two:
Sculpture Carved from a Block of Plaster

Materials

Plaster of Paris, paper cup or half-gallon milk or juice carton, sandpaper, plaster files, X-ACTO knife, kitchen knife.

Time

150 minutes steps 1-4, three to five days drying time before step 5.

Procedure

1. If using milk or juice cartons, have students remove the tops.

2. Have students prepare the plaster and pour it into the cup or carton.

3. Allow the plaster to become hard but still damp, then remove the cup or carton from the plaster.

4. Have students choose a realistic, abstract, or non-objective subject, or a picture of a sculpture to use as a subject, and begin carving the plaster while it is still damp, using X-ACTO and kitchen knives. Students should try to incorporate negative space into the piece.

5. After carving a general, rough design, allow the piece to dry completely. This may take several days.

6. When dry, use files and then sandpaper to refine the form.

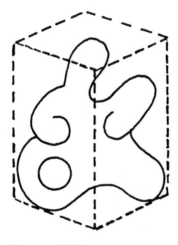

Figure 5.5.

Level Three:
Hand-Held Plaster Sculpture

Materials

Same as level two, but omit the cup or carton.

Time

200 minutes steps 1 through 4, three to five days drying time before step 5.

Procedure

1. Have students mix the plaster to a thick, creamy, smooth consistency.

2. Have students cup their hands to receive a blob of plaster. Students should hold the plaster in their hands until it begins to set.

   ■ *Warning!*
   Students should not dig their fingers into the plaster because it may be difficult to remove them as the plaster sets.

3. Have students remove their hands and allow the plaster to set until it hardens but is still damp.

4. Use X-ACTO and kitchen knives and plaster files to refine the shape. It is best to create a non-objective piece. The shape is dictated by the plaster as it continues to harden. Students should try to incorporate negative space into the piece.

5. When dry, use sandpaper to refine the surface.

Questions and Conclusions

1. Identify negative space in your plaster forms.

2. Explain how your plaster form illustrates the principles of a good three-dimensional sculpture: Variety, unity, interest, and truth in material.

3. Write a chemical equation for the formation of plaster of Paris from gypsum. (See Plaster of Paris: A Hot Item.)

4. Write a chemical equation for the formation of gypsum from plaster of Paris. (See Plaster of Paris: A Hot Item.)

Forming wet plaster

Completed piece

Figure 5.6.

Examples of Professional Sculpture

Crouching Man (stone), Andre Derain, 1907
The Newborn (marble), Constantin Brancusi, 1915
Princess X (marble), Constantin Brancusi, 1916
The Miracle (marble), Constantin Brancusi, 1924
Joie de Vivre (bronze), Jacques Lipchitz, 1927
Human Lunar Spectral (bronze), Jean Arp, 1957
Reclining Figure (stone), Henry Moore, 1929

Plaster of Paris: A Hot Item

The plaster used in Activity 5.4, plaster of Paris ($CaSO_4 \cdot 1/2H_2O$), has interesting chemical properties. It is derived from gypsum ($CaSO_4 \cdot 2H_2O$), which is used to make cement and pottery and, in a more purified form, chalkboard chalk. When gypsum is heated, it loses three-fourths of its water (H_2O) content and becomes plaster powder. (Comment: Liquid refers to a pure substance in the liquid state. The water in the $CaSO_4$ is loosely bonded to the $CaSO_4$ to form a crystalline solid.)

gypsum → plaster of Paris + water

$$CaSO_4 \cdot 2H_2O_{(s)} \rightarrow CaSO_4 \cdot 1/2H_2O_{(s)} + 3/2H_2O_{(g)}$$

In this reaction, water from the solid $_{(s)}$ gypsum is released in gas $_{(g)}$ form. It is an endothermic reaction (energy is absorbed). The reverse reaction, in which liquid $_{(l)}$ water is added to the plaster of Paris, is exothermic (energy is released):

plaster of Paris + water → gypsum

$$CaSO_4 \cdot 1/2H_2O_{(s)} + 3/2H_2O_{(l)} \rightarrow CaSO_4 \cdot 2H_2O_{(s)}$$

While hydrating plaster of Paris, students feel heat—the energy being released by the hydration of the plaster.

How Much Heat Is Released?

We can calculate just how much heat is released when plaster is mixed with water using a concept called *heat of reaction*. Heat of reaction, symbolized ΔH, is derived from the heat of formation, $\Delta H_{(f)}$, of the reactants and products in a chemical change. Heats of formation values, $\Delta H_{(f)}$, are compiled on special thermodynamic tables and expressed using the unit kilojoules per mole (kj/mole). The heats of formation of plaster of Paris, gypsum, and water are -1575.2 kj/mole, -2021.1 kj/mole, and -285.8 kj/mole, respectively. To find the heat of the reaction, it is necessary to subtract the heat of formation of the reactants from the heat of formation of the products:

$$\Delta H = \Sigma \Delta H_f \text{ Products - } \Sigma H \Delta_f \text{ Reactants}$$

For the formation of plaster of Paris, the calculation would be:

$$\Delta H = (-2021.1) - (-1575.2 - 428.7)$$

$$\Delta H = -17.2 \text{ kj/mole}$$

From the equation for the formation of plaster of Paris: $CaSO_4 \cdot 2H_2O_{(s)} \rightarrow CaSO_4 \cdot 1/2H_2O_{(s)} + 3/2\ H_2O_{(g)}$ it can be seen that 3/2 mole of H_2O is produced. Since $\Delta H_{(f)}$ values are given in kj/mole, the value for water (-285.8) must be multiplied by 3/2 before the ΔH value for the formation of plaster of Paris is calculated.

When ΔH is negative, the reaction is exothermic. When ΔH is positive, the reaction is endothermic. In the formation of plaster of Paris, the reaction is exothermic. 17.2 kj/mole plaster of Paris are released. There is enough energy released for students to feel the heat.

Other Macrosculpture Materials— Plastic Possibilities

Chemists have been combining small, simple hydrocarbon molecules into long-chain complex molecules for many years. The process is called polymerization and the resulting product is called a plastic. When a simple, small hydrocarbon molecule like ethene (C_2H_4) is polymerized, polyethylene results: $CH_2{=}CH_2 \rightarrow CH_2(CH_2)_nCH_2$. (Comment: The two horizontal bars denote a double bond between the carbon atoms.) This is the product that is used to make transparent wrap, flexible bottles, and thousands of other products. In addition, polyethylene makes an outstanding macrosculpture material. It can be molded into an endless variety of interesting shapes. It can be colored or left clear.

Polyethylene is formed by addition of C_2H_4 molecules, which are merely linked together without the elimination of any reactant atoms. When other polymers are formed, molecules are linked together and particular atoms break loose to form additional products. When water (H_2O) is the additional product, the reaction is called a condensation reaction. Often, the reactants are not simple hydrocarbons but are more complex organic molecules. The formation of nylon is a condensation polymerization reaction. In Activity 5.5, students will prepare a condensation polymer and use it to create a macrosculpture.

5.5

Preparation of a Polymer

Warning! Due to the toxicity of some reactants, this activity should be performed under a hood. (Groups of students can do this.)

Objectives

1. Students will learn how to prepare a plastic substance.

2. Students will write and explain the equation for the formation of nylon, a condensation polymer.

Materials

250 ml beaker, 50 ml beaker, 25 ml graduated cylinder, tweezers, cardboard, bare thread spool, seven pellets NaOH (sodium hydroxide), 1.3 g (25 drops) (hexamethylene diamine), 1.0 ml (sebacoyl chloride), 50.0 ml CCl_4 (carbon tetrachloride), distilled water, eye dropper, food coloring.

Time

120 minutes

Procedure

Have students prepare nylon, a condensation polymer:

1. Make a cardboard form in a shape to be used for a nylon thread sculpture (the nylon thread will be wrapped around the shape). The shape should be interesting and have a variety of negative space. It may be objective or non-objective.

2. Place seven pellets NaOH into 50.0 ml distilled water in a 50 ml beaker.

3. Add 1.3 g (25 drops) of hexamethylene diamine and a drop of food coloring.

4. Place 1.0 ml of sebacoyl chloride in 50.0 ml of carbon tetrachloride in a 250 ml beaker.

5. Slowly pour the water solution into the carbon tetrachloride solution. Pour it along the side of the larger beaker.

6. Using tweezers, grasp the center of the film (nylon) that forms at the interface of the two solutions. Slowly pull the nylon from the beaker.

7. Wrap the nylon thread around the cardboard form to make a sculpture. Thoroughly wash the sculpture.

8. Additional nylon thread should be wrapped around a bare thread spool, washed, and saved for Activity 5.6.

Questions and Conclusions

Level One

1. Write a word equation for the formation of nylon. Why is this reaction called a condensation reaction?

2. In the preparation of polyethylene, ethene molecules (C_2H_4) are bonded together to form a long carbon chain, with two hydrogen atoms bonded to each internal carbon atom and three hydrogen atoms bonded to the end carbon atoms. Draw polyethylene and explain why the formation of polyethylene is an addition reaction.

3. Explain how your nylon thread sculpture incorporates the elements of good three-dimensional composition (variety, unity, interest, truth in materials).

Level Two

1. Using a chemical equation for the formation of nylon from reactants adipic acid and hexamethylene diamine, explain why this is a condensation reaction (see Formulation of Nylon below).

2. Unsaturated hydrocarbons are more likely to form polymers by addition reactions than saturated hydrocarbons. Explain why.

3. Describe how threads such as nylon can be used to create a three-dimensional work of art.

4. Describe a design for a sculpture in which nylon would be the appropriate material to use.

Formation of Nylon

The formation of nylon using adipic acid and hexamethylenediamine takes place as follows:

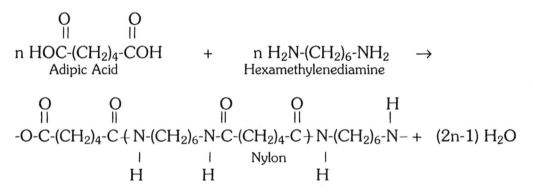

In Activity 5.5, we condensed hexamethylene diamine with sebacoyl chloride, another way of producing nylon. In the polymerization using adipic acid, it can be seen that we no longer have hydrocarbon molecules. Nitrogen (N) and oxygen (O) appear in the molecules combined. When we add nitrogen and oxygen atoms to hydrocarbon molecules, we create molecules with an immense number of different properties, both physical and chemical. When combined with hydrocarbon chains, the following groups of atoms, called functional groups, produce familiar substances (R represents a hydrocarbon chain of any length):

Table 5.2
Functional Groups

Functional Group Structure	Family Name	Examples
R-OH	Alcohol	Methanol: For rubbing
$$\begin{matrix} O \\ \| \\ R\text{-}C\text{-}OH \end{matrix}$$	Carboxylic Acid	Acetic Acid: Vinegar
R-O-R′	Ether	Diethyl Ether: Anesthetic
$$\begin{matrix} O \\ \| \\ R\text{-}C\text{-}H \end{matrix}$$	Aldehyde	Formaldehyde: Preservative
$$\begin{matrix} O \\ \| \\ R\text{-}C\text{-}R′ \end{matrix}$$	Ketone	Acetone: Solvent
$$\begin{matrix} O \\ \| \\ R\text{-}C\text{-}O\text{-}R′ \end{matrix}$$	Ester	Pentyl Acetate: Banana odor
$$\begin{matrix} H & R′ & R″ \\ \| & \| & \| \\ R\text{-}N\text{-}H & R\text{-}N\text{-}H & R\text{-}N\text{-}R′ \end{matrix}$$	Amine	Methylamine: Organic base

EXPANDING ON ORGANIC MOLECULES: FUNCTIONAL GROUPS MAKE A DIFFERENCE

Organic molecules have a wide variety of structures that can result in innumerable sizes, shapes, and varieties of microsculptures. Each functional group presents a new shape and size to a molecule, and within each family are endless opportunities for molecular types. For each functional group, a change in the number of carbon atoms in the hydrocarbon chain will affect the physical and chemical properties of the resulting substances. For example, methanol (CH_3OH), an alcohol with one carbon atom, is used for external purposes such as rubbing on the skin but is extremely poisonous if taken internally. Ethanol (C_2H_5OH), however, an alcohol with two carbon atoms, can be enjoyed, in moderation, as a beverage. What a world of difference one carbon atom makes. Just as the addition of one atom in a molecule changes the physical and chemical properties of a substance, the addition of one element in a macrosculpture changes the mass, volume, size, balance, and unity of the artwork.

THE KINETIC WORLD
OF MOBILES AND MOLECULES:
KINETIC SCULPTURE

The type of sculpture that incorporates motion and change into the artistic expression is called kinetic sculpture. We call some kinetic sculptures mobiles: The works of Alexander Calder immediately come to mind. Some of his mobiles are constructed of geometric and organic shapes connected by wires so that a slight breeze will move the shapes into an endless variety of positive and negative space relationships. Like a Calder mobile, molecules are in constant motion (except at absolute zero, a temperature at which, theoretically, all molecular motion ceases), behaving like microscopic mobile parts. In the solid state, they vibrate. In the liquid state, they rotate. In the gaseous state, they translate, moving from place to place while rotating and vibrating. Molecular motion represents nature's kinetic sculpture. In Activity 5.6, students will make a mobile that exhibits movement and balance, with a theme to provide unity.

5.6

Mobile Making

Objectives

Students will construct a mobile sculpture that exhibits the principles of good three-dimensional composition (variety, unity, interest, and truth in materials) using prepared nylon thread.

Materials

Large, colored glass or plastic beads; colored posterboard; X-ACTO knife; rigid 12- or 14-gauge wire; nylon sewing thread (prepared in Activity 5.5) or fishing line; examples of mobiles pictured in art books (see list at the end of this chapter); craft glue; needlenose pliers, wire cutters; ruler.

Time

150 minutes

Procedure

1. Use colored glass or plastic beads and cut additional shapes from colored posterboard, create several mobile pieces.

2. Look at examples of mobiles pictured in art books (Alexander Calder mobiles are engaging examples). If additional ideas are needed, visit a local library to find books about mobile construction.

3. Draw a picture of the mobile to be constructed. Students should show enough detail that construction will be possible using the drawing as a reference.

4. Cut rigid 12- or 14-gauge wire into lengths about two centimeters longer than necessary to construct the planned mobile. Make a loop at each end of each wire.

5. Using nylon sewing thread (prepared thread in Activity 5.5) or fishing line, tie pieces made from posterboard and colored beads to each loop and secure with a dot of glue.

6. Attach nylon thread or fishing line to the middle of each wire and move it back and forth to find the center of balance. Secure the thread to the wire at this point with a dot of glue.

7. Construct a balanced mobile, following the drawing. It is easiest to begin at the lowest section of the mobile, balance

Figure 5.7.

that section, and then work toward the top, balancing each additional section as it is added.

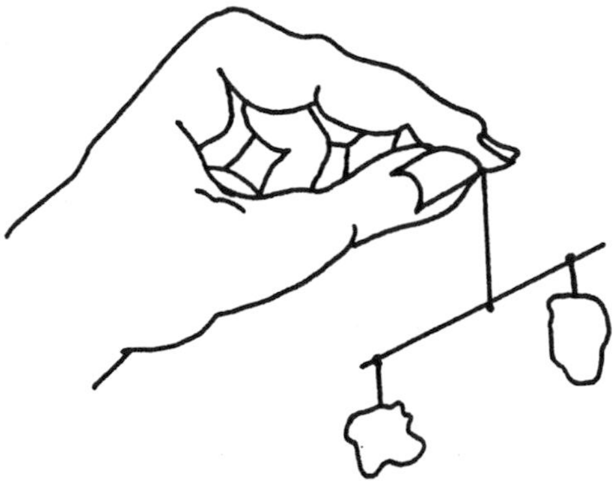

Questions and Conclusions

1. Discuss each of the elements of good composition in a three-dimensional sculpture (variety, unity, interest, and truth in materials) as it applies to your mobile.

2. Explain the new relationships in space that are created as your mobile moves. Consider positive and negative space.

3. Is a kinetic sculpture more complex than a motionless three-dimensional sculpture? Explain your answer.

4. Explain how the three-dimensional periodic table constructed in Activity 4.4 is a kinetic sculpture.

LINE

Line: A Dot Drawn Out

When a chemist looks at X-ray diffraction pictures of atoms, pictures for which X-rays are bounced off atoms, the chemist sees an array of dots in a definite pattern on an X-ray film. This indicates to the chemist that atoms, in a solid, are arranged in a precise order. When artists look at an X-ray diffraction film showing a precise arrangement of dots, they may recall a style of painting known as pointillism. In pointillism, an artist places tiny dots of many colors close together so that from a distance the viewer sees a merging of the dots into shapes and images in a variety of graduated colors. Lines are not used in such a work. The relationship between lines and dots is important to consider when the visual elements of a painting are examined. When is a line not a line? When it is a dot. By definition, a line is the path of a moving point, or dot. So a line is a mark made by a tool or instrument drawn across a surface.

A line can represent the edge of something. In the case of a work by Georges Seurat, the edge of a set of dots represents a line. A line can be used to separate one area from another. Line is used to communicate information in many ways: We write our name or a note to a friend using line. Artists draw with pencil, pen, and paint, using lines to form objects and express ideas. Line does not exist in nature; it is an invention, an abstraction developed to represent what we see and what we want to communicate. The eye interprets line when it is actually the edge of the viewed object.

The Personality of a Line

Line has personality, just like people. The personality of a line is expressed by its size, type, direction, location, and character. The character of the line can come from the medium. A charcoal line will be different in character from a wire line. Lines are short or long, wide or narrow, curved, straight, wavy, or jagged. They cross a painting's surface, move up and down, in and out, and back and forth. A line may unify or divide. Lines can show a variety of character, depending on the tool used to create the line. A brush stroke line is very different in character than one made with a pencil. Line can express emotion and feeling.

5.7
An Examination of Line in Art

Objective

1. Students will identify different characteristics of line as seen in example reproductions of professional two- and three-dimensional artwork and as seen in the film.

Materials

Reproductions of the following examples of line artwork may be used in a discussion and examination of line:

Two-Dimensional Artwork

Lavender Mist, Jackson Pollock, 1950
Big Painting, Roy Lichtenstein, 1965
The Red Tree, Piet Mondrian, 1908
The Jungle, Henri Rousseau, 1908
Any drawing by Leonardo da Vinci
Any Japanese brush painting
Any woodcut by Albrecht Dürer

Three-Dimensional Artwork

Linear Construction No. 2 (lucite and monofilament), Naum Gabo, 1970–71
Monument for V. Tatlin (fluorescent tube), Dan Flavin, 1966–69
Man Walking III (metal), Alberto Giacometti, 1960
Spiral Jetty (environmental sculpture, stone), Robert Smithson, 1970
Linear Construction Variation (plastic and nylon thread), Naum Gabo, 1942–43
Star Cage (steel), David Smith, 1950
1-2-3-4-5 (painted aluminum), Sol le Witt, 1980

16mm film

The Dot and the Line. 9 min. Wilmette, IL: Distributed by Films Inc., 1969

Time

60 minutes

Procedure

1. Have students view reproductions of the artwork suggested or similar works.

2. Divide the class into groups, each with an example reproduction or the film, and have them answer these questions:

   a. Describe the lines used in terms of size, type, direction, location, and character.

   b. What do you feel when looking at the lines in the work?

   c. Discuss the types of shapes and lines seen in the film *The Dot and the Line.*

   d. In *The Dot and the Line*, what feelings were expressed by the dot? By the line?

5.8
Descriptive Line

Objective

1. Students will use paper and writing materials to draw colored lines that express particular emotions.

Materials

8½-x-11-inch paper, ruler, colored markers or colored pencils.

Time

30 minutes

Procedure

1. Divide a sheet of paper into eight spaces. The spaces do not have to be equal in size or shape. Be creative!

2. Using the colors available, draw an expressive non-objective line or lines to express these feelings: Weariness, loneliness, happiness, fear, excitement, confusion, nervousness, and sadness.

Questions and Conclusions

1. How does color affect the emotion expressed by a line or lines?

2. How does the shape of a line or lines affect the emotion portrayed?

3. Look at one space on your paper. How did you use line to communicate a particular emotion?

4. How do the size and placement of a line or lines affect the emotion evoked?

5. Discuss how dots or contrasting colors can be used to suggest a line to the eye. Make a small sketch of a such a line.

Lines Take Us into the Third Dimension: A Study in Depth on a Flat Surface

We have been examining line as a way to define space and describe emotion. There is an additional function that line can serve in artistic expression—allowing the artist to represent the third dimension on a flat surface. Depth on a flat surface can be achieved through the use of two systems: Atmospheric perspective and linear perspective.

Atmospheric Perspective

In atmospheric perspective, line is not used. Perspective, distance, or space is achieved on a flat surface using the following techniques:

1. Objects are portrayed to be overlapping one another. Overlapping objects appear closer to the viewer than overlapped objects.

2. More detail is used for objects that would appear closer to the viewer than for objects that would appear more distant.

3. Greater intensity of color is used for objects that would appear closer to the viewer than for similar objects that would appear more distant.

4. Larger size is used for objects that would appear closer to the viewer than for objects that would appear more distant.

Examples of pictures illustrating these techniques can be found in magazines or may be demonstrated on a chalkboard or with the use of an overhead projector.

Linear Perspective

As the word *linear* suggests, line is used in linear perspective, a mechanical system developed centuries ago during the Italian Renaissance. The following terms outline this system:

Eye Level. The position at which the viewer's eyes are located in relationship to the subject viewed. Objects directly in front of the viewer are at the eye level of the viewer. Objects are above eye level, other objects are below eye level.

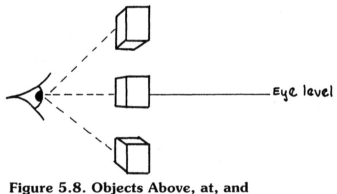

Figure 5.8. Objects Above, at, and Below Eye Level.

Horizon Line. The place in the distance where the sky and the earth appear to meet.

Vanishing Point. The point or points on the horizon line at which an object will disappear as it moves away from the viewer into the distance.

In one-point linear perspective, the lines of vision come together at one point on the horizon line. In two-point linear perspective, the lines of vision come together at two points on the horizon line.

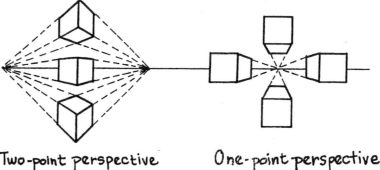

Two-point perspective   One-point perspective

Figure 5.9.

5.9

One- and Two-Point Linear Perspective— Discussion and Exercise

Objectives

1. Students will observe the procedure for creating one- and two-point linear perspective.

2. Students will use the procedures for creating linear perspective.

3. Students will identify the use of one- and two-point perspective in works of art by well-known professional artists.

4. Students will draw the guidelines to the vanishing point or points for objects in one- and two-point perspective.

Materials

Reproductions of artwork in one- and two-point perspective (see below), video about linear perspective or explaining how to draw in linear perspective (see list at the end of this chapter), 8½-x-11-inch paper, pencil, glue or tape, scissors, ruler, magazines.

Artwork in One-Point Perspective

The Parquet Layers, Gustave Callebotte, 1875
The Last Supper, Leonardo da Vinci, 1495–98
The Scream, Edvard Munch, 1893
Boulevard Monmartre Rainy Weather Afternoon, Camille Pissarro, 1897
Delivery of the Keys, Pietro Perugeno, 1482

Artwork in Two-Point Perspective

The Letter, Jan Vermeer, 1666
The Glass of Absinthe, Edgar Degas, 1876
The Dancing Couple, Jan Steen, 1663
Pope Pius VII in the Sistine Chapel, Jean Auguste Dominique Ingres, 1810

Time

150 minutes

Procedure

1. The teacher should show one of the videos and discuss linear perspective.

2. The teacher should show reproductions of artwork and ask the following questions:

   a. Does this picture use one- or two-point perspective?

   b. Where is the horizon line?

   c. Where is the subject in relation to the horizon line?

   d. Where is the vanishing point or points?

   e. What is the effect of the perspective on the composition?

3. Have students look through magazines to find a depiction of an object in one-point perspective and a depiction of an object in two-point perspective.

4. Have students cut out and tape or glue the pictures to two separate sheets of paper.

5. For each picture, have students use a ruler to draw a horizon line across the page in the proper position relative to the object depicted. The object will be above, at, or below the horizon line.

6. For each picture, have students determine the vanishing point or points for the object and draw guidelines to the point or points for the object.

5.10

Line As an Element of Three-Dimensional Sculpture

Objectives

1. Students will use nylon thread to create a three-dimensional sculpture incorporating line as an element of design.

2. Students will combine nylon thread with other materials to create sculptures.

3. Students will observe the principles of good three-dimensional composition.

Level One:
Non-Objective Geometric Sculpture

Materials

Various colors of posterboard, small hand-held hole punch, X-ACTO knife, illustration board, nylon thread prepared in Activity 5.5 (or purchased nylon thread), glue, scissors.

Time

60 minutes

Procedure

1. Have students choose a geometric shape and cut it from a piece of colored posterboard. The minimum size should be 6 x 6 inches.

2. Using an X-ACTO knife, cut a second shape from the center of the first shape, leaving a negative space. Discard the smaller shape. The center negative opening should be considerably smaller than the original shape. For example, if the larger shape is 6 x 6 inches, the smaller opening should be no larger than 3 x 3 inches.

3. Using a hand-held hole punch, punch holes around the edge or edges of the negative space.

4. Using nylon thread, weave a linear design into the negative space by threading it through the punched holes and across the space. Glue the ends of the thread into place.

5. Cut a square of illustration board to use as a base. A new shape may be used for the base, or its shape may be a repetition of one of the shapes already used.

6. Cut a slit in the center of the base and insert the sculpture.

7. Additional woven posterboard pieces may be added to create a more complex sculpture.

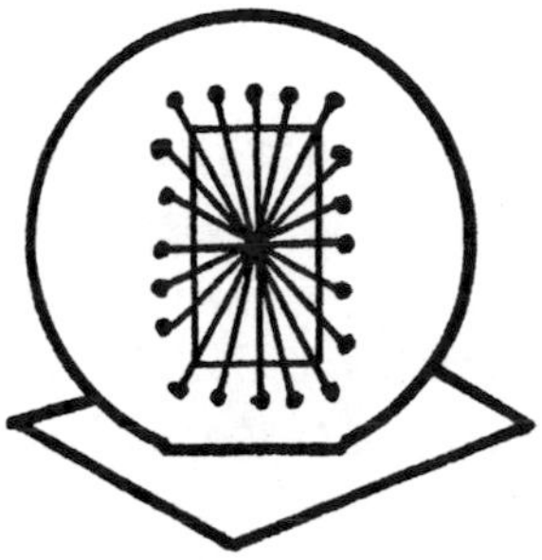

Figure 5.10.

Level Two: Modular Linear Sculpture

Materials

Craft glue, ⅛-square-inch strips of balsa wood, cardboard scraps, X-ACTO knife, colored posterboard, nylon thread prepared in Activity 5.5 (or purchased nylon thread).

Time

200 minutes

Procedure

1. Have students choose a module or shape as a theme (a shape such as a rectangle, triangle, or square works well).

2. Using the theme shape as the basis for all the shapes to be used in the sculpture, create a series of units (suggested number is seven or nine) in a variety of sizes and proportions from strips of balsa wood glued together. The shapes should be linear. Students should vary the size and proportion of the shapes, but all shapes should be variations of the theme shape.

Figure 5.11.

3. Using craft glue, attach completed units to one another, creating a linear sculpture.

4. Glue the sculpture to a base cut from colored posterboard.

5. To add a textured effect, choose three or more (but not all) of the units and wrap nylon thread around them, securing the thread with glue. Students should wrap the units in various directions. If preferred, shapes may be wrapped before the units are attached to one another.

Macrosculptures, three-dimensional works of art, are found just about anywhere people congregate. They make our world a pleasant and interesting place. Not all sculptures are made by artists: Plants and geologic formations provide us with natural three-dimensional macroscopic sculptures. Atoms and molecules are viewed at the microscopic level. We have been referring to these sculptures as microsculptures because they have never been viewed directly. We only see photographic imaging of refractive rays from these microsculptures—molecules, ions, and other combinations and forms of atoms—all of which have attributes of the visible macrosculptures: They provide interior negative as well as positive space for interesting viewing from every direction. They often show repetition and continuity of design. They are in constant motion, having kinetic properties of mobiles. Best of all, as chemical changes occur, these microsculptures change into new sculptures. Just imagine how a molecular microsculpture garden might appear to the human viewer: It certainly would not be boring!

REFERENCES

Arnason, H. H. *History of Modern Art: Painting, Sculpture, Architecture.* 3d ed. New York: Harry N. Abrams, 1986.

Cole, Alison. *Perspective.* London; New York: Dorling Kindersley, 1992.

Cortel, Tine, and Theo Stevens. *Basic Principles and Language of Fine Art,* trans. Tony Burrett and Carla van Splunteren. London: David Newton and Charles Abbot. New York: Distributed by Sterling, 1989.

DK Art School. *An Introduction to Perspective.* London; New York: Dorling Kindersley, 1991.

Greenberg, Jan, and Sandra Jordan. *The Sculpture's Eye.* New York: Delacorte Press, 1993.

Janson, H. W. *History of Art.* 4th ed. New York: Harry N. Abrams, 1991.

Kent, Sarah. *Composition.* London; New York: Dorling Kindersley, 1995.

Lynch, John. *How to Make Mobiles.* New York: Viking Press, 1966.

Meilach, Dona Z. *Creating with Plaster.* New York: Galahad Books, 1966.

Opie, Mary Jane. *Sculpture.* London; New York: Dorling Kindersley, 1994.

Selleck, Jack. *Elements of Design: Line.* Worcester, MA: Davis, 1974.

Walker, John. *The National Gallery of Art.* New York: Harry N. Abrams, 1975.

BOOKS ON MOBILES

1. Arnason, H. H. *Calder.* Princeton, NJ: Van Nostrand, 1966.

2. Lynch, John. *How to Make Mobiles.* New York: Viking Press, 1966.

3. Marchesseay, Daniel. *The Intimate World of Alexander Calder.* Solange Thierry, éditeur, Paris; New York: Distributed by Harry N. Abrams, 1989.

4. Schegger, T. M. *Make Your Own Mobiles.* New York: Sterling, 1971.

5. Wiley, Jack. *Designing and Constructing Mobiles.* Blue Ridge Summit, PA: Tab Books, 1985.

6. Zarchy, Harry. *Mobiles.* Cleveland, OH: World, 1966.

VIDEOS ON PERSPECTIVE

1. Brommer, Gerald. *Basic Perspective Drawing.* 29 min. 19 sec. Aspen, CO: Crystal, 1996.
    How to make one-point and two-point perspective drawings using boxes, landscapes, and buildings as subjects.

2. *Perspective.* Narrated by Marty Lewis. 8 min. 1996.
    Defines one-point, two-point, and atmospheric perspective and how to use them.

6

Jewelry

Heavy Metal

INTRODUCTION

We are in the midst of a frenzied jewelry-wearing revolution! The old rules for wearing jewelry are changing overnight. Men wear jewelry as conspicuously as women. Baseball players as well as other male athletes wear jewelry. Jewelry is often displayed by insertion into a wide variety of pierced body parts by both sexes. Jewelry is worn by men and women on all occasions and at any time of day or night.

Sculpture in Miniature

Jewelry, or pieces of metal, stone, or other materials worn for ornamental purposes, has existed for centuries and represents one of the oldest crafts known to humanity. Jewelry is a form of sculpture in miniature. Many pieces, if enlarged, would be successful decorative pieces. For our purposes, we will address jewelry made of metal, although many other materials, such as beads, feathers, fiber, stone, wood, clay, paper, leather, glass, and natural objects, are used to make a wide range of modern jewelry. The metals most suitable for jewelry are the heavy metals, metals of high density, such as gold, silver, and copper.

From the Beginning

Jewelry, in addition to being worn for ornamentation, has many other purposes. During early times, before the invention of the button and zipper, a brooch, pin, or buckle provided a means for attaching pieces of clothing. Jewelry held magical properties for ancient tribes. The earliest items date to the time of the Paleolithic peoples.[1] Many cultures of the ancient world, including those of Mesopotamia, Egypt, Greece, and Rome, created exquisite handmade pieces of gold and precious and semi-precious stones. In many cultures, jewelry represented status or wealth because of its rarity and value.

During the Middle Ages and into the Renaissance in Europe, jewelers became highly skilled in many jewelry-making techniques; they developed elaborate pieces of various metals, often set with a multitude of stones. Through the seventeenth and eighteenth centuries, jewelry was worn primarily by the rich and privileged. It was not until the early nineteenth century that techniques for electroplating base metals with a thin layer of gold or silver were developed. Improvements were also made in the quality of imitation stones.[2] This, in turn, led to the creation of inexpensive pieces of jewelry. By the late nineteenth century, all classes of people could afford inexpensive pieces of jewelry. Quality pieces, however, were still reserved for the privileged.

METALS:
A UNIQUE SET OF PHYSICAL AND
CHEMICAL PROPERTIES

In Chapter 4, we learned that the known elements can generally be divided into two classes, metals and nonmetals. On the periodic table, the elements are arranged by increasing atomic number in rows and columns. As these rows and columns are generated, the elements with metallic properties fall on the left side of the table and the elements without metallic properties fall on the right side of the table. In Activity 6.1, we will examine the physical and chemical properties of metals to understand why they are so often the material of choice in jewelry making.

6.1

The Physical and Chemical Properties of Metals

Objectives

1. Students will perform chemical experiments to discover and document the physical and chemical properties of various metals.

2. Students will find regularities in physical and chemical properties of metals as related to each metal's position on the periodic table, and then predict which metals might be useful for jewelry making.

Materials

Small samples of copper (Cu), tin (Sn), lead (Pb), antimony (Sb), bismuth (Bi), aluminum (Al), sodium (Na) (preserved under mineral oil), calcium (Ca), zinc (Zn), and iron (Fe); emery cloth; wooden mallet; tongs; Bunsen burner or candle; matches; 0–300°C thermometer; 5 ml of each of the following acids: 3.0 M H_2SO_4 (sulfuric acid), 3.0 M HCl (hydrochloric acid), and 3.0 M HNO_3 (nitric acid); voltmeter and electrodes; 100 ml graduated cylinder; centigram balance; thread; phenolphthalein solution; small test tubes; distilled water; eye dropper; a periodic table; Tables 6.1 and 6.2 (page 150).

Time

80 minutes

Procedure

Physical Properties

■ *Note:*
Use Table 6.1, page 150, to record physical properties.

A. Color:

1. Remove oxides and other contaminates from all the metals except sodium by polishing them with emery cloth.

2. Observe and record the color of each metal.

B. Malleability:

1. Hammer each metal except sodium with a wooden mallet.

2. Record the malleability of each metal.

C. Conductivity—Heat and Electricity:

1. Using tongs, heat a small piece of each of the following metals in the flame of a Bunsen burner or candle for three minutes: Aluminum, zinc, copper, lead, and tin.

2. Place a thermometer bulb on the surface of the metal, being careful not to touch the hot metal, and record the metal's temperature.

3. Using electrodes connected to a voltmeter, test the electrical conductivity of tin, lead, antimony, bismuth, aluminum, calcium, zinc, copper, and iron. Record the voltage generated by each completed circuit.

D. Density:

1. Determine the density of tin, lead, antimony, copper, zinc, and aluminum metals as follows:

   a. Mass to 0.10 g each metal sample. Record each mass.

   b. Fill a 100 ml graduated cylinder about one-third full with tap water. Record the volume of water in the cylinder to the 0.50 ml.

   c. Tie a thread around a metal sample. Carefully lower it into the graduated cylinder below the water level. Record the new volume of water. Repeat this process for each metal sample.

   d. Determine the volume of each metal by subtracting original water volume from final water volume. (This is a method for determining the volume of an irregular object by water displacement.)

   e. Calculate the density of each metal by dividing the metal's mass by the metal's volume.

Chemical Properties

■ *Note:*

Use Table 6.2, page 150, to record chemical properties.

A. Reaction of metal with oxygen:

1. Using tongs, burn a small sample of each of the following metals in the flame of a Bunsen burner or candle for about one minute: Copper, iron, aluminum, lead, and zinc.

2. Record the color of each metal.

B. Reaction of metal with water:

1. Place a small sample of each of the following metals into test tubes and add enough distilled water to cover each sample: Copper, tin, lead, antimony, bismuth, aluminum, calcium, zinc, and iron. Let the test tubes stand for several minutes, then record observations.

2. Under a hood, place a tiny piece of sodium (a cube about 2 x 2 millimeters) in 2 ml distilled water and observe the reaction. Record observations.

3. Add a few drops of phenolphthalein solution to the test tube and observe and record the results.

4. Add phenolphthalein solution to each metal-in-water solution and record results.

C. Reaction of metal with acid:

■ *Warning!*
Acids can be damaging to skin.

1. In small test tubes, react separately small pieces of copper, tin, lead, antimony, bismuth, aluminum, calcium, zinc, and iron, each with 2 ml 3.0 M HCl, then with 2 ml 3.0 M H_2SO_4, then with 2 ml of 3.0 M HNO_3. Record observations of these reactions.

Questions and Conclusions

Level One

1. On the periodic table, find each metal tested and circle it.

2. For each metal, list the color, conductivity (voltage for electrical conductivity and temperature, °C, for heat conductivity), and density. State any relationship observed between the metal's position on the periodic table and the physical properties listed. Do metals in the same family have similar physical properties?

3. Research the physical properties of other elements in the same family as the tested metals and describe any trends in physical properties.

4. Which families of the periodic table have the most chemically active metals? Explain your answer.

5. What combinations of metal plus water turned phenolphthalein red?

6. Considering the malleability of the metals tested, which metals would be good candidates for jewelry making?

7. How would a metal's ability to react with oxygen, water, or an acid affect its use in jewelry making?

Level Two

1. Why is sodium kept under mineral oil?

2. What families in the periodic table have the most chemically reactive metals?

3. What area of the periodic table is home to the least reactive metals?

4. When phenolphthalein turns red, a base is present. Explain how a metal plus water can produce a basic solution.

5. Why is most jewelry made of alloys and not pure metals? What metal is most often combined with silver to make an alloy useful in making silver jewelry?

6. Design a piece of jewelry and then describe pure metals or alloys that should be used to construct this jewelry. Explain your choice of metals.

Table 6.1
Physical Properties of Metals

Metal	Color	Mallability	Conductivity		Density
			Heat	**Electricity**	
Copper (Cu)					
Tin (Sn)				X	
Lead (Pb)				X	
Antimony (Sb)			X		
Bismuth (Bi)			X		X
Aluminum (Al)					
Sodium (Na)		X	X	X	X
Calcium (Ca)			X		X
Zinc (Zn)					
Iron (Fe)			X		X

Table 6.2
Chemical Properties of Metals

Metal	Reaction with H_2O	Reaction with O_2	Reaction with HCl	Reaction with H_2SO_4	Reaction with HNO_3
Copper (Cu)					
Tin (Sn)		X			
Lead (Pb)					
Antimony (Sb)	X	X			
Bismuth (Bi)		X			
Aluminum (Al)					
Sodium (Na)		X	X	X	X
Calcium (Ca)		X			
Zinc (Zn)	X				
Iron (Fe)	X				

The Physical and Chemical
Properties of Metals Revisited

We now know that metals are shiny, conduct heat and electricity, are malleable, and react with oxygen, water, and acids. Because they possess these physical and chemical properties in varying degrees, we must examine in more detail how these properties make metals the material of choice in jewelry making.

A Burning Bracelet

In Chapter 4, we learned that within a family on the periodic table, the elements have similar chemical and physical properties. From working with sodium (Na) in Activity 6.1, we understand that alkali metals are very soft. They can be cut with a table knife. Also, they are very reactive. Sodium reacts violently with water to produce hydrogen gas and, in the process, produces enough heat to ignite the hydrogen gas, as follows: $2Na_{(s)} + 2H_2O_{(l)} \rightarrow 2NaOH_{(aq)} + H_{2(g)}$. The sodium hydroxide (NaOH) is in the form of sodium ions (Na^+) and hydroxide ions (OH^-); the hydroxide ions are in excess and the solution is basic, as indicated by phenolphthalein turning red. Considering these physical and chemical properties of the alkali metals, we would not want a sodium bracelet. A bracelet that burns in air and reacts violently with water is not a desirable piece of jewelry. Jewelry made from alkali metals is not likely to become a popular commodity.

Other Reactive Metals: Alkaline Earth Metals

Alkaline earth metals are also improbable candidates for jewelry making. We see that calcium (Ca) forms a thick oxide crust in the presence of air, and also reacts with water to produce calcium hydroxide and hydrogen gas: $Ca_{(s)} + 2H_2O_{(l)} \rightarrow Ca(OH)_{2(aq)} + H_{2(g)}$. In addition, calcium is rather brittle. We would not be wise to seek out alkaline earth metals to make jewelry.

Transition Metals:
Voted the Most Likely to Succeed

The alkali metals are too reactive, the alkaline earth metals are somewhat reactive, but the transition metals are just right. We have examined some of the transition metals and see that they have potential in jewelry making. Copper (Cu), iron (Fe), and zinc (Zn) are malleable. They can be pounded into myriad shapes and thicknesses. In addition, they are not very reactive with air (oxygen), water, or non-oxidizing acids, such as hydrochloric acid (HCl).

Two Miles of Gold Thread

Because elaborate equipment is required to test metal ductility, we did not test the ductility of the copper, iron, and zinc in Activity 6.1. Ductility is a physical property of metals that allows them to be drawn or stretched into thin threads without the metal breaking. Two of the most ductile metals are gold and silver. One gram of gold can be drawn into a thread two miles long![3] Threads can be used as lines in art. We know that lines in art are used to communicate what we see and feel. A thread, used as a line, can enhance a sculpture or even serve as the sole material for the sculpture. Because many pieces of jewelry are sculptures in miniature, threads of gold and silver are excellent materials for creating attractive pieces of jewelry.

Metal Density and Jewelry Making

The density of a substance is the mass of the substance in a particular volume, expressed as g/cm^3 (grams per cubic centimeter). The more units, such as molecules, atoms, or ions, that exist in a given volume, the greater the density of a substance. A crafter designing a piece of metal jewelry will consider the density of the metal used. For example, a large earring of very dense metal would not fit comfortably in a small earlobe (in some African tribes, such as the Masai in Kenya, large, dense earrings are used to elongate earlobes). The densities of copper (Cu), iron (Fe), and zinc (Zn) are 8.92 g/cm^3, 7.86 g/cm^3, and 7.14 g/cm^3, respectively.[4] We can see that the density of copper is somewhat higher than the density of iron, which is higher than the density of zinc. However, all these metals would have the same usefulness when metal weight is a consideration in the design of jewelry. Considering the two metals most often used in jewelry making, silver (Ag) and gold (Au), silver has almost the same density as copper, but gold has a density of 19.32 g/cm^3. Jewelry made of pure gold can be very heavy.

Acids, Metals, and Jewelry

Acids are a part of our environment, present in food, in rain, and a component of skin moisture. It is necessary to consider the effect of acids on metals used to make jewelry. In Chapter 3, we learned that acids produce hydrogen ions (H^+) in aqueous solutions. Metal atoms tend to be effective reducing agents, losing electrons to become more stable. Some metals are better reducing agents than others. For example, zinc atoms lose electrons more easily than iron atoms, which, in turn, lose electrons more easily than copper atoms. Hydrogen ions will seize available electrons and convert to hydrogen gas (H_2). The more effective the metal is as a reducing agent, losing electrons, the more reactive the metal will be with an acid. Also, the stronger the acid, the more likely it is to react with the metal.

Of the three acids used in Activity 6.1, nitric acid (HNO_3) is the strongest. Sulfuric acid (H_2SO_4) is next in strength, and hydrochloric acid (HCl) is the weakest. It would follow that a nitrate ion (NO_3^-) is a stronger oxidizing agent than a sulfate ion (SO_4^{2-}). If we make a piece of jewelry from zinc and it comes in contact with nitric acid, too bad! The chemical reaction will permanently change the jewelry. However, copper metal, a weaker reducing agent than zinc, does not react with sulfuric acid. Copper can react with strong acids such as nitric acid. If these acids are present on skin, copper ions (Cu^{2+}) will form, turning the skin blue-green. In addition, if we had tested gold and silver, we would have found that they are even weaker reducing agents than copper and do not react with most acids. It is easy to understand why gold and silver are popular choices for precious jewelry. Not only are they not very chemically reactive, but also they can be polished to a radiant shine, they have a beautiful luster, and they can be textured in a variety of ways.

Alloys: Metal Mixtures

To make metals even more appropriate for jewelry making, we combine them to attain the most desirable physical properties of each. We melt two or more metals in specific proportions to form a metal solution called an alloy. Gold (Au) and silver (Ag) in their pure states are very soft and usually unsuitable for jewelry, which requires a harder metal to resist wear and tear. Sterling silver is an alloy of silver (92.5%) and copper (7.5%). Gold is sometimes used in jewelry as pure gold, known as 24-carat gold. More frequently, though, jewelry is made of 18-carat and 14-carat gold, containing 75.0% and 58.3% gold, respectively. The remaining 25.0% and 41.7%, respectively, consist of metals such as silver and copper.

Alloys: New Colors and New Strength

When a pure metal is changed to an alloy, new physical properties are imparted to the resulting alloy. Silver added to gold forms an alloy that appears greenish gold, and copper alloyed with gold creates an alloy that is reddish gold in color. "White" gold is an alloy of platinum (Pt) and gold. This combination is very durable and appropriate for delicate but strong settings for stones. Gold can also be alloyed with other metals to create additional colors, such as purple, gray, and blue-gold. Brass, often used in jewelry making, is an alloy of copper (Cu) and zinc (Zn). Depending on the amounts of copper and zinc, brass can have a yellow color or a reddish color. Nickel-silver contains no silver but is actually an alloy of copper, nickel (Ni), and zinc. Because of its strength and reasonable cost, nickel-silver is sometimes used for jewelry. Pewter is an alloy of copper and tin (Sn). Because of its low melting point and softness, it is not suitable for pieces such as rings, which require a more durable metal.

When making metal jewelry, the artisan is concerned with the melting point of a chosen metal, especially when they must solder together jewelry parts or melt the metal to pour it into a mold. Table 6.3 lists the melting points and approximate composition of various metals and alloys.

Table 6.3
Alloy and Metal Melting Points

Metal or Alloy	Melting Point	Composition
Gold (Au)	1945°F/1063°C	
Silver (Ag)	1761°F/961°C	
Sterling Silver (Ag, Cu) (Alloy)	1640°F/893°C	92.5% Silver, 7.5% Copper
Copper (Cu)	1980°F/1082°C	
Tin (Sn)	450°F/232°C	
Brass (Cu, Zn) (Alloy)	1503°F/817°C	79% Copper, 21% Zinc
Nickel Silver (Cu, Ni, 2n) (Alloy)	1959°F/1071°C	60% Copper, 20% Nickel, 20% Zinc
Pewter (Sn, Cu) (Alloy)	500°F/260°C	85% Tin, 15% Copper

In addition to the alloys listed in Table 6.3, bronze has been known since ancient times. Bronze is 70–95% copper, 1–25% zinc, and 1–18% tin. Bronze is not used extensively in jewelry, but it is used for casting sculptures and medals that must remain permanently in good condition. Another alloy, Wood's metal, made of 50% bismuth, 25% lead, 13% tin, and 12% cadmium, has such a low melting point, about 70°C, that it would not be suitable for jewelry use.[5]

How Metal Atoms Mix

When some alloys are formed, atoms of one metal replace atoms of another metal. These alloys are classified as substitution alloys. When a substitution alloy is formed, the atoms of metals forming the alloy are about the same size. Therefore, one kind of atom can fit into a space vacated by another atom. In sterling silver, about 7% of the atoms are copper. These copper atoms are randomly dispersed throughout the metallic crystalline silver atoms. Pewter and brass are other examples of substitution alloys.

Alloys can also be formed when much smaller atoms are introduced into spaces between the metallic crystalline atoms. In steel, small carbon (C) atoms occupy spaces between larger iron (Fe) atoms. This type of alloy is called an interstitial alloy. The strength of the steel is much greater than the strength of the iron. Steel is used for posts in earrings because it is relatively nonreactive and very strong. For the same reasons, steel is used in the construction of decorative belt buckles.

Metals and Electron Configuration

We know the physical properties of metals, that they are shiny, malleable, ductile, have high densities, and are usually gray or silver (except in the case of copper and gold). We know some of the chemical properties of metals, that many are reactive in air (oxygen), forming oxides, and that some react with acids, forming hydrogen gas. Now, we will examine the electron configuration of metals to explain these chemical and physical properties of this unique material called metal.

Alkali Metals: Chemical Reactivity

The alkali metals, as we have seen, are frisky little devils. If there is any doubt about this, watch potassium (K) burst into flame in the presence of air, or watch sodium (Na) react violently in water. As we learned in Chapter 4, there are some electron configurations that are very stable, mainly those having eight outermost electrons. The alkali metals have one outermost electron of which that they are anxious to dispose. These electrons are usually transferred to nonmetals, such as oxygen (O), chlorine (Cl), fluorine (F), and bromine (Br), with a release of energy that is pronounced and unforgettable.

As we move down the family of alkali metals on the periodic table, metal chemical reactivity increases. This increase in reactivity corresponds to an increase in atomic size. As atomic size increases, the outermost electrons are farther from the atomic nucleus. The positively charged protons in the atomic nucleus are trying to attract the negatively charged outermost electrons, but attractive force decreases as distance increases. This is analogous to a mother trying to keep her children home while the children, as they become more energetic, wander farther away and often eventually leave home. A child can leave home more easily when already distanced from home. Therefore, cesium (Cs), in which the outermost electron is far from the positive nucleus and can easily leave home, is much more chemically reactive than lithium (Li), in which the outermost electron is close to home, the nucleus.

The Alkaline Earth Metals: Chemical Reactivity

Though not as chemically reactive as the alkali metals, the alkaline earth metals lose or share two outermost electrons easily to obtain eight outermost electrons. Calcium (Ca) reacts with hydrogen gas (H_2) to produce calcium hydride (CaH_2), and with water (H_2O) to produce hydroxide ions (OH^-) and hydrogen gas (H_2):

$$Ca_{(s)} + H_{2(g)} \rightarrow CaH_{2(s)}$$

$$Ca_{(s)} + 2H_2O_{(l)} \rightarrow Ca^{2+}_{(aq)} + 2OH^-_{(aq)} + H_{2(g)}$$

Magnesium (Mg) and beryllium (Be) are not nearly as reactive as calcium. Beryllium does not react in water, and magnesium reacts in hot water to produce hydrogen gas as follows:

$$Mg_{(s)} + H_2O_{(l)} \rightarrow MgO_{(s)} + H_{2(g)}$$

Our theory regarding atomic size and reactivity holds true for the alkaline earth metals. As we move down a group on the periodic table, as the atomic size increases, the chemical reactivity increases. Calcium is more reactive than beryllium and magnesium. Neither the alkali metals nor the alkaline earth metals would be good candidates for jewelry making. We would not want to wear metal jewelry that might react violently to oxygen or water vapor in the air.

The Transition Metals: Chemical Reactivity

The transition metals are our premier metals for jewelry making. They have electron configurations that are different from the alkali metals and the alkaline earth metals. Therefore, transition metals exhibit different chemical and physical properties. It is necessary to determine just where electrons reside in transition-metal atoms so we can understand the properties of transition metals and how they bond. To understand these properties and manners of bonding, we must revisit the electron cloud atomic model.

The Electron Cloud Atomic Model

In Chapter 1, we learned that electrons are outside the atomic nucleus in probability areas that resemble clouds. We do not know exactly where these electrons are because they are in constant motion. Werner Heisenberg, in 1927, told us that it is impossible to know simultaneously the speed and position of an electron. He called this his uncertainty principle. Even though we cannot determine the exact position of an electron or how the electron moves in an atom, we can place an electron in an area outside the atomic nucleus where it is highly likely to be found, called a probability area.

Probability Areas: Orbitals

The first probability area, or orbital, is called an *s* orbital. It has a spherical shape and can hold two electrons. In fact, any single orbital can only hold two electrons (these electrons are spinning in opposite directions, however). Next, we have *p* orbitals, of which there are three, holding a total of six electrons. Each *p* orbital has an elongated figure-eight shape. The *d* orbitals come next and have complex shapes. There are, as you might have guessed, five *d* orbitals, holding 10 electrons altogether. Finally, we have the *f* orbitals, seven of them, with 14 electrons. (See Fig. 6.1, p. 156.)

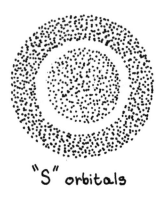

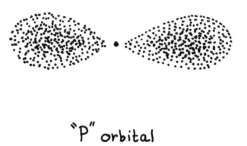

"S" orbitals   "P" orbital

Figure 6.1.

Energy Levels

The orbitals, as described, are placed in energy levels that denote the amount of energy in an electron. The greater the number of the energy level, n, the greater the energy of the electron and the farther the electron is from the nucleus. Therefore, when the energy level, n, for an electron is 1, the electron is closest to the nucleus and at its lowest energy level. Also, the first energy level has only one s orbital, with two electrons. The second energy level, farther from the nucleus, has one s and three p orbitals, each containing two electrons, for a total of eight electrons. The third energy level has one s orbital, three p orbitals, and five d orbitals, holding a total of 18 electrons. The fourth energy level has one s orbital, three p orbitals, five d orbitals, and seven f orbitals, holding a total of 32 electrons.

Placing Electrons in Orbitals

When the electrons in an atom are at their lowest possible energy levels, we call this the ground state: Electrons are placed into orbitals beginning at the first energy level, then the second energy level, next the third, and so on, until all the electrons in a particular atom are placed into orbitals. There is some variation in this pattern beginning at the third energy level, where electrons fill into the fourth energy level s orbital before they are placed into the third energy level d orbitals. When electrons are placed into the same orbitals at the same energy level, one electron is placed into each orbital and then the orbitals are filled with a second electron. For example, when five electrons are placed in the three p orbitals, one electron would be placed in each orbital and then the two remaining electrons would pair with a single electron, so two p orbitals would have two electrons and one p orbital would have one electron. Now we can place electrons in these orbitals and see how the electron placement affects bonding for and properties of the transition metals.

What Is Stable and What Is Unstable?

Particular electron configurations are very stable and others are not so stable. Helium (He) has only two electrons, which are in the first energy level in the s orbital, designated $1s^2$. This arrangement is quite stable. We know that helium is a nonreactive noble gas. We also know that eight is great! Eight outermost electrons make an atom or ion very stable. Considering the 10 electrons in neon (Ne), two are in the first energy level s orbital, two are in the second energy level *s* orbital, and six are in the second energy level *p* orbitals, or $1s^2 2s^2 2p^6$. Neon has eight outermost electrons and is nonreactive. All the noble gases, except helium, have eight outermost electrons, and all the noble gases are nonreactive. Therefore, one very stable electron configuration is filled outermost *s* and *p* orbitals. Another fairly stable arrangement is filled outermost *d* orbitals and half-filled *d* orbitals. Chromium (Cr) atoms should have four electrons in the *d* orbitals, but actually five electrons are one each in the five *d* orbitals, resulting in half-filled *d* orbitals. Manganese (Mn) atoms also have half-filled *d* orbitals, and copper (Cu), zinc (Zn), palladium (Pd), silver (Ag), and cadmium (Cd) have filled *d* orbitals—10 electrons in the five *d* orbitals. These elements having half-filled and filled *d* orbitals are among the least chemically reactive of all the known elements.

Alkali Metal and Alkaline Earth Metal Reactivity

The alkali metals have one outermost electron in an *s* orbital. This is a very unstable electron configuration, so the alkali metals are very reactive. The alkaline earth metals have two outermost electrons in an *s* orbital, making them somewhat reactive because an arrangement with eight outermost electrons is the most stable. The larger alkaline earth metals, strontium (Sr) and barium (Ba), are very reactive because those two outermost electrons are far from the nucleus.

In summary, it appears that the chemical activity of the elements is based primarily on electron configuration and then on outermost electron distance from the nucleus. Mostly because of their electron configuration, the transition metals, in the middle of the periodic table (next to the noble gases), are the most stable elements. They are not very reactive with other elements. This is why these transition metals, the so-called heavy metals, make such good jewelry material. However, other important factors are their shiny luster, ductility, and malleability.

Metallic Bonds: A Sea of Electrons

When we determined the crystalline structure of solids in Chapter 4, we noted that most transitional metals form crystals with atoms in a hexagonal-closest, face-centered, or body-centered arrangements. In the body-centered cubic structure, the spheres take up almost as much space as in the hexagonal-closest packing structure. Many of the metals used to make alloys used for jewelry, such as nickel, copper, zinc, silver, gold, platinum, and lead, have a face-centered cubic crystalline structures. Perhaps their similar crystalline structures promote an ease in forming alloys. In sterling silver, an atom of copper can fit nicely beside an atom of silver in the crystalline structure.

The crystalline structure of metals is often disturbed when metals are worked into pieces of jewelry. For example, the artisan might pound, pull, twist, bend, and cut a piece of gold to produce a single, unique bracelet or earring (students should examine jewelry that they are wearing to find evidence of metal manipulation). Metals do not shatter when they are pounded. There must be a particular bonding structure for metals that explains this behavior.

The electron sea model (see Fig. 6.2, p. 158) for metal bonding proposes a theory that explains observed metal properties. In this model, we can envision that metal bonds are formed when a uniform array of metal cations, positively charged metal ions, are surrounded by a sea of electrons. The electrons' attraction for the cations acts like a glue to keep the metal together

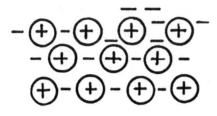

Figure 6.2. Electron Sea Model.

even when it is pulled into a wire or pounded into a thin sheet. This electron-cation attraction is strong, and the bonding is nondirectional. Therefore, cations can easily be moved around when metals are worked. Metals have high melting points, which indicates a strong bonding system. Metals can conduct electricity and heat through their mobile electrons. The electron sea model provides good evidence for the physical properties of metal.

METALWORKING TECHNIQUES

Metal for jewelry making comes in a variety of forms, including sheet, wire, ingot, and pellet. For handmade or fabricated pieces, made by sawing, pounding, twisting, bending, and soldering, sheet and wire forms are used. For casting or melting metal, which is then poured into a mold, ingot or pellets are the most common forms used. Sheet and wire forms can be obtained in various thicknesses, or gauges. The smaller the number of the gauge, the thicker the wire or sheet. Typical gauges for wire and sheet metal used in jewelry making range from 16- to 20-gauge in thickness.

Two Basic Metalworking Techniques: How to Do It

Fabrication. Fabrication is a method of jewelry making that involves the uniting together of parts, either by soldering, linking, or intertwining. An example of a fabricated piece would be one in which layers of metal are attached by heating. Solder is placed between the layers. Because the solder has a lower melting point than the metal, the solder melts first and attaches the sections of metal.

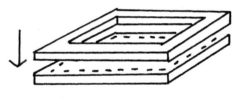

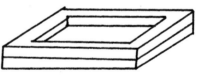

Figure 6.3. Fabrication.

Casting. Casting is a method of making jewelry that involves melting the metal and pouring, or pulling, it into a prepared mold. There are several methods of casting, including casting in molds made of plaster, sand, or other porous materials. A second method, the lost wax method, is not new, dating to 1000 B.C. It has been refined and updated over the years. The lost wax process is based on the principle that a model or pattern of the finished product is made in wax. This pattern is surrounded by a creamy investment plaster that hardens to form a mold. During the mold heating that follows, the wax pattern melts away and is "lost." Metal is then cast into the cavity left by the lost wax, thus duplicating the original wax pattern. The mold is then destroyed to recover the casting. For more information on the lost wax method, see the video list at the end of this chapter. A casting method is used when it is necessary to make several identical shapes or when the piece is too difficult to model directly in metal using the fabrication method.

Preliminary Preparation for Jewelry Making

Basic Equipment for Jewelry Making

Jeweler's saw and blades: 2/0, 1/0, and 1
Pliers: Flat, round, and needlenose
Needle files: Round, semicircular, and flat
Small vise
Hammer
Scribe for scratching designs
Wooden or rawhide mallet
Ring mandrel (steel rod)
Bench pin and C-clamp
Wire cutters
Punch and hand drill (small drill bits #53 and #57)
Medium and fine emery paper or cloth

Steel block
Propane torch
Charcoal block
Fireproof working surface
Easy silver solder (melts at 1325°F)
Tweezers
Scissors, for cutting solder
Flux
Flux brush
Pickle solution
Copper tongs

Proper Precautions for Jewelry Making

When working with materials for jewelry making, the following precautions should be taken:

Wear protective goggles.
Wear a protective apron.
Have proper ventilation.

Avoid breathing fumes.
Use reasonable care in handling tools
and materials.

6.2

One-Piece Adjustable Ring with Interrelated Design— A Fabricated Piece of Jewelry

Objectives

1. Students will design an adjustable ring so that a portion of an interrelated design appears at each end.

2. Students will saw, file, and prepare the adjustable ring for use in Activity 6.4.

3. Students will properly use jewelry making tools and equipment.

4. Students will exhibit a knowledge of good design in the creation of a jewelry piece.

Materials

Paper, pencil, scissors, jeweler's saw and #1 blades, C-clamp, 16- or 18-gauge sheet copper, scribe, needle files, ring mandrel, mallet, medium and fine emery paper. (See equipment list above for more details.)

Time

200 minutes

Procedure

1. Have students make several patterns using paper and pencil based on the following design idea: One end of the ring will contain a first part of the design and the other end of the ring will contain a second part of the design. When the ring is bent into a circle, the parts of the design will become interlocked. The side edges of the ring design may be straight or may also have a design. (See the list of design resources under "Resources" near the end of this chapter.)

2. Cut out the design and fit it around a finger, allowing enough negative space between the ends for adjustment.

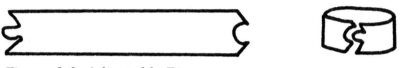

Figure 6.4. Adjustable Ring.

3. Transfer the design to a sheet of copper using a scribe to scratch the outline into the metal.

4. Attach the saw blade to the frame of the saw at one end. The teeth of the blade must be facing down, toward the saw handle. Apply pressure to the frame to achieve tension on the blade before attaching the opposite end.

5. Secure the bench pin to the surface of a table with the C-clamp and place the area of the metal to be sawed across the V of the pin. Saw out the design shape using a vertical sawing motion. Notice that the blade cuts only on the down stroke. When turning a corner, move the saw up and down while slowly turning the metal.

6. Use needle files to smooth the rough edges. Use flat files for flat areas and outside curves, and use semicircular and round files for inside curves.

7. Polish the copper, first with medium emery cloth and then with fine emery cloth, to remove scratches and create a brushed finish.

8. Bend the ring around the ring mandrel and complete the form by gently tapping with a mallet. Adjust the ring to fit a finger.

9. Save this ring for Activity 6.4, in which the ring will be electroplated.

ELECTROCHEMISTRY: PROTECTIVE COATS FOR METALS

Electrochemical Cells

Batteries are electrochemical cells. Where would we be without batteries? A battery is needed to start a car. Batteries power flashlights, move toys, and make watches work. Jewelry with lightbulb designs can use tiny batteries. A battery provides an electric current through oxidation-reduction reactions in which the flow of electrons is directed through a wire. The force of the electrons through the wire is measured in volts.

Electrochemical cells are made of two conducting electrodes, called the anode and the cathode. The oxidation reaction takes place at the anode, where electrons are released to flow

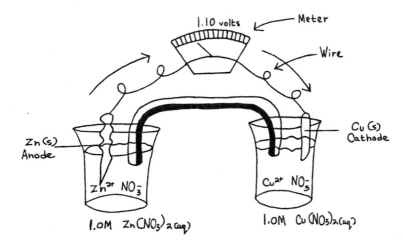

Figure 6.5. An Electrochemical Cell.

through a wire to the cathode. At the cathode, reduction take place. For the oxidation and reduction reactions to occur, the electrodes must be in a conducting solution called an electrolyte. The electrochemical cell voltage is dependent upon the types of materials, usually conducting metals, used as electrodes and the concentration of the electrolyte solution.

Because the oxidation reaction and reduction reactions occur simultaneously in an electrochemical cell, it is difficult to find the voltage produced from just one of these reactions. If the voltage produced at a particular electrode could be known, it would be possible to predict the overall voltage for most electrochemical cells. A standard voltage, $E°$, is determined for a reaction at one electrode by using a hydrogen electrode reaction assigned an $E°$ value of 0 as a comparison to all other reactions. A table of $E°$ values can be established experimentally by preparing an electrochemical cell with one hydrogen electrode (hydrogen gas is bubbled over platinum), and another electrode, zinc for example. The electrolyte solution has a 1 molar concentration. The cell voltage is read from a voltmeter. This entire voltage is assigned to the zinc reaction and, because oxidation occurs at the zinc electrode, the voltage is given a positive sign, $+0.76$ V. In this case, in a zinc electrode/hydrogen electrode cell, the voltage would be 0.76 V. A positive sign indicates that zinc loses electrons more easily than hydrogen.

Half Reactions

When $E°$ values are established for a number of substances, these values are placed in a table that shows an equation for the half reaction associated with each $E°$ value. Either the oxidation half reactions at the anodes or the reduction half reactions at the cathodes may be listed. For the zinc/hydrogen electrochemical cell described above, the half reactions would be as follows:

Oxidation: $Zn \rightarrow Zn^{2+} + 2e^-$

Reduction: $2H^+ + 2e^- \rightarrow H_2$

At the present time, tables of $E°$ values use reduction half reactions called standard reduction potentials. Because the value of $E°$ is affected by the concentration of the electrolyte solution, these values are given for 1 molar solutions. On a table of standard reduction potentials, we would find the $E°$ value for zinc to be -0.76 V, the negative value resulting because the zinc oxidation half reaction must be reversed for a reduction potential table: When the half reaction is reversed, the sign must also be reversed. Some standard reduction potential half reactions include the following:

$$Ag^+ + e^- \rightarrow Ag \ E° = 0.80 \ V \qquad Ni^{2+} + 2e^- \rightarrow Ni \ E° = -0.23 \ V$$

$$Cu^{2+} + 2e^- \rightarrow Cu \ E° = 0.34 \ V \qquad Zn^{2+} + 2e^- \rightarrow Zn \ E° = -0.76 \ V$$

$$2H^+ + 2e^- \rightarrow H_2 \ E° = 0.00 \ V$$

To calculate the $E°$, the voltage, of an electrochemical cell, the voltage for the oxidation half reaction at the anode is added to the voltage for the reduction half reaction at the cathode: $E°_{cell} = E°_{oxid.react.} + E°_{red.react.}$. For an electrochemical cell with zinc and copper electrodes, $E° = 0.76 + 0.34 = 1.10 \ V$. The sign for the zinc reduction potential half reaction is changed because the half reaction is reversed to show that oxidation occurs at the zinc electrode. The two half reactions can also be added to show the overall reaction in the electrochemical cell:

$$Zn \rightarrow Zn^{2+} + 2e^-$$
$$Cu^{2+} + 2e^- \rightarrow Cu$$

$$+ \ \overline{\phantom{Zn + Cu^{2+} \rightarrow Zn^{2+} + Cu}}$$

$$Zn + Cu^{2+} \rightarrow Zn^{2+} + Cu$$

The zinc anode is eroded as zinc metal changes to zinc ions, and the copper cathode gains mass as copper ions convert to copper metal, which is deposited on the copper cathode. The oxidation and reduction reactions, sometimes called redox reactions, in the electrochemical cell are spontaneous. The electrode most likely to lose electrons, the most effective reducing agent, which is zinc, becomes the anode, and the strongest oxidizing agent, which are the copper ions, is the cathode. In theory, a copper bracelet or earrings could be the cathode of this cell so that a copper coat could be deposited on the bracelet or earrings. In Activity 6.3, we will make an electrochemical cell and in Activity 6.4 we will observe the results when a piece of jewelry is coated with copper.

6.3

Making an Electrochemical Cell

Objectives

1. Students will construct an electrochemical cell and identify the anode, cathode, electrolyte, direction of current flow, and direction of ion flow.

2. Students will write balanced chemical half reactions and an overall redox reaction for the reaction that takes place in the electrochemical cell.

3. Students will discuss the pros and cons of coating a piece of jewelry in an electrochemical cell.

4. Students will calculate the voltage for their electrochemical cell and determine if their calculated voltage is the observed voltage. They will explain any differences between the two voltages.

Materials

For each group: Two 250 ml beakers, 200 ml 1.0 M $Cu(NO_3)_2$ (copper nitrate), 200 ml 1.0 M $Zn(NO_3)_2$ (zinc nitrate), zinc metal for an electrode, copper metal for an electrode, U-tube, cotton plugs, two conducting wires with alligator clips at both ends, 100 ml 1.0 M $NaNO_3$ (sodium nitrate), voltmeter.

Time

50 minutes

Procedure

1. Place 200 ml 1.0 M $Cu(NO_3)_2$ solution in a 250 ml beaker.
2. Place 200 ml 1.0 M $Zn(NO_3)_2$ solution in another 250 ml beaker.
3. Fill the U-tube entirely with 1.0 M $NaNO_3$ and plug the ends with cotton so that there are no air bubbles in the solution.
4. Invert the U-tube into the beakers so that one arm is in one beaker and the other arm is in the other beaker.
5. Place a copper electrode in the $Cu(NO_3)_2$ solution.
6. Place a zinc electrode in the $Zn(NO_3)_2$ solution.
7. Clip a conducting wire onto each electrode.
8. Connect the other ends of the conducting wires to a voltmeter.
9. Read the voltage generated by the electrochemical cell and record this voltage.
10. After the cell has been connected for several minutes, observe any changes in the solution colors and record these changes.
11. Wait several minutes, disconnect a wire, and remove the copper and zinc electrodes. Carefully observe the electrode surfaces and record any changes in color and texture. Look for changes in electrode size. Record all observations.
12. Remove the zinc electrode and record any changes in its appearance.

Questions and Conclusions

Level One

1. Which electrode is the anode? Which electrode is the cathode? (Answer: Zn is the anode, Cu is the cathode.)
2. Which electrode loses mass? Which electrode gains mass? (Answer: The anode loses mass, the cathode gains mass.)
3. Write the half reaction at the anode. Write the half reaction at the cathode. Add these reactions together to find the overall reaction. Be sure that you have written balanced equations for all the reactions. (Answer: At the anode: $Zn_{(s)} \rightarrow Zn^{2+}_{(aq)} + 2e^-$; at the cathode: $Cu^{2+}_{(aq)} + 2e^- \rightarrow Cu_{(s)}$; overall reaction: $Zn_{(s)} + Cu^{2+}_{(aq)} \rightarrow Zn^{2+}_{(aq)} + Cu_{(s)}$.)
4. After examining the electrodes, explain why an electrochemical cell would be a good way to coat metal and why it would be a bad way.

Level Two

1. Using half reactions and E° values, calculate the expected voltage for the cell that you constructed. If the observed voltage is different from the calculated voltage, explain this difference.

2. Explain the change in color in the $Cu(NO_3)_2$ (copper nitrate) electrolyte solution.

3. The Statue of Liberty was made of sheets of copper attached to an iron framework. Explain why the iron framework corroded so badly that the Statue of Liberty almost collapsed. How would you remodel the Statue of Liberty so that the metals would not corrode?

Electrolytic Cells

The plating of jewelry in an electrochemical cell is not very satisfactory. Because the reaction is spontaneous, there is not much control over the rate of plating. Metal is deposited unevenly. Also, often the metal does not adhere to the jewelry being coated and will flake off, leaving a mottled appearance. A better way to coat jewelry is in an electrolytic cell.

A Non-Spontaneous Reaction

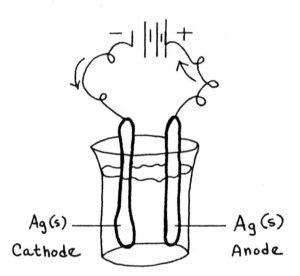

Figure 6.6. An Electrolytic Cell.

In the electrolytic cell (see Fig. 6.6), electricity is added to the cell from an outside source. This outside source of current can be from direct-current sources, such as a battery or generator. The hookup of the current source to the electrolytic cell electrodes determines which electrode will be the anode and which electrode will be the cathode. The electrode, where electrons flow into the electrolytic cell from the current source, is the cathode. At the cathode, ions or molecules undergo reduction. If metal ions are present in an electrolyte solution surrounding the cathode, they will gain electrons and deposit on the cathode as a metal coating or plating. Meanwhile, at the anode, electrons are produced when ions or molecules are losing electrons. If the anode is metallic, the metal atoms will leave surface of the anode and convert to metal ions, which become part of the electrolyte solution. As the cell operates in this manner, the anode gradually erodes.

Except for its source of outside current, the electrolytic cell has the same elements as the electrochemical cell: An anode and a cathode placed in an electrolyte in which cations, positive ions, move toward the cathode, and anions, negative ions, move toward the anode. The oxidation half reaction at the anode and the reduction half reaction at the cathode can be added together to find the overall redox reaction for the cell. The process is called electrolysis. If a coating of silver metal is desired on a piece of silver jewelry, electrolysis can be performed to coat or plate the silver jewelry in an electrolytic cell: The electrolyte silver nitrate ($AgNO_3$)

solution supplies a source of silver ions (Ag^+). The cathode is the silver jewelry, from which silver ions are reduced to silver metal. The anode is a silver metal strip that is oxidized to produce silver ions. The oxidation half reaction is the reverse of the reduction half reaction.

Electrolysis of Molten Sodium Chloride

An electrolysis reaction in which the oxidation reaction is not the reverse of the reduction reaction is the electrolysis of molten sodium chloride. Molten sodium chloride (NaCl), with calcium chloride ($CaCl_2$) added to decrease the melting point, is electrolyzed in a Downs cell, in which the sodium and chlorine products are separated so that sodium chloride does not reform. The following reactions occur:

Anode (oxidation): $2Cl^- \rightarrow Cl_2 + 2e^-$

Cathode (reduction): $Na^+ + e^- \rightarrow Na$

This is an example of how electrolysis is performed in an important industrial process.

6.4
Electroplating a Copper Ring

Objectives

1. Students will prepare a system for the electrolysis of a copper ring.
2. Students will identify the parts of the electrolysis system and explain the function of each part.
3. Students will operate their electrolysis system to plate a copper ring.
4. From experimental data, the students will determine and explain what conditions should exist for ideal jewelry electroplating.

Materials

For each group: 100 ml 1.0 M $CuSO_4 \cdot 5H_2O$ (copper sulfate), 100 ml 5% solution H_2SO_4 (sulfuric acid), copper rings made in Activity 6.2, strips of 18-gauge copper metal, 250 ml beaker, wax, source of 12-volt direct current, ammeter, three wires with alligator clips at both ends, fine emery cloth, hot plate.

Time

60 minutes

Procedure

A. Electroplating a metal object with copper:

1. Pour approximately 100 ml 1.0 M $CuSO_4 \cdot 5H_2O$ and approximately 100 ml (5%) H_2SO_4 into a 250 ml beaker.
2. Take a strip of copper and form it into an incomplete cylinder that can surround the object to be plated.
3. With wax, cover the areas on the copper ring that are not to be plated.

4. Using a wire with clips, clip the copper cylinder to the positive electrode of the current source, and clip the copper ring to the negative electrode of the current source. Connect the ammeter to the current source.

5. Place the copper cylinder and copper ring in the beaker containing the solutions. Be sure that both the cylinder and the bracelet are covered with the solutions.

6. Adjust the voltage to 6 volts and the ammeter to 0.5 amps.

7. Allow the electrolysis to proceed until the desired coating of copper is achieved. Record the amount of time it takes.

8. Examine the appearance of the copper plating and record observations.

9. Remove the wax by placing the ring in warm water and wiping off the wax. Using fine emery cloth, polish the ring.

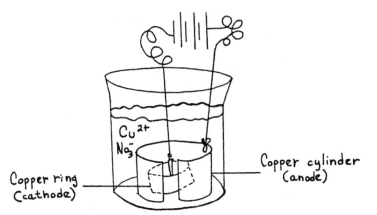

Figure 6.7. Copper Ring Electrolysis.

B. Perform the electrolysis in part A with the copper sulfate electrolyte heated to about 40°C.

Questions and Conclusions

Level One

1. Identify the anode, cathode, anions, and cations in the electrolysis performed in this activity.

2. Write the reduction half reaction and the oxidation half reaction for this electrolysis. (Answer: Reduction half reaction: $Cu^{2+}_{(aq)} + 2e^- \rightarrow Cu_{(s)}$. Oxidation half reaction: $Cu_{(s)} \rightarrow Cu^{2+}_{(aq)} + 2e^-$.)

3. Which electrode should always have the piece of jewelry to be plated? Why?

Level Two

1. In writing, compare the appearance of the objects plated at room temperature to those plated at a higher temperature. Discuss evenness, color, distribution of the copper, and any other observed properties.

2. Using this activity, predict the ideal temperature for electroplating a piece of jewelry with copper.

Electroplating is commonly performed to enhance the appearance of a piece of jewelry. Silver and gold are often plated onto cheaper metals to produce inexpensive jewelry that resembles more expensive varieties. The average person can spend less money and look great.

WIREWORK: LINE IN METAL

Because the bonding structure of metals consists of electrons in a sea of protons, in which the electrons act like glue to hold on to the protons, metals are malleable and ductile enough to be shaped into many forms, such as sheets and wires. Jewelry can be made from these and other forms of metal. Wire is one of the more popular forms for jewelry construction. With a minimum of tools, wire can be flattened, twisted, and woven into a variety of interesting pieces.

Wire for jewelry making can be purchased in a variety of metals and in a variety of thicknesses, or gauges. For jewelry making, 16-, 18-, 20-, 22-, and 24-gauge wires are most often used. Silver wire can be purchased in half-round, square, and round shapes.

6.5
Linear Jewelry

Objectives

1. Students will experiment with bending, twisting, and flattening wire.
2. Students will create a piece of linear jewelry using wire in various forms.
3. Students will learn to properly use tools to form wire pieces.
4. Students will employ good design in the creation of wire jewelry.

■ *Note:*
See the list design resources under "Resources" near the end of this chapter for design ideas.

Level One: A Simple Pendant

Materials

Pencil, paper, pliers (round, flat, and needlenose), wire cutters, hammer, steel block, hand drill, vice and eye screw for twisting wire, propane torch, emery paper, copper wire in various gauges from 16 to 24.

Time

90 minutes

Procedure

1. Have students experiment with a short length of 16- or 18-gauge wire, bending the wire with pliers to form curves and angles.

2. Flatten segments of the wire using the hammer and steel block.

Figure 6.8.

3. Twist two or more wires together, using the drill and hook to hold one end of the wires and the vice to hold the other end. Allow extra length for twisting. (See Fig. 6.8.)

NOTE: Twisting can make wire brittle, so care should be taken. To soften brittle, twisted wire so that it can be bent without breaking, the wire must be annealed. Annealing involves heating to a dull red and plunging the heated wire into water. Twisted wire should not be pounded to flatten it. Annealing is also used to soften pounded wire that is brittle.

4. Have students sketch several chemistry-related ideas for a simple pendant design using one continuous piece of wire.

5. Have students create a piece of jewelry from one continuous piece of wire, following the ideas sketched in step 4. A means of attachment to the chain or cord can be made by forming a loop at the top of the piece and binding it with a piece of 22- or 24-gauge wire.

Figure 6.9.

Level Two:
Pendant Using Several
Individual Pieces Joined Together

Materials

Same as level one, with the addition of glass, clay, or wooden beads.

Time

100 minutes

Procedure

1. Proceed with steps 1–3 from the procedure in level one.

2. Have students sketch several ideas for a pendant based on having several separate pieces of wire joined together, allowing for movement of the parts. Students should try to incorporate round pieces of wire as well as flattened and twisted variations. Incorporate beads for accent.

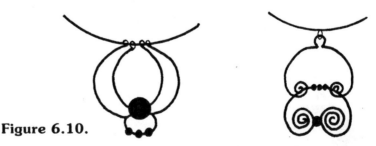

Figure 6.10.

3. Have students create a piece of jewelry using various gauges of wires and various methods, such as twisting, flattening, and pounding, following the ideas sketched in step 2.

REVISITING FABRICATION: SOLDERING AND COLORING

Soldering: One Plus One Equals One

Soldering is a procedure used to join two pieces of metal together using heat. This process is referred to as hard soldering and requires a much higher temperature than soft soldering. The solder used is made from an alloy of metals—tin-lead alloys for soft soldering at low temperatures and copper-zinc alloys for hard soldering at high temperatures. It is necessary that the solder melt at a lower temperature than the metals being soldered. Silver solder is typically used to solder most metals. Solder is cut into very small pieces because not much is needed to make a strong connection. (*Note:* When purchasing solder, make sure it is cadmium free. Cadmium vapor is toxic.)

Flux is a protective coating applied to a piece before soldering to help the solder flow and to prevent oxides from forming on the surface of the pieces to be soldered. Flux separates the surface of the piece from the air (oxygen). The solder is melted by applying heat from a propane torch or other source of intense heat. After the solder has melted onto the piece, it is placed in an acid solution, called pickle, to convert any oxides formed during soldering to soluble substances that can be easily removed. The commercial name of one pickle solution is Sparex. Heating the pickle solution in a heat-proof glass container will speed the cleaning process.

■ *Note:*
An appropriate video to help students understand the processes of jewelry making is *Basic Jewelry* (see "Resources" list near the end of this chapter).

 **6.1**

Soldering

Objectives

1. Students will observe the proper preparation of a piece for soldering.
2. Students will observe a proper soldering procedure.

Materials

Copper sheet metal, easy silver solder, scissors, propane torch, charcoal block, fireproof surface for soldering, flux, brush, pickle solution, copper tongs, tweezers. (See the list of basic equipment for jewelry making on p. 159 for details.)

Time

50 minutes

Procedure

1. The teacher should place a charcoal block on a fireproof surface.
2. Prepare two pieces of flat copper by cleaning them with emery paper. Do not touch the flat surfaces after they are cleaned.

3. Place the bottom copper piece on the charcoal block and apply flux with a brush to the top surface of this piece.

4. Clean solder with emery paper and cut it into small pieces, about $\frac{1}{16}$ inch wide. Place them on the fluxed piece surface along the edges.

5. With a brush, apply flux to the top and bottom surface of another copper piece and place this piece over the bottom piece.

6. Light a propane torch and rotate the flame around the outside of the piece. Keep rotating it until the flux turns white. At this point, direct heat can be applied to the solder areas.

7. Continue heating until the top piece appears to drop down. This indicates that the solder has begun to melt. A bright seam of metal can be seen around the edges. This means that the solder has flowed.

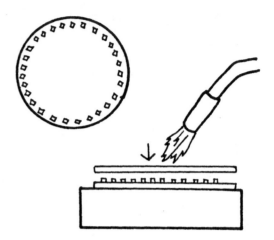

Figure 6.11. Solder Setup.

8. When the solder has flowed, remove the heat, grasp the piece with tweezers, and drop it into the pickle solution to clean it. Remove the soldered piece with copper tongs and rinse with water.

COLORING METALS:
A PLEASANT PATINA

When a piece of jewelry is fabricated, solder is the glue that holds together the individual pieces. After the object is assembled, a surface color may be desired. This surface color, or patina, may develop naturally upon exposure to the atmosphere or may be produced as the result of an anticipated chemical change. Usually, the patina will make the piece of jewelry more attractive than it was originally.

After metals are fabricated into jewelry pieces, a patina may be added by the artisan. The patina is usually considered ornamental and not protective. However, the chemical reactions to produce patinas are similar to those reactions that cause metals to form protective coats. These are oxidation-reduction reactions in which the metal atoms change to ions by losing electrons: They undergo oxidation. These metal ions can react with available anions, such as carbonates (CO_3^{2-}), oxides (O^{2-}), sulfides (S^{2-}), and sulfates (SO_4^{2-}), to form colored compounds that, in small amounts, give the metal an attractive patina and, in larger amounts, provide a protective coating to the metal. However, if the oxidation proceeds to erode a large portion of the metal, the design of the original piece of jewelry is not protected but will be destroyed. We call this process corrosion.

Patinas, Protective Coatings, and Corrosion

Patinas

Patinas add color and interest to works of art on public display, along with those items, such as jewelry, that are kept in a more controlled environment. Henry Moore's bronze *Reclining Figure*, 1963–1965, displayed in front of the Center for Performing Arts in New York City, is a beautiful blue color because the copper combines with sulfate to form copper sulfate ($CuSO_4$). The blue-green color of the Statue of Liberty comes from brochantite [$CuSO_4 \cdot 3Cu(OH)_2$] and antlerite [$CuSO_4 \cdot 2Cu(OH)_2$].[6] Copper can form a black patina as copper oxide (CuO) and also as copper sulfide (Cu_2S), and can form an olive-green patina as copper chloride ($CuCl_2$). In ornate silver jewelry, black silver sulfide (Ag_2S) can form in crevices in the design. This can delineate and emphasize the design, adding to the beauty of the jewelry.

Protective Coatings

Upon exposure to air, most metals tend to form an oxide coating. If colored, this oxide coating acts as a patina to enhance the appearance of the metal. The oxide coating can also act as protection against further chemical change with internal metal atoms. Particular types of steel are protected from rust formation by a coating of metal oxide. Aluminum forms aluminum oxide (Al_2O_3) or [$Al_2(OH)_6$], which provides a protective coating.

Corrosion

The corrosion of metals is an electrochemical process involving oxidation-reduction, or redox, reactions. When corrosion is addressed, it is often in the context of structural materials for buildings, bridges, and transportation vehicles, such as steel, an alloy of iron (Fe) and carbon (C). However, steel is also used for necklace and bracelet findings, such as clasps, and is often used for the post in an earring. When corrosion of iron occurs, the iron atoms are oxidized to iron ions (Fe^{2+}) and electrons are released. In a reduction reaction, the released electrons react with oxygen and water to form hydroxide ions (OH^-). Another oxidation reaction can occur when iron atoms react with hydroxide ions, producing iron (II) hydroxide ($Fe(OH)_2$) and releasing electrons. Finally, iron ions can react with oxygen and water to produce iron oxide (Fe_2O_3), commonly known as rust. The following equations describe these pathways to the corrosion of iron in steel:

Oxidation (anode reaction): $Fe \rightarrow Fe^{2+} + 2e^-$

or

$2Fe + 4OH^- \rightarrow 2Fe(OH)_2 + 4e^-$

Reduction (cathode reaction): $O_2 + 2H_2O + 4e^- \rightarrow 4OH^-$

Formation of rust: $4Fe^{2+} + O_2 + 6H_2O \rightarrow 2Fe_2O_3 + 2H_2O + 8H^+$

The Sacrificial Anode

When it is desirable to prevent corrosion of iron, a new anode, such as a zinc (Zn) or magnesium (Mg) strip, is connected to the surface of the iron. These metals are stronger reducing agents than iron and will be more easily oxidized. As oxidation occurs, the zinc or magnesium, rather than the iron, will furnish electrons. These "sacrificial anodes" will erode instead of the iron. They must be replaced periodically, but the iron will remain intact.

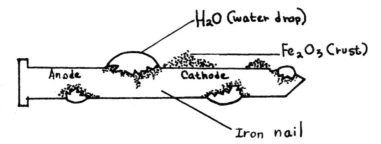

Figure 6.12. The Rusting Process.

In a piece of jewelry, such as an earring, the steel post is often placed into a silver or gold earring design. When the earring is worn, body fluids come into contact with the steel. *Voila!* We have a small electrochemical cell. The iron in the steel acts as the anode, the silver (Ag) or gold (Au) is the cathode, and the body fluids act as an electrolyte. Oxidation at the anode results in iron atoms converting to iron ions and releasing electrons. The anode is eroded. Some iron ions will travel to the gold or silver cathode region through skin moisture and react with oxygen in a reduction reaction, resulting in the formation of rust (Fe_2O_3), which can deposit on the silver or gold. Our earrings would not be very pretty, nor would they be wearable. Fortunately, steel compositions have been formulated so that the iron is tightly bonded and not available to participate in redox reactions. Steel posts are ideal for earring construction.

Coloring Metals:
In Nature and in the Laboratory

Some metals will react with substances available in the environment, such as oxygen, sulfur, and water vapor, to form colors, highlights, and shadings that are attractive to the eye. However, a natural change in color can take years. We can speed the process by placing a piece of metal jewelry into an appropriate chemical solution that will cause a chemical change resulting in a new color on the surface of the metal. There are hundreds of coloring chemicals such as copper sulfate and ammonium sulfide.

CASTING: THE PLOT THICKENS

Casting is used to produce jewelry that is too difficult or inappropriate for fabrication methods. There are two types of casting: Vacuum casting, using a lost wax mold (described on page 158); and gravity mold casting, using pewter. In both methods, the metal is melted and poured into a prepared mold.

Gravity Mold Casting: Gravity Pulls It Down

A gravity mold casting uses the force of gravity to produce the piece. A variety of materials can be used for the mold, including plaster, charcoal, and cuttlefish bone. Pewter is a metal often used in gravity mold casting. Pewter is an alloy consisting of about 84% tin and about 16% of another metal, such as copper. The copper adds strength to the alloy. Pewter is an easy metal to work with because of its relatively low melting point (500°F, 260°C). It is available in casting ingots or sheets from supply houses.

6.6

Plaster Gravity Mold Using Leaf Forms As a Subject Matter

Objectives

1. Students will design a pendant using leaf forms, employing the principles of good composition.
2. Students will carve and assemble a plaster mold for casting.
3. Students will melt and pour pewter metal into the mold, producing a pendant.
4. Students will use proper techniques to finish a pewter piece.

Materials

Paper, pencil, small (3 x 4 inch) cardboard box with lid, plaster of Paris or casting plaster, water, iron skimmer ladle, pewter in sheet or ingot form, wire (stove pipe), pliers, carving tools (simple knife, nail file, pencil, old dental tools, or anything that will carve plaster), wire cutters, propane torch, fireproof surface (casting container of sand), steel wool, jeweler's saw and blades, files, X-ACTO knife, C-clamp, leaves.

Time

200 minutes

Procedure

1. Have students mix plaster and pour into the top and the bottom sections of the box to a depth of at least 1 inch. Allow the plaster to set and dry. Each student will need two plaster pieces: One to carve and one for back of mold (see Figure 6.13).
2. Remove the box top and bottom from the plaster pieces. This should be done several days in advance of carving to allow the plaster to dry thoroughly.
3. Have the students collect a variety of leaves in different sizes and types. Arrange several leaves in an overlapping fashion and draw a picture of this arrangement. It is important to have several layers created for carving in the plaster. Students should try several arrangements, using a variety of sizes and shapes.
4. Transfer or draw the design on one of the plaster pieces. Allow a minimum of ½ inch as a border. Be sure the surface is completely flat.

5. Using carving tools, carve the design into the plaster. Remind students that the carved areas will become raised areas in the cast piece.

6. Carve a sprue or channel from the piece to the outer edge of the plaster.

7. Carve a sprue or channel in the flat side of the second piece. This channel will allow the metal to flow into the carved cavity. The sprue should be deep enough and long enough to touch the carved area of the first piece. Be sure that the sides that touch each other are completely flat to ensure a good cast. Secure the two sections with a C-clamp or wire.

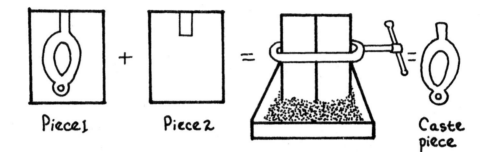

Piece 1   Piece 2   Caste piece

Figure 6.13.

8. Place the plaster mold on end in a bed of sand in a metal pan.

9. Place the pewter in the ladle and heat with a propane torch.

10. Pour the liquid pewter into the sprue opening. Allow the pewter to cool.

11. Remove the piece with pliers.

12. Saw off the sprue with a jeweler's saw. If any metal has run beyond the mold, this too should be removed.

13. File and polish the piece with fine steel wool.

HEAVY METAL

Whether we are referring to music or high-density metals, heavy metal brings to mind a material that plays an essential role in almost every phase of our daily lives. We use metals not only for jewelry but as the structural material for transportation vehicles and most buildings and bridges, and as conductors of electricity and heat. Our entire infrastructure depends on metals.

Gold (Au), silver (Ag), and copper (Cu) can occur freely in nature. However, most metals are combined with other elements and occur as ores. If the ore has a low melting point, ion mobility will allow the electrolysis of the ore to produce a pure metal. Most ores do not have low melting points. Until a process for separating a metal from its ore is developed, the metal remains scarce. In 1855, the cost of aluminum was $100,000 per pound. In 1890, the price dropped to $2 per pound—the Hall-Heroult process for isolating aluminum from its ore was discovered.[7] Today, we take the availability of pure metals for granted. After working with heavy metals in jewelry making, we should give these metals their proper respect.

Design

Bartholm, Lis. *Scandinavian Folk Design.* New York: Dover, 1988.

Brooks, Sue. *Nature Stencil Designs.* New York: Dover, 1996.

Cahier, Charles, and Arthur Martin. *376 Decorative Allover Patterns from Historic Tilework and Textiles.* New York: Dover, 1989.

Chapman, Kenneth M. *Pueblo Pottery Designs.* New York: Dover, 1995.

Davis, Courtney. *Celtic Designs and Motifs.* New York: Dover, 1991.

Horning, Clarence. *Traditional Japanese Crest Designs.* New York: Dover, 1986.

Wilson, Eva. *North American Indian Designs for Artists and Craftspeople.* New York: Dover, 1984.

Jewelry Supplies

Allcraft Tool and Supply Company, Inc.
666 Pacific Street
Brooklyn, NY 11217

Rio Grande
6901 Washington
Albuquerque, NM 87109

Sax Arts and Crafts
2405 S. Calhoun Road
New Berlin, WI 53151

Videos

Werger, Paulette. *Basic Jewelry.* 26 min. Artsmart Video. Aspen, CO: Crystal, 1988.
Demonstration of cutting, piercing, soldering, filing, and polishing techniques.

Cast Jewelry. 30 min. Artsmart Video. Aspen, CO: Crystal, 1988.
Demonstration of the lost wax casting method.

McCreight, Tim. *The Complete Metalsmith, with Tim McCreight.* 70 min. Brookfield, CT: Brookfield Craft Center.
Covers joining, butting, forming, and surface techniques.

REFERENCES

Ferre, R. Duane. *How to Make Wire Jewelry.* Radnor, PA: Chilton, 1980.

Kain, Jay D. *Cast Pewter Jewelry.* Worcester, MA: Davis, 1975.

Masterton, W., E. Slowinski, and C. Stanitski. *Chemical Principles.* 6th ed. Philadelphia: Saunders, 1985.

McGrath, Jinks. *Basic Jewelry Making Techniques.* Edison, NJ: Chartwell Books, 1993.

Morton, Philip. *Contemporary Jewelry.* Rev. ed. New York: Holt, Rinehart & Winston, 1976.

Redu, David. *Jewelry Making: A Manual of Techniques*. Wittshire, England: Crowood Press.

Sprintzen, Alice. *The Jeweler's Art: A Multimedia Approach*. Worcester, MA: Davis, 1995.

———. *Jewelry, Basic Techniques and Design*. Radnor, PA: Chilton, 1980.

von Neumann, Robert. *The Design and Creation of Jewelry*. Radnor, PA: Chilton, 1982.

Zumdahl, Steven S. *Chemistry*. 2d ed. Lexington, MA: D. C. Heath, 1989.

NOTES

1. Philip Morton, *Contemporary Jewelry*, rev. ed. (New York: Holt, Rinehart & Winston, 1976), 11.

2. Ibid., 33.

3. David Redu, *Jewelry Making: A Manual of Techniques* (Wittshire, England: Crowood Press, 1991), 36.

4. Steven S. Zumdahl, *Chemistry*, 2d ed. (Lexington, MA: D. C. Heath, 1989), 897.

5. W. Masterton, E. Slowinski, and C. Stanitski, *Chemical Principles*, 6th ed. (Philadelphia: Saunders, 1985), 239.

6. Zumdahl, *Chemistry*, 803.

7. Ibid., 810.

Two- and Three-Dimensional Works of Art Revisited

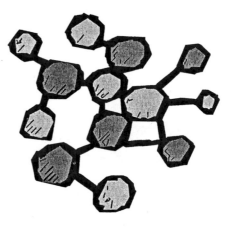

Putting Together the Pieces of the Puzzle

INTRODUCTION

In the preceding chapters, four of the five basics or elements of art were discussed in detail. You will remember the example of the jigsaw puzzle made up of many pieces of elements. When a jigsaw puzzle is assembled properly, a picture appears. So it is with the elements of art: Color, line, shape, texture, and light and dark contrast. When properly composed, these elements make a successful work of art. The composition of the artwork, whether two- or three-dimensional, should contain an effective balance of these basic elements, along with an eye-catching center of interest, an arrangement that promotes movement of the eye through the work, an interesting arrangement of space (both positive and negative), and a feeling of unity and harmony of the parts. These are the tools artists use to turn their ideas into reality. Whether the medium is paint, clay, or stone, the structural tools are the same.

In this chapter, the last of the five elements, light and dark contrast, or value contrast, will be examined in detail. Students will use value contrast, along with the other elements and principles of good composition, to create works of art that incorporate as subject matter molecular models depicting a variety of molecular geometric shapes. The artistic movements of fauvism, cubism, and surrealism will be explored and examined because their techniques are used to create "modern" art.

 Note:
It would be helpful to review with students the elements of art and principles of composition as seen in reproductions of the artwork listed in Chapter 1 beginning on p. 11 or in reproductions of similar artwork.

IT IS A RELIEF: BUT WHAT IS IT?

We have been working in two dimensions with paper and pencil or paint, and in three dimensions, "in the round," with clay and plaster. A three-dimensional piece can be seen from all angles, as we turn it or walk around it and study the play of light and shadow against its surfaces. In a mobile, the element of motion is added, allowing for an ever-changing combination of relationships between negative and positive space. Relief sculpture, unlike sculpture in the round, has a back and a front. The forms of the relief project into the third dimension from the front area. The surface may be a wall or a canvas or a piece of metal. The projection of shapes may be in low relief, raised only slightly from the main surface, or it may be in high relief, protruding considerably from the back surface.

Relief sculpture has been used since prehistoric times, and it is still popular today. It is frequently seen in architecture, where it is used as decoration on the exterior and interior walls of buildings. It is seen in ceramics and jewelry, and in many works of contemporary painting.

Examples of Relief Sculpture in Various Media

Dying Lioness from Nineveh (limestone; Iraq), 650 B.C.
Frieze of the Parthenon (marble, Athens), 440 B.C.
Column of Trojan (marble; Rome), A.D. 106–113
Gates of Paradise (bronze; door of the Bapistry, Florence, Italy), 1435
Singing Angels (marble), Luca Della Robbia, 1435
Musical Instruments (painted wood), Pablo Picasso, 1914
Target with Four Faces (canvas and plaster), Jasper Johns, 1955
Radiant White 952 (cardboard and plywood), Robert Rauschenberg, 1971

As can be seen from the list above, relief subject matter can be almost anything. We have faces, musical instruments, singing angels, a dying lioness, and mythical themes. Now we will try something new. For our purposes, it is appropriate that we use a chemistry theme for our relief construction. The varied and sometimes unique shapes of molecules will provide unusual and interesting material for the subject matter of a relief sculpture.

MOLECULAR SHAPES

When we studied organic molecules in Chapter Five, we realized that chains of carbon atoms with branches appear in a variety of shapes. Cyclic molecules were possible. Catalysts worked to change the rate of a chemical reaction because one molecule fit into another, like puzzle pieces. Catalysts worked because of the molecular shapes of the interacting molecules. Clearly, molecules have distinct shapes.

How Molecular Shapes Can Be Predicted: Using the Periodic Table

In chemistry, as well as in art, we look for organizational systems to help us understand our subject matter. The five elements of art—color, line, shape, texture, and value contrast—are guidelines for evaluating a work of art. The periodic table is the means for assembling information about the chemical elements. It provides the basis for determining the molecular shape of many molecules.

All the elements of a group A family have the same number of bonds when a molecule is formed. In addition, these bonds all originate in the same orbitals. In Chapter 6, we learned the names of the orbitals where the outermost electrons reside. These orbitals are the places where bonds form with other atoms. The shape and orientation of these orbitals determine the geometric shape of resulting molecules when a group A atom bonds with other atoms. Before this information is summarized, it is necessary to consider how some orbitals combine to form hybrid orbitals when bonds are formed.

Hybridization of Orbitals; Hybridization of Corn

Hybrid corn seed comes from corn plants that have particular properties worth preserving. One plant may produce sweet kernels; another may produce long ears. Cross-breeding of the two plants will produce seeds that grow sweet-kernel, long-eared corn. A better ear of corn is produced. When group IIA, IIIA, and IVA families bond, the s and p orbitals combine to form hybrid sp orbitals, where bonding occurs. The sp orbitals replace the individual s and p orbitals to provide more stable locations for the bonds and a more stable molecule. A better molecule is formed.

How Hybrid Orbitals Are Created

For the group IIA elements, the two outermost electrons are in an s orbital. When a bond is forming, these two electrons move 180° away from each other into new, hybrid sp orbitals made of one s and one p orbital. These atoms now have two bonding sites. For the group IIIA elements, the two outermost electrons are in an s orbital and the other outermost electron is in a p orbital. Three hybrid orbitals, sp^2 orbitals, are formed when bonding occurs. These sp^2 orbitals are made of one s orbital and two p orbitals and provide three bonding sites, with a 120° angle between each bonding site pair. Finally, the group IVA elements bond in sp^3 orbitals, which are made of one s and three p orbitals, providing four bonding sites, with a 109.5° angle between each bonding site pair. Molecules formed when atoms bond to IIA and IIIA elements are on a two-dimensional plane. When atoms bond to a IVA element, a three-dimensional molecule is formed.

Table 7.1
"A" Group Families: Bonding Orbitals and Shapes.

Family	Bond Number	Bonding Orbitals	Sample Molecule	Molecular Shape
IA (Alkali Metals)	1	s	LiH	Linear
IIA (Alkaline Earth Metals)	2	sp	MgH_2	Linear
IIIA	3	sp^2	BH_3	Triangular Planar
IVA	4	sp^3	CH_4	Tetrahedral
VA	3	p	NH_3	Pyramid
VIA	2	p	H_2S	Bent
VIIA (Halogens)	1	p	Cl_2	Linear

Molecular Polarity: The Shape of Groups of Molecules
(Covalent, Ionic, and Polar Covalent Bonds)

As we have seen, the orientation of atoms in a molecule, as determined by bonding orbitals, in turn determines the molecular shape. However, the type of bonds between atoms in a molecule along with the molecular shape of the molecule determines the polarity of a molecule. (A molecule is polar if it has a positive end and a negative end.) If a molecule is polar, it can attract other polar molecules to make a variety of structures including, but not limited to, chains, hexagons, and grids. Hydrogen fluoride molecules bond to form zigzag chains, water molecules bond to form open hexagons, and iodine chloride molecules bond to form grids. Bonded molecules make beautiful, three dimensional structures that have all of the elements of successful works of art.

In addition to molecular shape, intramolecular bond types also help to determine molecular polarity. Our discussion thus far has concerned covalent and polar covalent bonds. In covalent bonds, electrons are shared equally by both atoms forming the bond; in polar covalent bonds, electrons are shared unequally. Sharing an electron is like sharing a piece of pie. The piece of pie is either cut exactly down the middle—equal sharing, as in a covalent bond; or it is cut into one large and one small piece—unequal sharing, as in a polar covalent bond. In ionic bonds, electrons are pulled entirely to one atom; a bond results because the positive side of one atom attracts the negative side of another atom. The system for determining the type of bond that exists between two atoms depends on an atomic property called electronegativity.

Electronegativity

The electronegativity of an atom describes its ability in a molecule to attract bonding electrons to itself. Linus Pauling, a Nobel Prize–winning American scientist, developed an electronegativity scale in which each element is assigned a number. The greater the number, the greater the ability of the atom to attract an electron. The periodic table shows electronegativity trends: Electronegativity values decrease down a column (a group, or family) and increase across a row (or period). For the group A elements, electronegativity correlates to atomic radius. As the atomic radius increases, the electronegativity decreases. Down a column, the atomic radius increases and electronegativity decreases. Across a row, atomic radius decreases and electronegativity increases. As an atom becomes larger and outermost electrons move farther from the nucleus, the atom becomes less able to attract those outermost electrons. Electronegativity values range from a high of 4.0 for fluorine (F) to a low of 0.7 for francium (Fr).

Electronegativity Values: What Is the Difference?

The difference between the electronegativity values of the atoms forming a bond within a molecule is used to determine whether the bond is covalent, polar covalent, or ionic. Generally, an electronegativity difference from 0 to 0.4 indicates a covalent bond; a difference from 0.5 to 1.8 indicates a polar covalent bond; and a difference of 1.9 or greater indicates an ionic bond. For example, the electronegativity differences for the bonds Cl-Cl, H-O, and Na-Cl are 0, 1.4, and 2.1, respectively, indicating that the bond types are covalent, polar covalent, and ionic, respectively.

Intramolecular bonds (with molecular shape) determine molecular polarity. Molecular polarity, in turn, establishes whether or not one molecule will attract another molecule. If a IA or VIIA intramolecular bond is ionic, the molecule is polar. If a IA or VIIA intramolecular bond is covalent, the molecule is nonpolar. Polar molecules bond to each other (intermolecular bonds) to form an endless variety of geometric shapes that resemble beautiful three-dimensional sculptures.

Orbital Orientation

In Chapter 6, we learned that, in an atom, there is a spherical-shaped *s* orbital at any energy level outside the nucleus. In addition, there are three *p* orbitals at every energy level, except the first level, and each *p* orbital is shaped like a figure eight, with the atomic nucleus between the two lobes of the figure eight. Because the *s* orbital is spherical in shape, there is no particular orientation for electrons in the *s* orbital. However, the three *p* orbitals have definite orientations in space: They appear at right angles to one another. One *p* orbital appears on an *x*-coordinate axis, one appears on a *y*-coordinate axis, and one appears on a *z*-coordinate axis. When electrons in the *p* orbitals are involved in forming bonds with other atoms, the orientation of the *p* orbitals determines the resulting molecular shape.

					H 2.1	
Li 1.0	Be 1.5	B 2.0	C 2.5	N 3.0	O 3.5	F 4.0
Na 0.9	Mg 1.2	Al 1.5	Si 1.8	P 2.1	S 2.5	Cl 3.0
K 0.8	Ca 1.0	Ga 1.6	Ge 1.8	As 2.0	Se 2.4	Br 2.8
Rb 0.8	Sr 1.0	In 1.7	Sn 1.8	Sb 1.9	Te 2.1	I 2.5
Cs 0.7	Ba 0.9	Tl 1.8	Pb 1.9	Bi 1.9	Po 2.0	At 2.2
Fr 0.7	Ra 0.9					

Figure 7.1. Electronegativity Table.

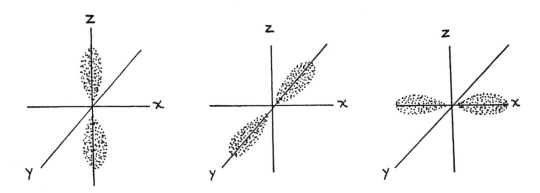

Figure 7.2. The Three *p* Orbitals.

In an atom, the hybridization of *s* and *p* orbitals to form *sp* orbitals provides electron probability areas where bonds can form to make a molecule more stable than if the bonding had occurred in the individual *s* and *p* orbitals. The *sp* orbitals have one large lobe and one small lobe and are aligned along *x*, *y*, and *z* coordinates so that four *sp* orbitals, called *sp*^{3} orbitals because they are made of one *s* and three *p* orbitals, result in a tetrahedral-shaped arrangement. When there are three *sp* orbitals, made of one *s* and two *p* orbitals, called sp^2 orbitals, the molecular has a triangular-planar shape. If there is bonding in two *sp* orbitals, made of one *s* and one *p* orbital, a linear molecule results.

Hybridization: A Theory That Explains Molecular Structure

When a group IIA atom bonds with two atoms to form a molecule, the molecular shape is linear. If a group VIA atom bonds with two atoms to form a molecule, the shape is bent. In each case, the molecule is made of three atoms. The different shapes result because the group IIA atom bonds in *sp* orbitals and the group VIA atom bonds in *p* orbitals. Group IIIA atoms bond with three atoms in sp^2 orbitals to form triangular-planar molecules; group VA atoms bond three atoms in *p* orbitals to form pyramid-shaped molecules. In each case, the resulting molecule is made of four atoms. Finally, group IVA atoms bond with four atoms in sp^3 orbitals to form tetrahedral-shaped molecules. Hybridization is a useful theory to explain the known structures of many molecules.

Molecular Shapes: Relief Subject Matter

Now we are ready to construct molecular models that will provide subject matter for a relief sculpture. The molecules can be arranged like pieces of a puzzle in a pleasing composition to form a unique work of art.

7.1
Making Molecular Models

Objectives

1. Students will predict molecular shapes and construct molecular models from molecular formulas.

2. Students will compare the bond angles and geometric shapes in their molecular models to actual angles and shapes.

3. Students will determine geometric shapes for their molecular models based on bonding orbitals.

4. Students will use electronegativity values to determine whether a bond is ionic, polar covalent, or covalent.

5. Students will arrange their molecular models into a composition to be used as the subject matter for a relief sculpture.

Materials

For each group: Ball-and-stick molecular-model building kit (need molecular bonding kit for correct bond angles), paper and pencil, protractor.

Time

50 minutes

Procedure

1. Have students review the following rules of bonding:

   a. Group IA atoms have one bond; group IIA atoms have two bonds (180° apart); group IIIA atoms have three bonds (120° apart); group IVA atoms have four bonds (109.5° apart); group VA atoms have three bonds (105° apart); group VIA atoms have two bonds (105° apart); group VIIA atoms have one bond.

   b. To allow each atom the correct number of bonds, it might be necessary to have double and/or triple bonds in a molecule.

   c. The central atom in a molecule having more than two atoms determines the shape of the molecule.

   d. When bonding occurs in *sp* orbitals, the atoms surrounding the central atom are as far as possible from one another.

2. The teacher should make a list on the chalkboard of the following molecules: H_2, NH_3, CCl_4, MgO, $AlCl_3$, H_2O, CO_2, N_2, C_2H_6, C_2H_2, C_2H_5OH.

3. Have students use a molecular-model building kit to make ball-and-stick models of the molecules listed on the chalkboard. The balls represent atoms and the sticks represent bonds.

4. After the models have been prepared, have students prepare a table as follows: List the molecules in step 2 in a vertical column along the left side of a sheet of paper. Across the top of the paper, write "Drawing of Molecule," "Geometric Shape," and "Bond Angle Degrees." Students should draw lines to create boxes in which the indicated items will be recorded.

5. Students should complete the table, drawing each molecule and predicting each geometric shape. They should use a protractor to measure the bond angles for each model. Students should discuss their answers and the teacher should provide correct answers.

Questions and Conclusions

Level One

1. Predict the shapes of the following molecules: H_2S (hydrogen sulfide), $CaCl_2$ (calcium chloride), CH_4 (methane), BF_3 (boron trifluoride), and KBr (potassium bromide).

2. Which of the molecular models had double bonds and which had triple bonds? Why are double bonds and triple bonds necessary in particular molecules?

3. Explain why some four-atom molecules, such as NH_3 (ammonia), have a pyramid shape and other four-atom molecules, such as $AlCl_3$ (aluminum chloride), have a triangular-planar shape.

4. What is the best way to arrange your molecular models to form a relief sculpture with interesting positive and negative space?

Level Two

1. For each of the molecules H_2S, $CaCl_2$, CH_4, BF_3, and KBr, name the bonding orbitals where intramolecular bonds are formed.

2. For each of the molecules H_2S, $CaCl_2$, CH_4, BF_3, and KBr, use electronegativity values to determine the type of each intramolecular bond: Ionic, polar covalent, or covalent. For each molecule, determine whether the molecule itself is polar or nonpolar, explaining your reasoning.

3. Explain why a molecule (such as H_2O [water]), that has two polar covalent bonds, is polar.

Molecules and Relief Sculptures

The molecules we have been studying are composed of atoms that usually bond in s, p, and sp orbitals. We can explain additional molecular shapes when we account for the hybridization of d orbitals with sp orbitals. In some molecules, such as phosphorus pentachloride (PCl_5), there are five sp^3d orbitals for bonding electrons. The PCl_5 molecule has a trigonal-bipyramidal shape (see Fig. 7.3). In other molecules, such as sulfur hexafluoride (SF_6), the six bonding orbitals are sp^3d^2 and the molecular shape is octahedral. Have students make models of PCl_5 and SF_6 to use (in addition to the models constructed in Activity 7.1) as the subject matter for a relief sculpture in Activity 7.2.

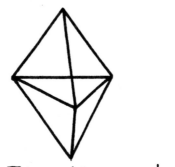 

Trigonal bipyramid   Octahedral

Figure 7.3. Trigonal-Bipyramidal and Octahedral Bonding Arrangements.

7.2

Relief Plaster Sculpture Using a Clay Mold

Objectives

1. Students will design relief sculptures based on previously constructed molecular models, emphasizing interesting negative and positive space, visual movement through shape, and visual texture applied to positive shapes.

2. Students will construct clay molds and cast plaster to create relief sculptures.

Level One:
Relief Plaster Sculpture Emphasizing Interesting
Positive and Negative Space

Materials

Pencil, paper, molecular models from Activity 7.1, nonhardening clay, clay tools, strips of cardboard to form a frame around a clay mold, cardboard for base, X-ACTO knife, ruler, tape, plaster of Paris, bowl, water.

Time

150 minutes

Procedure

1. Using the molecular model or models desired, have students draw a series of small preliminary sketches of the model or models, emphasizing interesting positive and negative space. A sketch need not be completely contained by the edges of the paper: Allow some parts of the drawing to touch the edge of the page, implying extension beyond the page. Students might try combining two or more models in one sketch. The typical shape for a sketch would be rectangular, but the outer shape might be square, circular, or triangular.

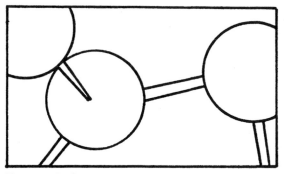

Figure 7.4.

2. Have students choose one of their sketches and prepare a clay mold:

   a. Flatten the clay to a 2-inch thickness.

   b. Cut a cardboard base in an appropriate shape and place the clay over it. Trim the clay and the base so that the edges are flush.

   > ■ *Note:*
   > Students should feel free to use any desired size and shape for the mold. Recommended size for a rectangular shape is 5 x 8 inches.

   c. Use clay tools or hands to make indentations in the clay. Students should not remove so much clay that the base is exposed, and they should make some areas high relief and some areas low relief, for variety. Remind students that the cast piece will be an inverted image of the mold: The deeper the carving in the mold, the higher the relief in the cast piece.

   d. Place cardboard strips around the outside of the mold, securing them with tape. The strips should rise at least one inch above the highest part of the clay. In the cast piece, this elevated portion will form the base. Secure the bottom edge of the outside of the mold with clay to prevent plaster leakage.

3. Mix plaster of Paris with water in the bowl and pour it into the mold. Allow the plaster to completely set.

> ■ *Note:*
> The plaster may be colored, if desired, by adding a small amount of liquid tempera paint to the mixture.

4. Remove the frame and the cardboard bottom. Peel the clay off the mold. (The clay can be reused.)

5. Have students title their piece, using a variation or combination of the names of the molecules modeled.

Level Two:
Relief Plaster Sculpture Emphasizing
Positive and Negative Space and Visual Movement

Materials

Same as level one.

Time

150 minutes

Procedure

1. Have students draw preliminary sketches as in level one. In addition to emphasizing interesting positive and negative space, students should try to create a sense of visual movement across, up, down, in, out, around, and so forth. This sense of movement can be intensified by exaggerating the components of the models (e.g., varying the sizes and shapes of their components).

2. Proceed with steps 2–5 from the procedure in level one.

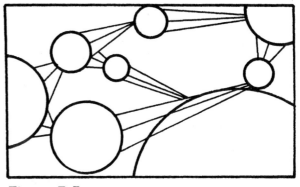

Figure 7.5.

Level Three:
Relief Plaster Sculpture Emphasizing Positive and
Negative Space, Visual Movement, and Visual Texture

Materials

Same as level one.

Time

150 minutes

Procedure

1. Have student draw preliminary sketches as in level two, applying visual texture to the positive shapes in the composition. These textures should reinforce the movement of the positive shapes.

2. Proceed with steps 2–5 from the procedure in level one.

Figure 7.6.

THE LAST PIECE TO THE PUZZLE

The Value of Contrast, the Contrast of Value

Contrast of value is an important tool of the artist. Without contrast, a work would lack definition. Whether in color or in black and white, a contrast between light and dark helps the eye focus on particular areas of a work. Contrast of value can be seen all around us: A dark-colored tree against a light-colored building; a white full moon against a black night sky; areas of a sculpture highlighted by a light source while other areas are plunged into darkness. Shapes are distinguished from each other by value.

In X-ray diffraction pictures, atomic nuclei reflect X-rays on to photographic film, resulting in a pattern of dark-colored spots against a light-colored background. This value contrast in the picture allows the scientist to determine the position of atoms in a crystal or in a molecule. There are many uses for light-dark contrast.

The use of light-dark contrast to suggest three dimensions was first successfully accomplished during the fifteenth century by Italian painters. The term often used to describe the effect of light colors against dark colors is the Italian word *chiaroscuro*, from *chiaro*, meaning "light," and *oscuro*, meaning "dark."

Well-Known Examples of Value Contrast

Any work by Rembrandt van Rijn, seventeenth century
Any work by Jan Vermeer, seventeenth century
Death of Marat, Jacques-Louis David, 1793
The Bathers, Georges Seurat, 1883–84
Anxiety, Edvard Munch, 1896
The Old Guitarist, Pablo Picasso, 1903
Melancholy and Mystery of a Street, Giorgio de Chirico, 1914
Self Portrait, Max Beckmann, 1927
Whaam, Roy Lichtenstein, 1963

Change in the Works:
New Ways of Seeing

By 1700, 13 elements had been discovered or isolated in a pure form. Copper (Cu), gold (Au), silver (Ag), mercury (Hg), and lead (Pb) were among these elements. In 1896, 26 elements were known, including sulfur (S), oxygen (O), and aluminum (Al). By 1908, 81 elements were known, and by 1993, 109 elements had been isolated or synthesized. The late nineteenth century was a time of great discovery and enlightenment in chemistry.

In art, the twentieth century was a time of many changes. Many artists turned from realistic interpretations of the world to more individual ways of seeing things. Artists began to alter their subject matter by distorting or changing what they viewed. Others drew upon their imagination and upon dreams to express themselves. Many of the examples in this and previous chapters show how varied and personal their works can be. Throughout all centuries, however, the tools of the artist (line, color, texture, shape, and value contrast) and the principles of good composition (strong center of interest or focal point; movement of the eye through the composition; balance of parts; interesting negative and positive space; and unity and harmony) continue to shape the world of art.

Fauvism, Cubism, and Surrealism

Some artists, such as Henri Matisse, chose to use bold colors not natural to the subject, distortion, simplification, and visual texture to describe their ideas. Because of the shocking effect of the works of Matisse, and the works of other expressive artists of the early twentieth century, the artists were given the name *fauves*, meaning "wild beasts." Others, such as Pablo Picasso, chose to break down their subjects into simple geometric forms, calling their form of abstraction *cubism*. Still others, such as Salvador Dali and Rene Magritte, chose to draw upon dreams and fantasy to express their views in a style called *surrealism*.

7.3
A Discussion of Fauvism, Cubism, and Surrealism

Objectives

1. Students will view reproductions of work by Matisse, Picasso, Dali, and Magritte.
2. Students will discuss how each artist expresses their ideas based on the definition of each style, the meaning of the title of the work, and how the title is seen in the picture.
3. Students will discuss how each artist uses the elements of art and the principles of good composition.
4. Students will compare and contrast the styles of these artists.

Materials

Slides (or photographs) of work by Matisse, Picasso, Dali, and Magritte; slide projector.

Time

50 minutes

Procedure

1. The teacher should list the elements of art and the principles of good composition in a prominent location.

2. Discuss the characteristics of fauvism, cubism, and surrealism (a discussion follows this activity) with students.

3. Show the students reproductions of works by Matisse, Picasso, Dali, and Magritte (and other artists of the fauvist, cubist, and surrealist movements).

4. Have students compare and contrast the works of artists from the three movements, in terms of style and subject matter. Have the students discuss how each artist expresses his ideas based on the definition of each style and how he uses the elements of art and the principles of good composition.

   ■ *Note:*
   It may be helpful to have students research Matisse, Picasso, Dali, and Magritte (and other fauvist, cubist, and surrealist artists) and share with the class what they learn.

Fauvism: 1900 to 1920. Some of the artists involved in the fauvist movement were Henri Matisse, Andre Derain, and Raoul Dufy. They used bold colors that were not natural to the subject and made use of visual texture to enrich the painting surface. They painted simplified shapes without realistic shading, and their paintings had flat areas of color. These "wild beasts" broke the rules and shocked the art world.

Cubism: 1900 to 1950. Some of the artists involved in the cubist movement were Pablo Picasso, Georges Braque, and Juan Gris. They broke down form into geometric parts and were not interested in color. For them, form and shapes were more important. They used multiple views of the same object, painting objects as seen from many angles at the same time. Their art was a form of abstraction taken from reality but changed by the artist.

Surrealism: 1920 to the Present. Artists who have been involved in the surrealist movement include Salvador Dali, Joan Miro, Rene Magritte, and Max Ernst. Surrealism combines realism, the subconscious, and the dream world. Imaginative objects, the real and unreal, exist in the same picture. This movement was inspired by Sigmund Freud's study of the subconscious. The surrealistic artists are also excellent technicians. A surrealistic painting, for example, usually suggests a specific mood (e.g., eerie, sad, playful, mysterious).

These artists, intentionally or unintentionally, stepped into the world of atoms, molecules and subatomic particles and incorporated theories concerning atomic and subatomic particles into their works of art. The simplified shapes of fauvism might resemble our concept of the arrangement of particles in a crystalline solid—a uniform display of the crystal particles. The geometric shapes in cubist paintings often resemble the geometric shapes of molecules. The dream-world shapes of the surrealists often resemble molecules or atoms floating, as in a gaseous phase, or intermingling to resemble the liquid or solid phases of matter. Shapes resembling electron-cloud probability areas are seen in works of Salvador Dali and Joan Miro. The imagination of fauvist, cubist, and surrealist artists has resulted in an unintentional interpretation of the structure of matter.

Examples of Fauvist, Cubist, and Surrealist Paintings

Fauvist Paintings

> *Green Stripe (Madame Matisse)*, Henri Matisse, 1905
> *Open Window, Collioure*, Henri Matisse, 1905
> *Indian Model in the Studio at L'Impasse Guelma*, Raoul Dufy, 1928
> *Oriental Rugs*, Henri Matisse, 1906
> *Spanish Still Life*, Henri Matisse, 1906

Cubist Paintings

> *Girl with Mandolin*, Pablo Picasso, 1910
> *Accordionist*, Pablo Picasso, 1911
> *Card Player*, Pablo Picasso, 1913–14
> *Violin and Palette*, Georges Braque, 1909–10
> *Portrait of Picasso*, Juan Gris, 1912

Surrealist Paintings

> *The Persistence of Memory*, Salvador Dali, 1931
> *The Harlequin's Carnival*, Joan Miro, 1924–25
> *Europe After the Rain*, Max Ernst, 1940–42
> *The Castle of the Pyrenees*, Rene Magritte, 1959
> *Inventions of the Monsters*, Salvador Dali, 1937

7.4

Series of Four Drawings with Emphasis on Value Contrast—Fauvism, Cubism, and Surrealism

Objectives

1. Students will apply the principles and techniques of value contrast, fauvism, cubism, and surrealism in creating drawings of molecular models.

2. Students will apply the principles of good composition to their drawings.

Materials

6-x-16-inch white drawing paper, ruler, pencil, eraser, selection of molecular models, posterboard or other heavy mounting surface large enough to hold a set of four drawings, rubber cement, colored pencils, scratch paper, magazines, scissors.

Time

300 minutes

Procedure

1. Have students chose one or more molecular models to use as the subject for a series of four drawings. Students should arrange the models into a composition in preparation for a drawing.

2. Divide the white drawing paper into four 4-x-6-inch rectangles.

3. A black pencil should be used for the first drawing (leftmost rectangle), which will be realistic, emphasizing value contrast:

   a. Lightly sketch an outline of the molecular-model composition, drawing it as it actually appears.

   b. Using the edge of the pencil point, add shading values (light-dark contrast). Try to define the edges of the shapes using only shading, and try to achieve a realistic, three-dimensional effect. When complete, the drawing should have no outlining, and the subject should appear against a lighter- or darker-colored background.

4. A colored pencil should be used for the second drawing, which will be fauvist: Using the principles of fauvism, interpret the molecular-model composition in the second rectangle. Use the principles of good composition and the following techniques:

   a. Distort or alter the size and shape of parts.

   b. Add visual texture to some parts.

   c. Simplify the shapes.

   d. Incorporate "flat" areas of color and avoid three-dimensional (realistic) shading.

5. A black lead pencil should be used for the third drawing, which will be cubist:

   a. Using the same molecular models, create a composition that rests upon a table. Using a magazine as a source for interesting ideas, add at least two more objects to the composition (e.g., molecular models with a toy and a book; molecular models with a microscope and a textbook).

   b. On scratch paper, make a quick sketch of a cubist interpretation of the composition. Show all of the table or only part of it.

   c. In the third rectangle, interpret the items in the sketch by breaking down the shapes of the objects into their closest geometric shape or shapes (see Fig. 7.7). Interpreting the basic forms is important, not the color. If desired, use multiple views of the objects (see Fig. 7.8, p. 192).

**Figure 7.7. A Face
Drawn in Cubist Style.**

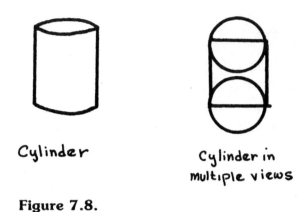

Cylinder   Cylinder in
                            multiple views

Figure 7.8.

    d. Shade the shapes with values of gray for contrast. Try to avoid outline alone to separate shapes from one another.

6. A colored pencil or black pencil should be used for the fourth drawing, which will be surrealistic:

    a. Using the molecular models as the center of interest, create a surrealistic or fantasy composition in the fourth rectangle.

    b. Create an unusual setting or location for the molecular models, such as underwater or on top of a mountain, or combine the molecular models with something else, such as the hood ornament of a car or the head of an animal. All objects and settings depicted (including the models) should be drawn in a realistic manner.

    c. Add other realistically depicted objects to the composition, as desired.

7. Cut out all four pictures and use rubber cement to mount them on posterboard or some other heavy mounting surface. Label the first drawing Realistic. Label each subsequent drawing with the name of the movement represented.

THE PUZZLE
IS COMPLETED

    We have studied color, line, shape, texture, and value contrast as the elements that, together, make a complete work of art. These are the puzzle pieces that fit together to make the entire picture. There are many ways to use these pieces to compose a work of art. In the next chapter, we will use new techniques to organize the five elements into a pleasing work of art. The same puzzle pieces will be placed together in new ways with interesting results.

REFERENCES

Arnason, H. H. *History of Modern Art: Painting, Sculpture, Architecture*. 3d ed. New York: Harry N. Abrams, 1986.

Baker, Rachel. *All About Art*. New Haven, CT: Fine Arts, 1971.

Essers, Volkman. *Henri Matisse: 1869–1954; Master of Colour*. Koln, West Germany: Benedikt Taschen, 1987.

Janson, H. W. *History of Art*. 4th ed. New York: Harry N. Abrams, 1991.

Ocvirk, Otto G. *Art Fundamentals: Theory and Practice*. Dubuque, IA: Wm. C. Brown, 1975.

Picon, Gaetan. *Surrealists and Surrealism*. New York: Skira Rizzoli, 1977.

Porzio, Domenico, and Marco Valsecchi. *Pablo Picasso: Man and His Work*. Secaucus, NJ: Chartwell Books, 1974.

Photography

A Picture Is Worth a Thousand Words

INTRODUCTION

Picture This

Picture this: A world without photography. Magazines, books, and newspapers are filled with photographs of current events. Advertisers bombard us with photographs of famous people and new products. In advertising, it is well known that a picture is worth a thousand words. What would a wedding or a graduation be without someone taking pictures to capture a memory of the event? However, life without photography was the case before the 1830s, when L. J. M. Daguerre, a French painter and stage designer created a process named after him—the daguerreotype. In this process, a reverse image, reversed by the lens of a camera, was projected onto a specially treated plate (see p. 196), which was then developed, and the image was fixed (made permanent), producing the final picture. The disadvantage of this first daguerrotype was the length of time the plate had to be exposed to produce the image. Samuel F. B. Morse, better known for the invention of the telegraph, was instrumental in improving the daguerreotype. He was able to decrease the exposure time, creating a more user-friendly procedure. By 1840, the daguerreotype was widely accepted and in use in America. However, the final image was not in color; artists were employed to color the images by hand to achieve a realistic effect.

■ *Note:*
A suggested example to introduce students to daguerreotype is *Girl with a Portrait of Washington*, Southworth and Hawes, mid-19th century. Also, any examples of daguerreotype from books listed in the "References" section at the end of this chapter may be used.

A Record of Going West and Wars

At the same time that the daguerreotype was in use, William Henry Fox Talbot, an English chemist, was developing a process using glass negatives and paper prints. This process, although slow to overtake the popular daguerrotype, was, by 1860, being used extensively to record many historical events, such as the Civil War and the move westward by the pioneers. Photography was used not only to record people and important events but also provided a means of more accurately recording events previously unobserved, such as the motion, in separate steps, of a running horse, or a human jumping. It gave artists a new tool for recording what they saw. However, photography as an art form in its own right was not realized until much later.

Cameras for the Average Person

In 1888, the camera moved into the hands of the average person when George Eastman developed the Kodak, a small camera for making quick, simple exposures, or "snapshots." The Kodak was made to be used with a roll of film.[1] Heavy, awkward photographic plates for recording images were no longer needed, so the camera was no longer a tool only for professionals.

Later developments expanded the possibilities provided by the camera. In 1924, for example, the Leica camera provided 35mm photography. It was small, unobtrusive, and quick, making it easier to take pictures that were difficult to take with the traditional camera.

THE CHEMISTRY BEHIND THE ART OF PHOTOGRAPHY

Historically, the development of photography as an art parallels the advancement of our knowledge concerning light-sensitive chemicals and our ability to control these chemicals. Photography is the art of painting with light. To make a photo, light from an image must strike a chemical substance. The chemical darkens in degrees proportional to the quantity of light that the chemical is exposed to. Even before the 1830s, scientists were experimenting with chemicals that changed in appearance upon exposure to light.

Silver Provides the Answer

In 1727, a German physicist, Heinrick Schulze, discovered that silver nitrate ($AgNO_3$) and other silver salts darkened upon exposure to light. Thomas Wedgwood, son of the English potter Josiah Wedgwood, was the first to make practical use of the phenomenon. In 1802, he published a paper that described a paper soaked in silver nitrate that was used to make photograms, pictures made without a camera (see Activity 8.3). Objects were placed on the paper, and light, striking the area surrounding the objects, reduced the silver ions (Ag^+) to silver metal (Ag), darkening the area exposed to light. The areas beneath the objects were not exposed to light and remained unchanged. Unfortunately, one major problem remained: The photograms produced were not permanent. Any exposure of the entire photogram to ordinary light turned the entire photogram black.

Photo Permanency: How Is It Done?

L. J. M. Daguerre, in the 1830s, solved the problem of photo permanency. His specially treated plate was a sheet of copper (Cu) plated on one side with silver. The silver was oxidized with iodine (I) vapor to produce silver ions:

$$2Ag_{(s)} + I_{2\,(g)} \rightarrow 2Ag^+_{\,(aq)} + 2I^-_{\,(aq)}$$

with half reactions:

$$\text{Oxidation: } Ag_{(s)} \rightarrow Ag^+_{\,(aq)} + e^-$$

$$\text{Reduction: } I_{2\,(g)} + 2e^- \rightarrow 2I^-_{\,(aq)}$$

■ *Note:*
$_{(s)}$ indicates a solid, $_{(g)}$ gas, and $_{(aq)}$ aqueous.

After exposure to reflected light, the plate was exposed to mercury (Hg) vapor, converting the silver ions to silver atoms and producing an image:

$$2Ag^+_{\,(aq)} + Hg_{(g)} \rightarrow 2Ag_{(s)} + Hg^{2+}_{\,(aq)}$$

with half reactions:

$$Hg_{(g)} \rightarrow Hg^{2+}_{\,(aq)} + 2e^- \text{ (oxidation)}$$

$$Ag^+_{\,(aq)} + e^- \rightarrow Ag_{(s)} \text{ (reduction)}$$

Daguerre used sodium thiosulfate ($Na_2S_2O_3$) to make the photo permanent. Today, we still use sodium thiosulfate for this purpose, but we call it hypo. The sodium thiosulfate removes unexposed silver bromide (AgBr) as follows:

$$Ag^+_{\,(aq)} + 2S_2O_3^{2-}_{\,(aq)} \rightarrow Ag(S_2O_3)_2^{3-}_{\,(aq)}$$

or

$$AgBr_{(s)} + 2S_2O_3^{2-}_{\,(aq)} \rightarrow Ag(S_2O_3)_2^{3-}_{\,(aq)} + Br^-_{\,(aq)}$$

Even though we still use light-sensitive silver salts in film to produce an image and sodium thiosulfate to preserve the image, we do not encourage iodine and mercury vapor use for film development. In hat making, mercury vapor was commonly used for felt enhancement. Constant inhalation of mercury vapor is not good for brain cells, as is evidenced in the Mad Hatter's story in *Alice in Wonderland*. Chapter 10 addresses the issue of chemical hazards in art.

Changing Solubility Preserves the Image

If the solubility of silver bromide or any slightly soluble silver salt could not be increased, we would not be able to fix a photographic image. When sodium thiosulfate reacts with insoluble silver bromide, the silver complex produced, $Ag(S_2O_3)_2^{3-}$, is quite soluble in water and can be washed away. Certain molecules or ions, called ligands, have an unbounded outermost electron pair that can be used to bond a metal ion, usually a transition-metal ion such as a silver ion, to form a complex ion that is often quite soluble in water. When children have excess lead ions (Pb^{2+}) in their body tissues, a ligand that bonds lead ions is given to the child to remove the excess lead ions.

General Rules of Solubility

The general rules of solubility help us to predict whether or not a substance is soluble in water. If one gram of a substance can dissolve in water to make 100 grams of solution, we say that the substance is soluble. If less than one gram but more than 0.1 gram can dissolve, the substance is slightly soluble. If a substance can only dissolve in water if less than 0.1 gram is present, we say that the substance is insoluble. These criteria for solubility of substances are determined at 25°C. The following rules summarize the solubility of a large number of substances:

1. Most alkali metal and ammonium (NH_4^+) compounds are soluble.

2. Most nitrate (NO_3^-), acetate ($C_2H_3O_2^-$), and chlorate (ClO_3^-) compounds are soluble.

3. Most chloride compounds are soluble, except silver chloride ($AgCl$), lead chloride ($PbCl_2$), and mercury I chloride (Hg_2Cl_2).

4. Most hydroxide compounds are insoluble, except alkali metal hydroxides and barium hydroxide [$Ba(OH)_2$], which are soluble, and calcium hydroxide [$Ca(OH)_2$] and strontium hydroxide [$Sr(OH)_2$], which are slightly soluble.

5. Most sulfate compounds are soluble, except lead sulfate ($PbSO_4$) and barium sulfate ($BaSO_4$), which are insoluble, and silver sulfate (Ag_2SO_4) and calcium sulfate ($CaSO_4$), which are slightly soluble.

6. Most carbonate (CO_3^{2-}), phosphate (PO_4^{3-}), and sulfide (S^{2-}) compounds are insoluble.

To understand why the addition of thiosulfate ions ($S_2O_3^{2-}$) to silver ions (Ag^+) is an extremely efficient way to remove unexposed silver ions on photographic film, it is necessary to investigate the concept of equilibrium.

Equilibrium: What Is Equal?

When a substance is dissolved in water to form a saturated solution (see Chapter 2 "Types of Solutions"), some of the substance remains undissolved, so we know we have reached the saturation point. Present in the solution would be the dissolved ions and a small portion of the undissolved substance. When all these substances are present, we can say that we have reached equilibrium. To have equilibrium, the rate of the substance dissolving has to equal the rate of the dissolved ions reforming the original substance. To show that a system is at equilibrium, we use a double arrow in the equation ⇔. When sodium thiosulfate reacts with silver ions to form a complex, and the reaction reaches equilibrium, the equation is written as follows:

$$Ag^+_{(aq)} + 2S_2O_3^{2-}{}_{(aq)} \Leftrightarrow Ag(S_2O_3)_2^{3-}$$

Equilibrium Concentrations

At equilibrium, depending on the temperature of the reaction, almost any concentration of the substances present can exist. If, at equilibrium in the reaction between sodium thiosulfate and silver ions, mostly silver ions and thiosulfate ions are present, we would not be successful in removing the silver ions to preserve a photo image. We need a system that shows us which substances are in excess at equilibrium, the reactants or products. It is possible to have equal concentrations of reactants and products at equilibrium, but this is usually not the case. At equilibrium, forward and reverse reaction rates are equal, not the amounts of reactants and products. At equilibrium, the rate of reactants making products equals the rate of products making reactants.

A System for
Determining Equilibrium Concentrations

When we consider a system at equilibrium, we find that if, at a specific temperature, we arrange the reactant and product concentrations expressed in moles per liter in a particular way, no matter what these concentrations are, a constant value results. This constant value is called the equilibrium constant and, for solubility, is given the symbol K_{sp}. The general formula to find the K_{sp} is the product (multiplication) of the concentrations of the products expressed in moles per liter over the product of the concentrations of the reactants expressed in moles per liter. Also, to find the constant, coefficients in the dissolving equation become exponents. Once we know the K_{sp} for the solubility of a substance, we can know precisely how soluble that substance is. When we are looking for a fixing agent for film development, we need a substance that will combine with silver ions and form a very insoluble product. The K_{sp} for a substance is determined from an equation as follows:

For $AgCl_{(s)} \rightarrow Ag^+_{(aq)} + Cl^-_{(aq)}$, the K_{sp} expression is

$$K_{sp} = \frac{[Ag^+][Cl^-]}{[AgCl]}$$

The brackets represent concentration in moles per liter. Because the constant, the K_{sp}, is dependent on concentration, we remove solids such as silver chloride ($AgCl$) from the expression. The concentration of a solid is constant. The density of a solid is a way to express the solid's concentration. Therefore, the K_{sp} of a solid dissolving is simply the product of the concentration of the ions produced.

For $AgCl$, the K_{sp} expression is:

$$K_{sp} = [Ag^+][Cl^-]$$

It can be seen that the higher the value for the K_{sp}, the greater the solubility of the substance.

Constants for
Film Fixing Substances

Using the same general formula that we used for K_{sp}, we can examine constants for the formation of complex ions and determine what would be the best substance to use as a film fixer; in other words, what substance can remove a large number of silver ions from the unexposed portion of the film. We use the symbol K_f for the formation constant of a complex ion. We know that thiosulfate ions are combined with silver ions to form the $Ag(S_2O_3)_2^{3-}$ complex:

For $Ag^+_{(aq)} + 2S_2O_3^{2-}_{(aq)} \rightarrow Ag(S_2O_3)_2^{3-}_{(aq)}$, the K_f expression is

$$K_f = \frac{[Ag(S_2O_3)_2^{3-}]}{[Ag^+][S_2O_3^{2-}]^2}$$

The K_f value at 25°C for $Ag(S_2O_3)_2^{3-}$ is 2.9×10^{13}. This extremely large value tells us that at equilibrium, there will be mostly $Ag(S_2O_3)_2^{3-}$ ions present.

The K_f value for the $Ag(CN)_2^-$ complex ion is 5.6×10^{18}. Cyanide ions (CN^-) would be better removers of silver ions than thiosulfate ions. However, most of us know that cyanide is a deadly poison if inhaled or ingested. In the play *Arsenic and Old Lace*, it was used very effectively to rid the cast of unwanted characters. Refining the process of film developing, which included not only the discovery of proper fixing solutions but also the development of film surfaces and developers that were reliable, helped to plunge us into the age of modern photography.

MODERN PHOTOGRAPHY

Photography Comes of Age: Art and Photography

Alfred Stieglitz (1864–1946) is widely considered to be the founder of modern photography. He took photography from being just a means of recording what we see and raised it to an art form. His photographs include not only artistic and personal images of what he saw, but also abstract images beyond realistic subject matter. These abstract images began in the 1920s with his cloud compositions.

Nature photography was raised to an art form by the most famous of the American nature photographers of the twentieth century, Ansel Adams (1902–1984). He is considered to be the master technician of black-and-white photography. His nature scenes still represent some of the most beautiful pictures ever taken.

With the creation of many new magazines and newspapers during the early portion of the twentieth century, photography grew into its own as a means of recording the visual images of the times, such as the Depression, the growth of industry, life in the city, and World War II. These events were recorded on film by photojournalists. As many new magazines and newspapers appeared, there came an increase in advertising and a need for the photographer to illustrate everything from baby booties to sleek new cars.

After World War II, photography as an art form took two directions: Some photographers turned from realism to abstraction and fantasy, as seen in the work of Minor White (1908–1976) and Bill Brandt (1904–1983). Others, such as Robert Frank (1924–), used realism and words to portray a personal view of American culture.

Works by Significant Photographers

Portrait (I) 1918 Georgia O'Keeffe, Alfred Stieglitz, 1918
   (or any cloud photograph by Alfred Stieglitz)
Moonrise, Ansel Adams, 1941 (or any nature photograph by Ansel Adams)
Migrant Mother (Depression era), Dorothea Lange, 1936
Fort Peck Dam (first cover of *Life* magazine), Margaret Bourke-White, 1936
Ritual Branch (abstraction), Minor White, 1958 (or any work by Minor White)
London Child (fantasy), Bill Brandt, 1955 (or any work by Bill Brandt)
Santa Fe, New Mexico (realism), Robert Frank, 1955–56 (or any work by Robert Frank)

Picture Perfect

Anyone can click the shutter of a camera, but will a good picture result? As in other forms of art, composition is an important element in photography. A photograph is judged by how well the picture is composed. Composition has already been discussed in relationship to other art forms (see Chapter 1), but a brief review of composition basics, focusing on their application to photography, follows:

1. Strong center of interest or focal point

   This is what the photographer wants the viewer to look at first. The entire subject, however, need not be shown; closeups of only a portion of the subject can sometimes be very effective. Also, the center of interest need not be at the center of the picture. Try moving it off-center, up or down, or to either side. The subject can be framed in a number of ways just by moving the camera.

2. Movement of the eye through the picture

   The viewer's eye should move through the picture easily. Avoid having confusing lines in the background that move in too many directions. Simplicity is the key. Too much confusion in the background may overwhelm the focus of the picture.

3. Balance of parts—symmetrical (equal) or asymmetrical (unequal)

   If the subject is placed off-center in the picture, another visual element should be used to balance the subject. Sometimes, visual balance can be achieved by framing. In a landscape, for instance, a tree branch can often be used to add interest in the foreground, to balance a subject, and to add depth to the picture.

4. Interesting negative and positive space

   The subject is important, but so is the space around the subject. Do not let the negative space dominate the composition. If necessary, move in closer to the subject. The photographer has control over what appears in the picture and where it appears. Do not "cut off" feet or the tops of heads, and be aware of where objects are in relation to one another. If photographing a person, for example, avoid having the person stand in such a way that a tree behind the person appears to be growing from his or her head.

5. Unity and harmony

   Everything in the composition should complement everything else. Move in closer to the subject, if necessary, and avoid any distracting elements. It is the photographer's responsibility to ensure a good composition. (Before taking a picture, many photographers use their hands to make a frame around the subject. This helps them ensure a better composition before they shoot the photo.)

8.1

Analysis of Photographs

Objectives

1. Students will identify the principles of good composition as observed in magazine or student-supplied photographs.

2. Students will discuss how the principles of good composition have been used effectively or ineffectively in the photographs.

3. Students will suggest ways to improve existing photos if they feel improvement is needed.

Materials

Photographs or magazines containing photos.

Time

50 minutes

Procedure

1. Have students bring to class several photographs that they have taken or photographs taken by friends or family. If no photographs are available, the students should look through magazines and find photographs that they think are well composed and some that they think are not well composed.

2. Either individually in writing, or in a class group discussion, have students answer the following questions for each photograph:

   a. What is the center of interest in the picture?

   b. Is the center of interest well identified or obvious? If not, how can it be improved?

   c. Does the photograph have any shortcomings as far as the composition is concerned? If so, what are they? How can they be corrected?

   d. How does the eye move through the composition? Should something be added or removed to improve the picture?

   e. Has framing been used? If so, is it effective?

   f. In what ways could the subject be framed in the photograph for an effective composition?

   g. If a student's photograph is being evaluated, ask the student to explain how the photograph could be improved if it were retaken.

THE PHOTOGRAM:
PICTURE WITHOUT A CAMERA

Following World War II, a group of artists called the dadaists, frustrated and disenchanted with the establishment and society, reacted against tradition by moving art in a new direction, away from the accepted forms. One of the techniques that became popular with these artists was the photogram. Christian Schad, a member of the Dadaist group, began by creating images cut from paper, which he put together in groups and laid out on light-sensitive paper. He then exposed the paper to light for a specific period of time and developed his prints. Later, in 1921, the artist Man Ray used some of these same methods to create what he called Rayographs. Another artist of the period, Moholy-Nagy, who also experimented with these shadow pictures, called them photograms.[2]

When making a photogram, the medium is light. Pictures can be created using any object, solid or transparent, that is exposed to light after being placed on light-sensitive paper. Objects can be exposed in one position, moved, and exposed again for a different amount of time for a repeat effect. Transparent and translucent objects can be used, as well as linear and solid objects, to achieve a variety of effects.

8.2

Photography—Printing Negatives and Making Photograms

Objectives

1. Students will prepare a developing solution and use the solution to make photograms.

2. Students will explore a variety of techniques to achieve unique photogram compositions (using a variety of two- and three-dimensional objects, creating a feeling of depth through overlapping and multiple exposure of objects, etc.).

3. Students will explain the use of some of the chemicals needed to make a print from a negative or to make a photogram.

Materials

Na_2SO_3 (sodium sulfite), hydroquinone (paradihydroxybenzene), $Na_2CO_3 \cdot H_2O$ (sodium carbonate), KBr (potassium bromide), concentrated $HC_2H_3O_2$ (acetic acid), Kodak fixing solution, Elon, gram balance, 1-liter volumetric flask distilled water, photographic printing paper, trays, scissors, tongs, solid or translucent two- and three-dimensional objects for making a photogram (e.g., wire mesh, lace, jewelry pieces, twigs, leaves, flowers), 60-watt lightbulb, darkroom and safelight, automatic stirrer, 250 ml beaker, 50 ml graduated cylinder.

Time

100 minutes

Procedure

(Note: All discarded solutions should be placed in containers provided for hazardous waste collection.)

 Note:
Distilled water should be used for all chemical dilutions.

A. Have students prepare a solution for developing paper:

1. In a 1 liter volumetric flask, combine the following chemicals:
   3.0 g Elon
   45.0 g Na_2SO_3
   12.0 g hydroquinone
   80.0 g $Na_2CO_3 \cdot H_2O$
   2.0 g KBr

2. Add distilled water to make 1 liter of developing solution. Agitate until dissolved, using an automatic stirrer.

B. Have students prepare a stop-bath solution:

1. In a 250 ml beaker, combine 15.5 ml of concentrated $HC_2H_3O_2$ with 40.0 ml distilled water to make a 28% solution of acetic acid.

   ■ *Warning!*
   Concentrated $HC_2H_3O_2$ is damaging to skin. Always add concentrated acid to water.

2. In a 1 liter volumetric flask, combine 48 ml 28% $HC_2H_3O_2$ solution and enough distilled water to make 1 liter of solution.

C. Have students make prints:

1. In a darkroom under a safelight, open a package of printing paper and cut a test strip about 1-inch wide.

2. Cover the strip to block all light. Turn on a light bulb (a 60-watt bulb works well) and gradually remove the cover from the strip, exposing portions of the strip for gradually longer periods of time. Keep track of the time for each exposure (exposures might be made in five-second increments, for example, but some experimentation is necessary).

3. Dilute the prepared developing solution 1 to 1 using distilled water.

4. Place the test strip in the diluted developing solution in developing tray. Developing time will vary from 45–60 seconds.

5. Observe the test strip to determine the proper amount of time for light exposure to make a clear, detailed print.

6. With the safelight still on, remove another piece of printing paper.

7. Place objects on the paper, composing them to make an attractive picture (use the principles of good composition: Try to achieve movement of the eye through the composition, interesting positive and negative space, and a strong center of interest). Experiment with a variety of objects and arrangements, using a variety of sizes, shapes, and textures. Objects might be overlapped to create a feeling of depth. The objects do not need to lie

flat on the surface of the paper. Negatives may also be used. If only negatives are used, the result will be a proof sheet, which is used to examine negative-size prints of the photos (a discussion follows this activity).

8. Expose the prepared photogram to light for the appropriate amount of time to make a clear, detailed print. Multiple exposures might be made as new objects are added or removed. The light source might be flashed on and off at different angles. Positive shapes will appear light in the photogram and negative shapes will appear dark. Prepare two copies of the photogram (one copy will be used in Activity 8.3).

9. Place the exposed photogram in diluted developing solution in a developing tray. Tongs should be used for handling the printing paper. Agitate the paper until a clear print appears, then remove the paper.

10. Wash the paper in a tray containing stop-bath solution for 30 seconds.

11. Next, wash the paper in a tray containing Kodak fixing solution for 5–10 minutes.

12. Wash the paper in running tap water for 30 minutes.

13. Finally, air dry the photogram.

14. All of the solutions can be reused several times and then disposed of according to acceptable waste disposal procedures.

Questions and Conclusions

Level One

1. Examine the finished photogram and evaluate it for the following:
   a. fog
   b. clarity
   c. contrast
   d. density
   e. spotting

2. Considering the procedure for making a photogram, discuss how problems concerning photogram quality, such as fogging, spotting, and unintentional blurry images, can be prevented.

3. Explain how making a photogram differs from making a photograph.

Level Two

1. Suggest various materials and describe new techniques that might be used to make photograms. If possible, make a photogram using some of these materials and techniques. New techniques might include light exposure using a flashlight or projecting the light from a variety of angles.

2. If a proof sheet is prepared, critique the photos appearing on the proof sheet, in terms of light-dark contrast.

3. Using oxidation and reduction reactions and your knowledge of acids and bases, describe the chemical changes needed to prepare a photogram.

4. Research the use of KBr and Na_2SO_3 in the developing solution and the use of $HC_2H_3O_2$ in the stop bath.

Proof Sheets: A Way to Examine Prints

Film negatives can be printed with the aid of an enlarger or by direct contact printing. The enlarger is a projector with a lens. Light from the projector is sent through a negative, then through a lens, and then onto photographic paper, on which the negative image is focused and enlarged. After the paper is exposed, it is printed.

In contact printing, the enlarger is eliminated. The negatives are placed on print paper and exposed to light for a predetermined time. This is how photograms were made in Activity 8.2. The printed contact sheet can be examined with a magnifying glass to determine the best photos, which can be printed again with the aid of an enlarger. This system allows the photographer to make several exposures of the same picture and then decide which photos are worth enlarging.

Pen-and-Ink Drawings

In Activity 8.3, a photogram will be used as a model for a pen-and-ink drawing. The pen-and-ink technique is a linear drawing technique. To create the effect of shading, a series of lines placed close together create the effect of darkness, a technique called hatching. Using crisscrossing lines is a second technique for shading with pen-and-ink drawings, called cross-hatching. A third shading technique is stippling, also referred to as dot density: The closer together the dots, the darker the area appears.

Figure 8.1.   Hatching   Crosshatching   Stippling

Well-Known Artists Famous for Pen-and-Ink Drawings

Leonardo da Vinci (1452–1519)	Albrecht Dürer (1471–1528)
Rembrandt van Rijn (1606–1669)	Hans Holbein (1497–1543)
Vincent van Gogh (1853–1890)	Aubrey Beardsley (1872–1898)
Pablo Picasso (1881–1973)	

8.3

Photogram and Pen-and-Ink Drawings— Same Subject, Different Media

Objectives

1. Students will apply the principles of good composition to pen-and-ink drawings based on their photograms.

2. Students will explore various pen-and-ink techniques in creating an inverse image of a photogram.

3. Students will properly use and care for pen-and-ink materials.

Materials

Photograms made in Activity 8.2; typing paper (for preliminary drawing); bristol board, index paper, or any hard-surfaced white paper (for final drawing); pencil; nib straight pen and pen holder; technical pen (Rapidograph); appropriate ink (India ink for straight pen and special Rapidograph ink for Rapidograph pen); commercial pen cleaner (for cleaning India ink); scissors.

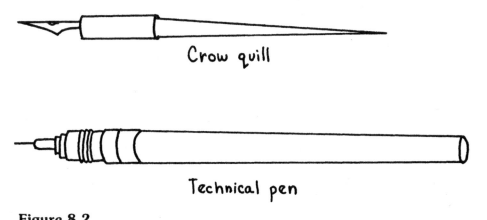

Crow quill

Technical pen

Figure 8.2.

Time

150 minutes

Procedure

1. Have students use typing paper and India ink (with a straight pen) or special ink (with a Rapidograph technical pen) to experiment with the three shading techniques—hatching, cross-hatching, and stippling. Students should choose a simple shape (circle or square) and draw it three times on the typing paper. Shade the shapes using the techniques, one for each shape.

2. Have students cut the paper that will be used for final drawing to the same size as the photogram. Have students use a pencil to draw a composition similar to or the same as the one in the photogram. They should draw lightly and observe the principles of good composition.

3. Have students use a straight pen or rapidograph to shade the shapes in the composition, using one or all of the pen-and-ink techniques practiced. Students should not use an outline in ink to separate one shape from another. The shading should define the shapes.

   ■ *Note:*
   The pen-and-ink drawing should be an inverse image of the photogram. The objects will be in black ink and the background will remain white. If using a straight pen, it is important to clean it after each use in a solution of pen cleaner and water. If using the Rapidograph pen, be sure to replace the cap after each use to prevent the ink from drying.

Adding Color to a
Black-and-White Photograph

Before color film was available, it was popular to tone black-and-white photographs to make the black, white, and gray areas sepia, tan, blue, or green. Toning is still practiced today to provide a new richness to a photograph. It can make black areas appear richer and more dramatic or duller, without affecting white areas.

In the toning process, a bleaching or oxidizing by potassium ferricyanide [$K_3Fe(CN)_6$] of metallic silver atoms (Ag) on exposed portions of a photograph produces silver ions (Ag^+), which are combined with sulfide ions (S^{2-}) to form very insoluble silver sulfide (Ag_2S). Silver sulfide has a K_{sp} of 6×10^{-50}. The silver sulfide provides brown or sepia tones to the photograph by replacing the metallic silver that produced the black and gray tones.

A PICTURE IS
WORTH TEN THOUSAND WORDS

With modern technology, we can take photographs using a digital camera and input the resulting data into computers, cropping and adjusting our photographs as we proceed. We might then use our computer printer to print the desired photographs. No film is needed. No chemicals are needed. No darkroom is needed. Wait a minute! How much computer memory is required for a single picture, perhaps a scenic view in Yellowstone Park? One photograph can require more computer memory than ten thousand words. However, with the development of new, increased-memory computer chips, digital photography may be the way of the future. Still, no matter how the photograph is made, it will be worth at least a thousand words.

REFERENCES

Brown, Milton W. et al. *American Art*. New York: Harry N. Abrams, 1988.

Ebbing, Darrell D. *General Chemistry*. Boston: Houghton Mifflin, 1984.

Hayes, Colin. *The Complete Guide to Painting and Drawing Techniques and Materials*. New York: Mayflower Books, 1978.

Janson, H. W., and Anthony F. Janson. *History of Art for Young People*. 5th ed. New York: Harry N. Abrams, 1997.

Lohan, Frank. *Pen and Ink Techniques*. Chicago: Contemporary Books, 1978.

Swedlund, Charles. *Photography: A Handbook of History, Materials and Processes*. New York: Holt, Rinehart & Winston, 1974.

Turner, Peter. *History of Photography*. New York: Exeter Books, 1987.

NOTES

1. Milton W. Brown et al., *American Art* (New York: Harry N. Abrams, 1988), 335.

2. Norman S. Weinberger, *The Art of the Photogram: Photography Without a Camera* (New York: Caplinger, 1981), 17.

CHAPTER 9

The Art of Forgery

Art Conservation and Restoration

INTRODUCTION: IS IT OR ISN'T IT?

We have all seen paintings in museums that have been signed by artists such as Rembrandt or Picasso, and we assume that these works are the original and "real" thing made by the artist whose signature appears on the painting. As with Coca Cola, we must question whether or not we are looking at the real thing. Even museums can be fooled by highly skilled forgers. Since ancient times, works of art have been forged to deceive the public, collectors, and sometimes even the experts.

What do we mean by the word *forgery*? Technically speaking, a forgery is a copy of a work of art done in the exact manner of the original style of the artist with the intent of passing the work off as the original. The intent is to deceive. A forgery differs from a legitimate copy in that a copy is not meant to be presented as the original. Many artists, as part of their learning process, will copy the works of the masters to develop skill and learn from great works of art. Often, young artists will be allowed to make a copy from a museum original, on location, setting up their easels in the museum gallery in front of the original. Throughout history, artists have copied famous works of art often for persons who would have liked to own the original but could not afford it or, for other reasons, could not obtain it for themselves. The next best thing, then, would be a well-executed copy. In a copy of this nature, the medium, size, and appearance are as close to the original as possible. Copies are not meant to defraud but are made merely as a facsimile of the original, and they do not claim to be the original.

Legitimate copies are, in a sense, reproductions of the original. The term *reproduction* also refers to a mechanically made version of an original. Usually, a copy is made so that the work can be illustrated in a book or magazine, or sold in volume to those who want a relatively inexpensive example of the work for themselves. Often, the size of the reproduction is reduced to accommodate the page size of a book, a postcard, or a print. Ceramic and sculpture are also made as reproductions in various sizes and materials different from the originals.

FAKES OR FORGERIES
THROUGHOUT THE AGES

Forgery of works of art has existed throughout the history of the world. However, by the nineteenth century, forgery was big business. Some European art dealers actually established factories and employed artists to paint forgeries, which they sold to unscrupulous dealers, who in turn sold them to American collectors for high prices as originals done by well-known artists.[1] Forgery, by this time, was regarded as a crime.

Related to this topic, many paintings done by followers or students of famous artists, in "the style of the master" and unsigned, were frequently assumed to be painted by the artists themselves. They were not meant to be forgeries, but they were sometimes mistaken for the work of the artist. Many of these works were later correctly identified as done by others, "in the style of." In recent years, it has been discovered that many paintings originally attributed to Rembrandt van Rijn were not painted by Rembrandt. It is often difficult to pinpoint the artist's work. Many times, especially during the sixteenth and seventeenth centuries, well-known artists would frequently paint only significant parts of a work, then assign students in their workshops to paint the portions of lesser importance.

Trompe l'Oeil:
Fool the Eye but Not a Forgery

Forgery is meant to fool viewers into thinking that they are looking at the real painting or sculpture produced by a famous artist. *Trompe l'oeil* (tromp-loy) is a French term referring to a type of art meant to fool the eye into believing it is seeing not a work of art but reality. The work, frequently a painting, is done in such a way that it appears as if the viewer could actually reach out and touch the objects depicted. *Trompe l'oeil* works have existed since the time of the Romans: The walls of their villas were painted realistically with scenes that appeared to extend beyond the wall into a garden or courtyard. Throughout the ages, even to the present day, the idea of fooling the eye has appeared in paintings and sculptures. During the seventeenth and eighteenth centuries, ceilings in churches and mansions of Europe were often painted with clouds and angels so real that the ceiling *became* the sky.

Today, with computer-controlled lights and sounds, a ceiling painted with clouds can not only mimic the appearance of a sky but can also exhibit meteorologic events, such as storms with lightning and thunder. Such a modern *trompe l'oeil* ceiling exists in Las Vegas at the Caesar's Palace ancient-Rome theme complex in the shopping mall.

Examples of Trompe l'Oeil Works

Any fresco wall-painting from a Roman villa
Any work by American artist William Michael Harnett, nineteenth century
Still Life with Bird, Francis van Myerop, 1670
Flower Piece with Curtain, Adrian van der Spelt, 1658
St. Ignatius Carried into Paradise (ceiling painting), Andrea del Pozzo, 1685

Real or Fake? Solving the Mystery—
Investigation Pays Off

How do we determine if a work of art is what it claims to be? The methods of investigation range from the opinion of the experienced eye of the expert to state-of-the-art scientific tests. Before 1930, scientific investigation was unknown. The art experts relied upon their knowledge of art, and maybe a magnifying glass, to find the fakes. Today, experts use their personal knowledge along with X-ray, ultraviolet, and infrared electromagnetic radiation; spectroscopy; radioactive dating; and the microscope, among other tools for detecting forgeries.

WAYS TO DETECT
ART FORGERIES

A forgery presents many clues: Is the surface consistent with the age of the paint? Are the brush strokes typical of those used by the artist? Are the colors, the shading, and the style of the figures consistent with those the artist typically used? Are the paper (or canvas) and supports consistent with the age of the work?

A chemical analysis of the materials used in a work can be done. In an oil painting, for example, a sample of the pigment can provide the expert with much information: Is the paint consistent with the apparent age of the painting? Many pigments, such as burnt sienna and raw umber, have been used since ancient times, but others, such as alizarin crimson, the cadmiums, and cerulean blue, were developed in the nineteenth century. Hansa yellow and phthalocyanine blue were not developed until the 1930s. If cerulean blue appears in a painting allegedly produced in the sixteenth century, something is afoot. At best, a recent touchup of an old master has occurred; at worst, the painting is a forgery.

In Activity 9.1, students will perform a qualitative analysis to detect the presence of certain ions that, in turn, may reveal an art forgery. The ions could come from paints that were not available at the time of the artwork. In the qualitative analysis, metal ions are separated by chemical means and identified by the products produced. Qualitative analysis is an engaging opportunity for students to develop experience with chemical change and separation through filtration. Today, however, a chemist analyzes a substance to detect ion content using quantitative analytical computerized instruments.

9.1

Qualitative Analysis and the
Detection of Art Forgeries

Objectives

1. Students will perform a qualitative analysis to identify silver, lead, and mercury ions.

2. Students will write a balanced chemical equation for each reaction that takes place in the qualitative analysis.

3. Students will explain how qualitative analysis can be used to detect art forgeries.

Materials

0.1 M $Pb(NO_3)_2$ (lead nitrate), 0.1 M $Ag(NO_3)$ (silver nitrate), 0.1 M $Hg_2(NO_3)_2$ (mercury I nitrate), 6.0 M HNO_3 (nitric acid), 6.0 M NH_4OH (ammonium hydroxide), 6.0 M HCl (hydrochloric acid), 0.1 M K_2CrO_4 (potassium chromate), small test tubes, hot plate, 250 ml beaker, eye dropper, distilled water, 10 ml graduated cylinder, stirring rod.

Time

45 minutes

Procedure

(Note: Discard all solutions in a container for hazardous waste pick-up.)

1. In order to record data, prepare a data table as follows: On the left side of a sheet of paper, make a vertical list of the substances added: HCl; hot H_2O; K_2CrO_4; NH_4OH; HNO_3. Across the top of the paper, list the ions tested: Pb^{2+}; Ag^+; Hg_2^{2+}. Make lines to create boxes where data will be recorded.

2. Pour 2.0 ml 0.1 M $Pb(NO_3)_2$ into a test tube, 2.0 ml 0.1 M $Ag(NO_3)$ into a second test tube, and 2.0 ml $Hg_2(NO_3)_2$ into a third test tube.

3. Add 20 drops 6.0 M HCl to each test tube. Record the results in your data table.

4. Let the precipitates settle. Decant the liquid portions.

5. To each precipitate, add 2.0 ml distilled water.

6. Place the three test tubes into a hot water bath. Agitate the test tubes and leave them in the hot water for about five minutes. Record the results in your data table.

7. For the test tube in which the precipitate has dissolved, pour some of the liquid into a small test tube and add a few drops of 0.1 M K_2CrO_4 to the liquid. Record the results in your data table.

8. Allow the liquid in the two remaining test tubes to cool, then decant and discard some of the liquid from each.

9. Add 3 ml 6.0 M NH_4OH to each precipitate and stir with a stirring rod. Record the results in your data table.

10. To the test tube in which a change occurred, add 4.0 ml 6.0 M HNO_3. Record the results in your data table.

Questions and Conclusions

■ *Note:*
A detailed discussion follows this activity.

Level One

1. Write balanced ionic equations for the reactions in step 2 of the procedure.
2. Write a balanced ionic equation for the addition of K_2CrO_4 to the liquid in step 7 of the procedure.
3. How could finding the presence of lead ions (Pb^{2+}) in a chip of paint removed from a work of art help determine whether or not the work of art is a forgery?

Level Two

1. List lead chloride ($PbCl_2$), silver chloride ($AgCl$), and mercury I chloride (Hg_2Cl_2) in order of decreasing solubility in water.
2. Imagine that a mixture of lead, silver, and copper ions (Pb^{2+}, Ag^+, Cu^{2+}) are thought to be present in a chip of paint taken from a work of art. Write a procedure for using qualitative analysis to detect these ions in the paint chip. Use reference books to find substances that will form a precipitate with copper and not with silver and lead.
3. Describe several ways that a work of art can be analyzed to determine whether it is a forgery or real.

In qualitative analysis, silver, mercury, and lead ions (Ag^+, Hg_2^{2+}, Pb^{2+}) are known as group I ions. Other ions fall into other qualitative analysis groups, depending on the solubility of the ions. Tin, cadmium, and mercury II ions (Sn^{2+}, Cd^{2+}, Hg^{2+}) are in group II. To detect their presence, these ions are precipitated as metal sulfides in an acidic solution. In analysis of a painting to detect a forgery, the presence of tin ions can indicate that cerulean blue pigment was used in the painting; the presence of cadmium ions indicates cadmium red is present; and the presence of mercury II ion can indicate that cadmium vermilion red pigment was used in the painting. Because these pigments have been available only since the nineteenth century, their presence in a pre-nineteenth-century painting would indicate a forgery.

In Activity 9.1, the group I ions were precipitated as insoluble chlorides as indicated in the following equations:

$$Ag^+_{(aq)} + Cl^-_{(aq)} \rightarrow AgCl_{(s)}$$

$$Hg_2^{2+}_{(aq)} + 2Cl^-_{(aq)} \rightarrow Hg_2Cl_{2(s)}$$

$$Pb^{2+}_{(aq)} + 2Cl^-_{(aq)} \rightarrow PbCl_{2(s)}$$

The lead chloride ($PbCl_2$) precipitate is soluble in hot water, so when the three solids are placed in a hot water bath, the mercury I chloride (Hg_2Cl_2) and the silver chloride ($AgCl$) residues remain and the lead chloride dissolves in hot water. To test for the presence of lead ion in the filtrate, chromate ion, CrO_4^{-2}, from K_2CrO_4, can be added to the filtrate:

$$Pb^{2+}_{(aq)} + CrO_4^{2-}_{(aq)} \rightarrow PbCrO_{4(s)}$$

The appearance of a yellow precipitate, lead chromate ($PbCrO_4$), indicates the presence of lead ions. To separate silver ions and mercury I ions, ammonium hydroxide (NH_4OH), which converts to NH_3, is added to the precipitates:

$$AgCl_{(s)} + 2NH_{3(aq)} \rightarrow Ag(NH_3)_2^+_{(aq)} + Cl^-_{(aq)}$$

The silver chloride ($AgCl$) is dissolved as the stable silver-ammonia-complex ion [$Ag(NH_3)_2^+$] is formed. Meanwhile, the mercury II chloride ($HgCl_2$) is undergoing oxidation and reduction at the same time! Mercury metal (Hg) and mercury II amido chloride ($HgNH_2Cl$) are formed and appear, respectively, black and gray in color:

$$2NH_{3(aq)} + Hg_2Cl_{2(s)} \rightarrow HgNH_2Cl_{(s)} + Hg_{(l)} + NH_4^+_{(aq)} + Cl^-_{(aq)}$$

The mercury substances are filtered and silver ions (Ag^+) are detected in the filtrate by adding hydrochloric acid (HCl), which releases the silver ions from the silver-ammonia-complex ion [$Ag(NH_3)_2^+$], allowing the silver ions to combine with chloride ions (Cl^-) to form silver chloride precipitate ($AgCl$):

$$Ag(NH_3)_2^+_{(aq)} + Cl^-_{(aq)} + 2H^+_{(aq)} \rightarrow 2NH_4^+_{(aq)} + AgCl_{(s)}$$

Either through instrumental analysis or qualitative analysis, the forensic chemist can reveal the presence of ions in a paint chip from an artwork and use the ion information to detect an art forgery.

THREE IMPORTANT
ART MOVEMENTS

The works of Claude Monet, Vincent van Gogh, and Jackson Pollock represent, respectively, impressionism, post-impressionism, and abstract expressionism. Even though it would be difficult to forge paintings by these well-known artists, forgeries still appear.

Impressionism

During the latter part of the nineteenth century, a group of French artists began to approach painting in a new and revolutionary way. They painted their canvases using short strokes of different colors. They believed that color should be mixed by the artist "in the eye of the viewer" and not on the canvas. This would capture the true color and light of nature in a new and vivid way. In the greens of grass, for example, many colors, including blues and yellows, combine in the eye of the viewer to give the impression of green on the canvas. This new technique was not readily accepted by the critics or the public of the time, who were accustomed to a more realistic approach to painting—clearer, sharpened edges and carefully blended colors. One critic, Louis Leroy, commented that this way of painting only gave the impression of form and subject. The word *impressionism* became popular as a name for this style.

Examples of French Impressionism

Any oil painting by Claude Monet (1840–1926), Auguste Renoir (1841–1919),
   and Edgar Degas (1834–1917)
Any later oil painting (after 1870) by Edouard Manet (1832–1883)

Impressionism Videos

Impressionists: Rebels in Art. 18 min. Washington, DC: Elaine Joselovitz Museum One, 1987.
Monet: Legacy of Light Portrait of an Artist Series. 28 min. Boston: Museum of Fine Arts, 1989.

Post-Impressionism

Following impressionism, a group of artists, in the late nineteenth and early twentieth centuries, took from the impressionists the use of short strokes and the brighter colors. To this they added their own ingredient—a strong personal quality that resulted in an emotion-filled interpretation of the subject matter. One such post-impressionist was Vincent van Gogh. His work was filled not only with emotion but also with texture and intense color.

Examples of Work by Vincent van Gogh (1853–1890)

The Starry Night (oil), 1889
The Night Cafe (oil), 1888
Any Vincent van Gogh self-portrait

Abstract Expressionism

During the 1940s and 1950s, a group of artists created a style of modern art painting that was spontaneous and filled with action. Jackson Pollock was one of these artists interested in the act and movement of painting. He applied his paint to large canvases with a sweeping motion of his arm and hand. The subject matter for him was non-objective (see Chapter 3). The results were paintings made of lines of interwoven color, moving in all directions across the canvas.

Examples of Work by Jackson Pollock (1912–1956)

Lavender Mist (oil, enamel, and aluminum paint), 1950
Ocean Greyness (oil), 1953
Night Ceremony (oil), 1944

■ *Note:*
Have students use a magnifying glass to examine copies of works by van Gogh, Monet, and Pollock, closely observing the brush strokes of each painter.

In Activity 9.2, students will prepare a "forged" painting and a "real" painting. They will study the styles and composition used by van Gogh, Monet, and Pollock and then analyze the prepared paintings to determine which one is a "forgery" and which one is "real." If it is not practical for the students to prepare the paintings, they can be obtained from:

Kemtec Educational Services
9889 Crescent Park Drive
West Chester, OH 45069

9.2

Using Three Methods to Detect Art Forgeries

Objectives

1. Students will compare and contrast the painting styles of Vincent van Gogh, Claude Monet, and Jackson Pollock, then prepare a "forged" painting and a "real" painting in each style.

2. Students will distinguish between an "art forgery" and the "real" painting and discuss methods of detecting art forgeries.

3. Students will detect an "art forgery" through chemical, ultraviolet, and paint-chip analyses.

Materials

Acrylic paints; drawing pencil; 2-x-3-inch pieces of foam board; $Pb(NO_3)_2$ (crystalline lead nitrate); tweezers; razor blades or an X-ACTO knife; fluorescent paints; 0.1 M K_2CrO_4 (potassium chromate) solution; small test tube; paintbrush for acrylic paints;

a source of ultraviolet light (e.g., plant grow-light); book containing reproductions of works by van Gogh, Monet, and Pollock; Table 9.1 (page 216).

Time

150 minutes

Procedure

■ *Note:*
This activity can be done in groups, dividing the tasks among the group members.

1. Have students find reproductions of paintings by van Gogh, Monet, and Pollock and select one painting that will be copied as an "art forgery" and as a "real" painting.

2. Have students list the differences and similarities among the composition and styles used by the three artists.

3. Have students prepare an "art forgery":

   a. On a 2-x-3-inch piece of foam board, make a pencil sketch of the selected painting.

   b. Using acrylic paint, paint the sketched picture in a technique opposite from the artist's technique. If it was known that the artist used mixed paints, the paints should be layered. If the artist used layered paints, the paints should be mixed. The paint should be applied in a variety of thicknesses.

   c. When the acrylic paint is dry, apply small dots or lines of fluorescent paint to the surface of the acrylic paint, using the same color as the color of the acrylic paint.

   d. Let the painting dry.

4. Have students prepare a "real" painting:

   a. Make another pencil sketch of the same painting on a piece of 2-x-3-inch foam board. This sketch should be identical to the previous sketch.

   b. Using acrylic paint, paint the sketched picture in the artist's style. However, the paint in four or five areas of the painting should be thickened to make small nodules. Proceed with the next step as soon as the nodules have been painted.

   c. Using tweezers, embed a small crystal of $Pb(NO_3)_2$ in each paint nodule, covering the crystals with the acrylic paint.

   d. Let the painting dry.

   ■ *Note:*

   The teacher should match the paintings into sets of two paintings, one "art forgery" and one "real" painting. For the detection of the art forgery, each student or each group should use one matched pair. The students should not know which painting is the "forgery" and which painting is "real."

5. Detection of an "art forgery":

    a. **Using Ultraviolet Light to Detect Art Forgeries.** Examine the paintings and make note of any differences or similarities between the paintings. Place each picture under an ultraviolet light and make note of any differences in the appearance. Record the identity of the painting that shows evidence of the presence of fluorescent paint.

    b. **Using Chemical Means to Detect Art Forgeries.** Remove a small chip of paint from a raised nodule of each painting (leave one nodule for the next detection method). In a test tube, drop one chip from one painting into 5 ml 0.1 M K_2CrO_4. Then drop the chip from the other painting into another test tube containing 5 ml 0.1 M K_2CrO_4. Shake the test tube vigorously several times and look for the appearance of a yellow precipitate. Record the identity of the painting whose paint produces a yellow precipitate.

    c. **Using Paint-Chip Analysis to Detect Art Forgeries.** Remove a paint chip from a raised nodule of each painting. Using a razor blade or an X-ACTO knife, make very thin slices through each chip. From the slices, try to determine whether the artist used mixed paints or layered paints. Record the painting style for each painting.

6. Have students use Table 9.1 and the results from the analyses to determine which painting is "real" and which painting is a "forgery."

Table 9.1
Characteristics of a "Forgery" and a "Real" Painting

	Fluorescent Light	**Precipitate**	**Chip Analysis**
Real Painting	No fluorescent paint	Yellow precipitate	Either layer or mix
Forgery	Fluorescent paint present	No precipitate	Either layer or mix

Questions and Conclusions

Level One

1. Vincent van Gogh, Claude Monet, and Jackson Pollock represent the movements of impressionism, post-impressionism, and modern art. Discuss the major characteristics of the artwork from each of these periods. Find reproductions of other works of art created by the impressionists, post-impressionists, and modern artists. Explain the principles of composition as expressed by each artist using the works of art as examples.

2. Define *art forgery*.

3. In the chemical analysis, we assumed that paints containing lead ions would not be present in a modern painting. However, in some paints, we may still find today chrome yellow pigment containing lead chromate and molybdate orange pigment containing lead chromate, lead molybdate, and lead sulfate. Lead-based paints

were commonly used by artists as late as the mid-twentieth century. Write chemical formulas for each of these lead compounds used in paint pigments. Which formula represents the yellow precipitate produced in this activity? (Answer: $PbCrO_4$, $PbMoO_4$, $PbSO_4$. The yellow precipitate is $PbCrO_4$.)

Level Two

1. List several reasons why it would be difficult to make a forgery of a painting by Vincent van Gogh, Claude Monet, or Jackson Pollock.

2. In addition to chemicals, ultraviolet, and paint-chip analyses, what other methods can be used to detect an art forgery?

3. Write a balanced ionic equation for the production of the yellow precipitate.

4. Find stories about detecting art forgeries and write a report about one such story, explaining the means used to prove that the artwork was a forgery.

In Activity 9.2, it is assumed that lead ions are not found in modern paint pigments, but this is not entirely the case. Even though lead-based paints are prohibited from use in house painting, lead compounds still appear in some art paints. Some red, yellow, and white pigments contain lead compounds. Hazards in art will be discussed in Chapter 10.

METHODS USED
TO DETECT ART FORGERIES

Fluorescence

By shining violet or ultraviolet light on a painting, the presence of fluorescent paints can be detected. These paints will glow after being exposed to the violet or ultraviolet light. The molecules in the fluorescent paints absorb radiation and emit characteristic energy waves that identify these molecules. Fluorescent paints are products of modern technology and would not appear in old paintings. The presence of fluorescent paints usually indicates an art forgery.

Spectroscopy

Spectroscopy is another method used to detect art forgeries. In spectroscopy, electromagnetic radiation is applied to the substance or substances under consideration. The resulting spectra are recorded to identify the chemical composition of the substance or substances. When a spectrophotometer is used, the radiation, usually visible and invisible ultraviolet waves, can be applied to a solution in a tube and the absorption of radiation is noted. For this type of analysis, a spectrophotometer must be available.

X-Rays

The use of X-rays in detecting art forgeries deserves mention. X-rays have shorter wavelengths than ultraviolet waves. These short-wavelength, high-energy waves can penetrate the canvas of a painting and reveal a painting underneath. In addition, the artist's brush strokes can be examined and compared to those in other works by the same artist.

Neutron Activation Analysis

Neutron activation is a method to detect as little as 10^{-12} gram of particular elements without destroying any of the artwork being investigated. This method of element detection is extremely valuable when an art forgery is suspected. Several paintings by the same artist can be analyzed for similarities in the paint composition. A different set of paint substances for one painting would place that painting under suspicion as being an art forgery.

In neutron activation analysis, the sample is bombarded with a beam of neutrons, some of which are absorbed into sample nuclei. These sample nuclei are now radioactive. They emit electromagnetic radiation, gamma rays. Each isotope is represented by a specific energy and frequency of gamma ray, which identifies the isotope and, thus, the element. In this method of detecting art forgeries, the sample is not changed and its composition can be accurately assessed.

Radioactive Dating

To understand how radioactive substances can be used to determine the age of an object, it is necessary to understand radioactivity, the spontaneous or forced breakdown or rearrangement of the atomic nucleus, with a release of radiation. We have discussed chemical changes in atoms in which outer electrons are shared, partially shared, or transferred, but the atomic nucleus remains intact. Here, we are considering nuclear changes and the products produced, including radiation. We need a system of symbols to represent these nuclear changes.

Nuclear Symbols

In Chapter 1, we learned about neutrons, uncharged particles, and protons, positively charged particles. These are the particles that will change in number when there is a nuclear change. The mass of an atom is largely determined by the protons and neutrons in the nucleus (a neutron is slightly heavier than a proton, but an electron's mass is negligible at one two-thousandth the mass of a proton or neutron). The relative masses of neutrons, protons, and electrons are 1, 1, and 0, respectively. The mass number of an atom is the total number of protons and neutrons in that atom. We can symbolize the mass of a nucleus by writing the name of the element and the mass number after the name, connected by a hyphen (e.g., iodine-131, strontium-90, uranium-235). In a nuclear equation, the symbol for the element is used, with the mass number written as a superscript before the symbol and the number of protons written as a subscript also before the symbol (e.g., $^{131}I_{53}$, $^{90}Sr_{38}$, $^{235}U_{92}$).

Nuclear Equations

In a nuclear equation, mass numbers and number of protons add up to the same total on either side of the equation. Also, in addition to atomic nuclei particles (protons and neutrons), called nucleons, other particles are emitted or absorbed in the nuclear change. Some of these particles include the following:

Beta Particle	$^{0}e_{-1}$	Neutron	$^{1}n_{0}$
Positron	$^{0}e_{1}$	Alpha Particle	$^{4}He_{2}$
Proton	$^{1}H_{1}$	Deuteron	$^{2}H_{1}$

For example, in the spontaneous decay of uranium-238, thorium-234 is formed and an alpha particle is emitted:

$$^{238}U_{92} \rightarrow {}^{234}Th_{90} + {}^4He_2$$

It can be seen that the mass numbers on either side of the equation add up to the same number, 238, and that 92 protons are accounted for in the equation's product and reactant sides. This is a balanced nuclear equation. Actually, some mass is converted into energy, but the amount of mass is very small. From Albert Einstein's equation $E = mc^2$, very little mass, m, is needed to produce a tremendous amount of energy, E, because c is the speed of light, 3×10^8 m/sec. This energy was evidenced when an atomic bomb was exploded over Hiroshima, Japan, during World War II. The fuel for that bomb was uranium-235.

Balancing Nuclear Equations

There are many ways that nuclear changes occur. Emission of alpha particles is one result of nuclear decay:

$$^{222}Rn_{86} \rightarrow {}^{218}Po_{84} + {}^4He_2$$

Emission of beta particles can also result from a nuclear change:

$$^{227}Ac_{89} \rightarrow {}^{227}Th_{90} + {}^0e_{-1}$$

In addition, positrons can be emitted in a nuclear change:

$$^{38}K_{19} \rightarrow {}^{38}Ar_{18} + {}^0e_1$$

Also, electrons can be captured:

$$^{73}As_{33} + {}^0e_{-1} \rightarrow {}^{73}Ge_{32}$$

It can be seen that students can easily balance and complete nuclear equations if they are familiar with the symbols for nuclear particles and know the method of nuclear decay, such as alpha particle emission or electron capture.

Isotopes

Isotopes are atoms of the same element that have different masses because of different numbers of neutrons. Uranium-238 atoms have 146 neutrons in their nuclei; uranium-235 atoms have 143 neutrons in their nuclei. Some isotopes are very stable; others decay spontaneously in a short period of time.

Half Life

Isotopes that decay spontaneously have different rates of decay. Some radioactive isotopes decay in fractions of a second; others will not decay for thousands of years. External factors, such as pressure and temperature, under normal conditions, have no effect on the rate of decay. When we consider how long it takes for spontaneous decay of atomic nuclei, we measure this time in something called half life. Half life is the time it takes for half a sample of radioactive nuclei to decay into other substances. The rate of decay, grams of radioactive nuclei remaining after a period of time, depends on the original number of radioactive nuclei present in the sample. For example, for iodine-131, the half life is 8.07 days. If we have 1.0 gram of iodine-131 today, we will have 0.5 gram after 8.07 days, 0.25 gram after 16.14 days, and 0.125 gram after 24.21 days. The half life of an isotope can be as short as 0.000164 second, the half life of polonium-214, or as long as 4.47 x 10^9 years, the half life of uranium-238.[2]

Half Life and Radioactive Dating

The age of an art object can provide a valuable clue as to whether the object is real or a forgery. Because the half life for a specific isotope is constant, half life can be used to find the age of an object. The isotope put to use for radioactive dating is carbon-14. The half life of carbon-14 is 5,730 years. The amount of carbon-14 in our atmosphere remains fairly constant. When an object such as a plant is alive, it absorbs CO_2. The carbon atoms in the CO_2 are made of a specific ratio of carbon-14 atoms to carbon-12 atoms. The carbon-14 atoms decay by emission of beta particles:

$$^{14}C_6 \rightarrow {}^{14}N_7 + {}^0e_{-1}$$

After the living tree is harvested to provide wood for a painting surface, or perhaps for a painting support or frame, CO_2 uptake ceases and the ratio of $^{14}C_6$ to $^{12}C_6$ begins to decrease. A piece of wood from an art object can be analyzed for carbon-14 content. If it is found that the ratio of carbon-14 to carbon-12 is one half that found presently in living trees, it can be assumed that the age of the object is approximately 5,730 years, the amount of time for half a sample of carbon-14 to decay.

The art of forgery is alive and well today. At a recent auction of art objects in New York City, it was determined that most of the objects were forgeries. Modern scientific methods, such as those outlined in this chapter, are available for the detection of an art forgery. It takes an alert collector of art objects to suspect an art forgery. Once there is a suspicion, the scientist can go to work to establish the truth of the matter.

CONSERVATION AND RESTORATION

Lasting Treasures

Great works of art, whether they are paintings, drawings, sculptures, or other forms of the visual arts, are all susceptible to the effects of aging, temperature and humidity changes, and exposure to light. In some cases, natural disasters such as fire or flood can damage works of art. In the early 1990s, a fire raged through a wing of Windsor Castle in England, damaging many valuable works of art.

Conservation

Conservation involves cleaning the work, analyzing the work for any damage, restoring the damaged areas, and preserving the original as much as possible. Many of the techniques used in investigating an art forgery are used in the conservation of artwork. The same scientific methods are used to analyze damage as are used to detect forgeries.

Restoration or Preservation?

Whether the work is restored or merely preserved depends on several factors: What is the extent of the damage? Is the work very valuable? Can the restoration be done without destroying the integrity of the work? In the case of oil paintings, age cracks may appear, or the canvas may become torn or begin to sag and pull away from the support. Bits of paint may flake off, and varnish may darken with age, hiding the true colors of the work.

Organic Molecules Do the Job

In Chapter 5, we studied organic compounds, those compounds containing carbon atoms, which are found in many living sources. Some carbon compounds are useful cleaning compounds; they can be used to effectively clean and restore works of art. Alcohols, such as ethyl, isopropyl, and benzyl alcohols, are used to remove unwanted paint and varnish, lacquer, or shellac. Aliphatic hydrocarbons (e.g., n-hexane) are paint and lacquer thinners and degreasers. Aromatic hydrocarbons such as xylene, toluene, and benzene remove paint and varnish and act as ink and plastic solvents. Chlorinated hydrocarbons, such as carbon tetrachloride, are plastic and wax solvents. The trick to using these restoration chemicals is to remove unwanted substances but leave intact the artist's original materials. The hazards of using these materials are discussed in Chapter 10.

A Job for a Professional

If restoration or preservation is required, a professional is consulted to slow the deterioration, thus giving the work an extended life. With some works of art, this is difficult. Many modern works are made of materials that are difficult to preserve and restore, such as newspaper, poor-quality paint, and experimental materials that may be glued to the surface or mixed with the paint. Many pictures are painted on a poorly prepared surface using very heavy applications of paint; in time, the paint will begin to fall off the canvas or other working surface. It is the task of the restorer to do whatever possible to preserve as much of the work as possible.

A Stitch in Time

For the consumer, proper care and maintenance can prevent many of the causes of damage. Proper storage and methods of hanging are important. Watercolor paintings and other works on paper, for instance, should be matted and framed behind glass to protect them. Acid-free mat board should be used. Special glass that filters out harmful light rays that may fade the work is also recommended. Many articles and books about the care and maintenance of art of all types are available (see "References" at the end of this chapter).

THE MARRIAGE OF ART AND CHEMISTRY

Art forgeries are detected by chemical means. Art restoration and conservation is accomplished through applying the principles of solution chemistry. We have a true and faithful marriage of art and chemistry when we restore or conserve artwork and when we discover art forgeries. In these endeavors, art and chemistry will never be divorced.

REFERENCES

Arnason, H. H. *History of Modern Art: Painting, Sculpture, Architecture*. 3d ed. New York: Harry N. Abrams, 1986.

Barron, John N. *The Language of Painting*. Cleveland, OH: World, 1967.

Courthion, Pierre. *Impressionism*. New York: Abradale Press; Harry N. Abrams, 1983.

Herbert, Robert L. *Impressionism: Art, Leisure, and Parisian Society*. New Haven, CT: Yale University Press, 1988.

Keck, Caroline K. *How to Take Care of Your Paintings*. New York: Charles Scribner's Sons, 1978.

Kelly, Francis. *Art Restoration*. New York: McGraw-Hill, 1972.

McQuarrie, Donald A., and Peter A. Rock. *General Chemistry*. New York: W. H. Freeman, 1984.

Milman, Miriam. *Trompe-l'Oeil Painting*. New York: Rizzoli, 1983.

Minneapolis Institute of Arts. *Fakes and Forgeries*. Boston: Museum Publications of America, 1973.

Taubes, Frederic. *The Painter's Dictionary of Materials and Methods*. New York: Watson-Guptill, 1979.

Waldron, Ann. *True or False? Amazing Art Forgeries*. New York: Hastings House, 1983.

NOTES

1. Ann Waldron, *True or False? Amazing Art Forgeries* (New York: Hastings House, 1983), 12.

2. Donald A. McQuarrie and Peter A. Rock, *General Chemistry* (New York: W. H. Freeman, 1984), 951.

CHAPTER
10

Chemical Hazards in Art

INTRODUCTION

Artists often insist that they must feel and breathe their materials to create art. There can be no interference between the artist and the art materials. However, the artist sickened by toxic material will not be able to create anything.

As early as 1713, Bernardini Ramazzini, the father of occupational medicine, observed that artisans who worked with paints, stone, and metal had physical problems and short life expectancies. In modern times, it is suspected that van Gogh's craziness and Goya's illness may have been the result of lead poisoning. It is known that van Gogh used leaded yellow paint for his numerous sunflower paintings and was careless with his paints, leaving them open to dry and scatter into his environment. He could easily have ingested lead paint chips.

There are two reasons why artists are particularly vulnerable to diseases caused by exposure to toxic materials. First of all, artists, by the nature of their work, may have daily, long-term contact with materials that are highly toxic. Second, art materials are used as aerosols, powders, dusts, and in solution, from which maximum physical absorption and adsorption are possible. An artist can inhale aerosols. Powders and dusts are also inhaled and, in addition, can be absorbed through the skin. Solutions and many solvents evaporate into the air for the artist to inhale over long periods of time. This chemical assault, day after day, causes a variety of illnesses. In the following section on artists' illnesses, all the chemicals cited are used by artists as they draw and paint, sculpt, work with metals, or develop and print photos—in general, as they engage in any art-associated activity.

ARTISTS' ILLNESSES

Skin Illnesses

Toxic solvents, such as methyl alcohol, benzene, and chlorinated hydrocarbons, can penetrate the skin through cuts and abrasions. On contact, these solvents cause chronic dermatitis and allergic skin reactions in susceptible individuals.

Eye Illnesses

Materials such as methyl alcohol, acids, ammonia, irritating gases, mercury compounds, and photography developers can cause eye irritation if splashed into the eye. With prolonged contact, eye inflammation and even cataracts can result.

Respiratory Illnesses

Gases such as sulfur dioxide, nitrogen dioxide, hydrogen chloride vapor, and ozone can cause lung damage from minimal exposure. When glazed pottery is fired in a kiln, toxic emissions containing carbon monoxide, formaldehyde, sulfur dioxide and trioxide, chlorine, fluorine, and metal particles can be released and inhaled. Chronic and acute respiratory diseases result. Also, inhaling these substances can increase susceptibility to respiratory infection and even pneumonia and lung cancer.

Circulatory System Illnesses

Constriction of blood vessels, arrhythmia, and even aplastic anemia, caused by ethyl alcohol, methylene chloride, and benzene, respectively, are circulatory system diseases that result from misuse of these chemical substances. Methylene chloride, a paint solvent, reacts in the body to produce carbon monoxide, which replaces oxygen in the hemoglobin molecule. This can cause carbon monoxide poisoning, which can be fatal.

Nervous System Illnesses

Solvents, such as chlorinated hydrocarbons, toluene, and xylene, can cause a feeling of euphoria, but they can be deadly toxins. Small, daily doses may cause dizziness, mental confusion, and fatigue; high doses will cause permanent damage to the central nervous system. Lead, mercury, and manganese ion poisoning will alter and destroy central and peripheral nerve function and cause personality changes.

A KNOWLEDGE OF CHEMISTRY WILL PREVAIL

Even though it appears that artists are doomed by their materials, a knowledge of chemistry and some simple precautions can minimize art material dangers. In *Art in Chemistry; Chemistry in Art*, students learn about the physical and chemical properties of the chemicals in art materials and, thus, should know how these chemicals can be manipulated or changed to provide a safer environment for producing a work of art. The prognosis for the physical well-being of artists is not as dire as it would appear.

CHEMICAL HAZARDS ASSOCIATED WITH SPECIFIC ART TECHNIQUES

Painting and Drawing

Pigments and Dyes

Pigments and dyes provide paint and ink colors. Many highly toxic pigments, such as copper acetate (blue-green), arsenic trisulfide (yellow), and mercury II iodide (red), are no longer used. However, other hazardous pigment compounds, such as lead carbonate, mercury II sulfide, and cadmium sulfide, are still used today. These compounds present a danger to the artists who use their mouths to make a brush more pointed.

Organic and Inorganic Pigments

Inorganic pigments are found in the earth. Iron and lead oxides provide earth colors. Copper calcium silicate and cobalt stannate provide blues. The colors burnt sienna and burnt umber come from iron oxides. Green pigments come from chromic oxide, calcinated cobalt, and zinc and aluminum oxides. Red pigments come from cadmium sulfide, cadmium selenide, and barium sulfate. All these chemical compounds come from the earth.

Cave dwellers, Native Americans, and the Ndebele people of southern Africa all have something in common. They all have used inorganic pigments from the earth to make a variety of paints. With these paints, they have painted walls to tell stories, to establish community status, and to embrace the beauty of the environment.

Organic pigments are found in living or once-living objects or can be laboratory-synthesized compounds. Charcoal from organic materials provides black pigment for paints. Complex organic molecules can be synthesized as red, blue, green, and yellow pigments. In the past, dyes were often made from aniline derived from coal tar. Because these dyes were toxic, azo compounds replaced aniline compounds. Azo dye compounds almost always have an $-SO_3^-Na^+$ group and $-N=N-$ bonding that brings together two aromatic rings.

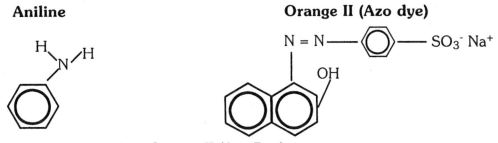

Figure 10.1. Aniline Orange II (Azo Dye).

In Chapter 2, we prepared inorganic and organic pigments for paints. An inorganic pigment was prepared by grinding cinnabar or azurite. Lead chromate, a yellow pigment, was prepared by precipitation, and organic pigment, carbon, was deposited on an evaporating dish during the incomplete combustion of a hydrocarbon.

Hazards and Help—Painting

Some paint pigments are toxic; others are not. We do not know the long-term hazards of using many synthetic pigments. Some are thought to cause cancer and birth defects. Others might cause lung disease.

Paints become hazardous when they are ingested, inhaled, or when they come in direct contact with the skin, especially skin sores or cuts. Precautions should be taken regularly while paints are used. It is not wise to lick a paintbrush to make a pointed end. Powdered pigments used to make paints and paint droplets, possible from air brushes, should not be inhaled. A face mask protects against inhaling paints. There should be no eating or drinking during painting. Using gloves when handling powdered pigments and mixing paints is advisable.

Care should be taken to avoid inhaling powder when grinding minerals or when using dried lead chromate (see Activity 2.3). Hands should be thoroughly washed after any pigment contact. A one-time direct contact with prepared pigments should not be hazardous to the user's health.

When a painting is finished, the artist often applies varnish or lacquer to the painting surface. Varnishes, and often paints, are thinned with turpentine. Turpentine can be used to remove surface varnish. Turpentine is moderately toxic if inhaled or ingested. Carbon tetrachloride, toluene, and methyl alcohol are also used to remove varnish. Carbon tetrachloride and toluene are highly toxic if routinely inhaled.

A complete list of paint and ink pigments, their chemical compositions, and their hazardous effects, is found in *Artists Beware* and *The Artist's Complete Health and Safety Guide* (see "References" at the end of this chapter).

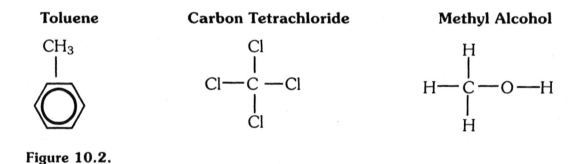

Toluene   **Carbon Tetrachloride**   **Methyl Alcohol**

Figure 10.2.

Ceramics

Artist often have to touch and feel their materials to create their artwork. Potters become intimate with their materials. They must manipulate and handle their clay to produce desired results. Direct contact with these materials for extended periods of time can be dangerous to the potter's health.

In Chapter 4, we learned that clay is made of minerals, including potassium, aluminum, and silicon oxides. Barium and other metal oxides, vermiculite, and mold controllers are often added to clay to enhance clay properties. If dry clay is mixed with water, large amounts of silica can be released into the air.

Hazards and Help

Many years of inhaling clay dust can be hazardous to the potter's health. If the clay dust contains silica, silicosis and a variety of lung-related illnesses can result. Clay dust can also contain harmful bacteria and molds.

In addition, clay wedging, throwing, and building can cause hand and wrist injuries, including median nerve damage resulting in carpal tunnel syndrome (identified by numbness in the thumb and first three fingers).

To minimize clay dust inhalation, it is best to buy premixed clay. Potters should change clothes before leaving their work area. Fresh clay should be used to minimize bacteria and mold growth. To avoid median nerve damage and resulting carpal tunnel syndrome, the potter's wrist should be unflexed frequently. A face mask can be worn when clay dust is present.

Glazes

In Activity 4.3, we prepared and applied glazes to clay slabs. The glazes were composed mostly of silicon dioxide, along with aluminum and potassium oxides (to reduce the melting point) and compounds such as copper oxide and iron oxide (colorants).

Hazards and Help

Metal oxides such as copper oxide and iron oxide have replaced lead compounds in glazes. Lead compounds should not be used in glaze compositions because lead inhalation or ingestion can cause nervous system and brain damage, organ damage, and anemia.

Glazes should be prepared where adequate ventilation is available. If glazes are routinely prepared from powders, a face mask should be used. Another option, if available, is to use a plain-opening exhaust hood or wear a toxic-dust respirator approved by the National Institute for Occupational Safety and Health. Also, gloves should be worn during the preparation and application because glaze substances can be irritating to the skin.

National Institute for Occupational Safety and Health (NIOSH)
4676 Columbia Parkway
Cincinnati, OH 45226-1998
1-800-35NIOSH

Firing

Because of obvious (and not-so-obvious) dangers involved, it is the art teacher who does the firing in the activities in Chapter 4. In schools, electric kilns are usually chosen for firing because fuel-fired kilns require wood, natural gas, oil, coke, coal, or charcoal as fuel and chimney ventilation systems. Electric kilns also require ventilation systems, such as negative pressure systems and a canopy hood, but the placement is more flexible than room placement for a fuel-fired kiln with a chimney ventilation system.

Hazards and Help

Many byproducts of bisque firing are highly toxic if inhaled, so all kilns must be vented. Carbon monoxide, sulfur dioxide and trioxide, chlorine, and fluorine are just some of the gases released in kiln firings. Metal ions such as cadmium, copper, chromium, and precious metal ions including silver and gold, appear in metal fumes at high temperatures and can be inhaled or deposited in the kiln to be released in future firings.

Heat is also a hazard produced by kiln firing. Electric kilns should be off the floor with adequate space surrounding the kiln to prevent heat buildup and fire. The heat produced can cause burns, eye damage, and possibly accelerate cataract development.

Constant exposure to kiln firings may cause chronic lung problems, such as emphysema. Carbon monoxide poisoning can occur (symptoms are lethargy and a continuing headache). Proper ventilation can prevent most kiln-induced health problems.

Jewelry Making and Metalworking

Metals can be shaped and designed into an immense variety of jewelry pieces. In Chapter 6, we sawed and soldered metal and cast molten metal to produce pieces of jewelry. Using electrolysis, we added metal coatings to the jewelry pieces. It is necessary to consider health precautions that should be taken regarding metalwork.

Soldering

Joining silver pieces with silver solder requires temperatures of 316–760°C. At these temperatures, impurities in the silver solder, such as antimony and cadmium, are released. The flux may contain fluoride compounds, such as potassium fluoride and boron trifluoride, or other boron compounds.

Casting

Metals, usually gold and silver, are often cast to make rings and other small jewelry pieces. In lost wax casting, a wax pattern for a jewelry piece is burned out of a mold. A large variety of waxes, such as beeswax, paraffin, and tallow, can be used. The waxes can release formaldehyde and acrolein.

Pouring liquid metal into the mold requires a steady hand and constant attention. When the mold containing liquid metal is placed in a centrifuge, hot metal can fly out of the centrifuge. This is why it is preferable to use the vacuum casting method, for which a centrifuge is not needed.

Metal Colorants

Metal colorants such as copper sulfate, ferricyanide, and ferrocyanide compounds can be irritating or highly toxic. If a colorant reacts with the metal, irritating acid fumes can be released.

Hazards and Help

In soldering, zinc chloride and other metal chloride fluxes are the safest, and fluoride fluxes, such as boron trifluoride, are the most hazardous. However, zinc chloride fumes can be irritating. Fluoride gases can cause lung damage and, with long-term exposure, bone and teeth damage. While soldering, a safe flux should be chosen and fluxes should not be mixed. Goggles and gloves should be worn. An exhaust system is needed to quickly remove toxic gases.

When an artist or metalworker is casting, burns are easily acquired. Asbestos gloves and goggles, of course, will minimize hand and eye burns. During centrifugal casting, a shield around the centrifuge protects against flying metal. The metalworker should be sure that the centrifuge is in balance before starting the centrifuge.

Applying colorants to metals should be done in a well-ventilated room. Copper sulfate can release irritating sulfur dioxide, and ferricyanide or ferrocyanide compounds with acid and/or heat will release hydrogen cyanide gas. Needless to say, these combinations should not be used to color metal.

Sterling silver, silver, and copper, or gold, can be used to cast a jewelry piece with a minimal amount of health hazard. Alloys with large amounts of cadmium, chromium, nickel, antimony, and arsenic should not be used.

Photography

Many photographers use commercial processing and avoid contact with hazardous chemicals. However, when photographers do their own processing, they come into direct contact, often for long periods of time, with a large variety of chemicals.

Hazards and Help—Developers

Because developing solutions are placed in large trays with an immense surface area exposed to the user, there can be considerable eye, skin, and lung contact between the photographer and the solution. Developing solutions can cause skin rashes, irritate eyes, and enhance respiratory allergies.

Metol (monomethyl p aminophenol sulfate), used in most developing solutions, can cause severe skin irritation and allergies. Phenidone-based developers are less toxic to the skin than metol, amidol, or pyrogallol. When developing powders are mixed, inhalation is a concern.

There are many ways to protect the user from developer hazards. A face mask will protect against inhalation of developer powder, which can be quite toxic. Eating small amounts of developer powder can be fatal to adults. Therefore, it is prudent to not eat where photos are being processed. Using liquid developer should minimize inhalation dangers. When handling negatives or prints in solutions, tongs should be used. In the darkroom, an apron and goggles should be worn when developing solutions are handled. Any developing solution that splashes onto the skin or into an eye should be immediately washed with copious amounts of water and checked by school health personnel.

Hazards and Help—Stop Baths

Standard stop bath is 28% acetic acid. A pH indicator is added, usually bromcresol purple, which is yellow below pH 5.2 and blue above pH 6.8. When the stop bath is blue, the hydrogen ion concentration is too low to be effective. Dilute acetic acid is an irritant to the skin and can cause allergic reactions and chronic bronchitis.

Adequate ventilation in the darkroom will eliminate acid fumes. The photographer should wear goggles, an apron, and plastic gloves, and should use tongs when handling negatives and prints in a stop bath.

Hazards and Help—Fixers

Sodium thiosulfate, sodium hydrogen sulfite, and aluminum potassium sulfate are used to remove remaining light-sensitive silver bromide or silver chloride, maintain an acid pH, and harden the negative or print finish.

Sodium thiosulfate and aluminum potassium sulfate are not very toxic upon skin and eye contact, and sodium thiosulfate is moderately toxic if inhaled, as is sodium hydrogen sulfite. However, sodium hydrogen sulfite is toxic if ingested.

As with developers and the stop bath, having adequate ventilation; wearing goggles, aprons, and gloves; and avoiding inhalation or ingestion of fixer solutions will minimize health risks.

Hazards and Help—Toners

Because gold and silver salt toners are very expensive, selenium toners in diluted, commercially prepared form are presently used. If the toner is heated, poisonous hydrogen sulfide gas can be released.

Because selenium powder and sodium selenite are extremely toxic, they can only be used under a fume hood with local exhaust ventilation. In addition, goggles, rubber gloves, an apron, and a dust mask should be worn. If the toner is heated, local exhaust ventilation should be provided.

THE POISON IS IN THE DOSE BUT ALL IS NOT LOST

In general, the longer the exposure to a toxic substance, the greater the risk of health problems. Also, the concentration of a substance determines its degree of toxicity.

Artists and chemists should not despair. They can continue to create and investigate without fear of failing health or instant injury to their well-being. With a knowledge of the chemicals and chemistry involved in their materials, artists can select proper alternatives to harmful materials. In fact, an artist might invent a new, better process or material for accomplishing a result by informed experimentation with different chemical combinations. *Art in Chemistry; Chemistry in Art* should help the artist to be more creative than ever before!

PRECAUTIONS TO PREVENT HEALTH PROBLEMS

Table 10.1 should be used to determine what precautions can be taken in particular *Art in Chemistry; Chemistry in Art* activities. However, if a substance is not listed, attention should still be paid to the proper use of that substance.

The information in Table 10.1 reflects currently available information concerning chemicals used in both art and chemistry. It should be understood that the authors and publisher can take no responsibility for the use or misuse of any information provided herein. Readers should use common sense and seek advice from the medical profession, regulation agencies, and associated professionals concerning specific hazards and problems.

Table 10.1
Materials Used in *Art in Chemistry; Chemistry in Art*
Activities and Demonstrations

Chemical or Art Material	Activities and Demonstrations	Hazards	Precautions
Acetic acid ($HC_2H_3O_2$)	8.2	Concentrated: can cause severe burns, dermatitis, ulcers, eye irritation. Dilute: Not very toxic.	Use fume hood for concentrated amounts (any). Wear goggles, apron, gloves.
Acids: Sulfuric (H_2SO_4), Hydrochloric (HC1), Nitric (HNO_3)	6.1, 6.4, 9.1	Highly irritating to eyes, skin, respiratory system. Can release toxic gases when reacted with metals.	Wear face mask, goggles. Use under hood with exhaust.
Acrylic paints	2.2, 9.2	Drying acrylic paints release ammonia (NH_3) and formaldehyde, which irritate nose and eyes.	Use with good ventilation.
Ammonium carbonate [$(NH_4)_2CO_3$]	2.4	Can release ammonia (NH_3)	Use with good ventilation.
Ammonium dichromate [$(NH_4)_2Cr_2O_7$]	Demo 1.2	Moderately toxic. Releases ammonia (NH_3). Potent animal carcinogen.	Use under hood with local ventilation. Wear goggles.

Chemical or Art Material	Activities and Demonstrations	Hazards	Precautions
Hydroquinone (paradihydroxybenzene)	8.2	Moderately toxic to skin, eyes, respiratory system. Suspected carcinogen.	Wear dust mask, goggles, apron during mixing. Use with local exhaust ventilation.
Lead nitrate [$Pb(NO_3)_2$]	2.3, 9.1, 9.2	Moderately toxic. Causes reduced mental acuity (neurotixin).	Avoid contact for long periods of time. Wear face mask with powder contact.
Markers	1.5, 1.6, 1.9, 1.10, 1.11, 1.13, 4.9, 5.9	Toxic solvents. Water-based are safest.	Use with good ventilation.
Matches	1.4, 2.1, 2.3, 6.1 Demos 1.2, 1.5, 4.1	Can cause burns. Inhaling sulfur fumes can cause throat and lung irritation.	Blow out quickly. Use with good ventilation.
Mercury I nitrate [$Hg_2(NO_3)_2$]	9.1	Skin irritation. Can be absorbed through the skin to cause neurological system problems.	Use with local exhaust ventilation. Wear dust mask, goggles, apron, gloves.
Methyl alcohol (CH_3OH)	Demos 1.2, 10.1	Toxic in high doses or chronic exposure.	Avoid skin and eye contact. Never ingest.
Sodium metal (Na)	6.1	Can burst into flame in air. Can cause burns and eye injuries.	Wear goggles, apron, gloves.
Silicon dioxide (SiO_2)	4.3	Can cause silicosis and lung diseases.	Wear plastic gloves, face mask. Do not inhale.
Silver nitrate ($AgNO_3$)	4.1, 8.2, 9.1	Stains and burns skin. Irritates mucous membrane. Can cause blindness if splashed in eyes.	Wear plastic gloves, goggles.

Chemical or Art Material	Activities and Demonstrations	Hazards	Precautions
Sodium carbonate (Na_2CO_3)	3.1, 6.7, 8.2	Moderately toxic. May cause skin and eye irritation.	Use with local exhaust ventilation. Wear dust mask, goggles, apron, gloves.
Sodium hypochlorite (NaHClO) (bleach)	3.4	Can cause severe eye, skin, and mucous membrane damage. Can release chlorine gas (Cl_2).	Wear gloves, goggles. Use with local exhaust ventilation.
Sodium sulfite (Na_2SO_3)	8.2	Not very toxic. May irritate skin, eyes, lungs. Ingestion in large amounts can be deadly.	Wear dust mask goggles, apron during mixing. Use with local exhaust ventilation.
Sulfur (S)	1.16	Toxic if inhaled or burned. Can produce sulfar dioxide (SO_2) and sulfar trioxide (SO_3), which are skin and eye irritants.	Do not inhale. Wear face mask. Do not burn.
Turpentine	2.4	Can cause dermatitis, asthma, kidney and bladder damage.	Use under hood with exhaust system.
Wax	2.4, 6.4, 10.1	Hot wax can release formaldehyde and acrolein, which irritate skin and eyes.	Use with good ventilation.

CHEMICAL HAZARDS FOR THE CHEMIST

Chemists are subject to the same hazards as artists when experiencing long-term, direct contact with toxic chemicals. In addition, some highly toxic chemicals can be deadly on single contact. Chemical warfare makes use of this knowledge. Fortunately, most chemists and artists will never come in contact with such chemicals.

The artist and the chemist should take the same precautions when chemical substances are present. As can be seen from Table 10.1, it is prudent to wear goggles and a fireproof apron when working with any chemicals. Because many chemicals are skin irritants, the use of gloves is wise. If powders or gases are present, a face mask protects lung and nasal tissue.

10.1

There Is a Right Way and a Wrong Way—How to Properly Use Chemical Materials in Art Projects

Objectives

1. Students will observe and evaluate the proper and improper way to handle chemical materials used in art projects.
2. Students will describe the molecular or ionic makeup of hazardous materials used in art projects.
3. Students will suggest substitute materials for hazardous art materials.
4. Students will experiment with methods of restoring a work of art.

Materials

Photography developing trays, old negatives, tongs, cube of wax, crucible, oil paints, varnish, methyl alcohol, surface for oil painting, paintbrushes for oil painting, soft white cloth, goggles, fireproof aprons, gloves, Table 10.1.

Time

100 minutes (two class periods about one week apart)

Procedure

A. The teacher should demonstrate the proper and improper use of chemicals in photo development:

1. Put on an apron, goggles, and gloves.
2. Fill two developing trays with water. The water represents developing solution.
3. Place a negative in the water.
4. Using tongs, remove the negative and transfer it to the next tray without dropping "chemicals" onto the surface of the table.

5. Using tongs, transfer the negative to a sink and run water on the negative.

6. Repeat the process, without wearing an apron, goggles, or gloves; using the tongs improperly; and dropping "chemicals" onto the surface of the table.

7. Have students record five correct procedures and five incorrect procedures that they observed.

B. The teacher should demonstrate the proper and improper use of metalworking materials:

1. Put on an apron, goggles, and gloves.

2. Add water to a crucible. The water represents molten metal.

3. Make a tunnel in a wax cube.

4. Using tongs to handle the crucible, pour the "molten metal" into the tunnel in the wax cube.

5. Repeat the above process, without wearing gloves, an apron, or goggles; and using the tongs improperly and pour the "molten metal" around the wax cube.

6. Have students record five correct and five incorrect procedures that they observed.

C. Have students prepare an oil painting, apply a varnish finish, and remove the "dirty" varnish with methyl alcohol:

1. Have students wear aprons and goggles.

2. Have students prepare an oil painting, using the principles of good composition. The oil paint should be applied thinly.

3. When the paint is dry, have students apply a thin coat of varnish to the oil paint. This should be done under a hood with a running exhaust fan. Students should wear gloves, aprons, and goggles.

4. Add a small amount of dirt or dust to a small area of the wet varnish.

5. When the varnish is dry, have students remove the "dirty" varnish methyl alcohol. The methyl alcohol should be absorbed by a soft cloth and gently rubbed onto the varnish to be removed. Care should be taken not to remove paint. This should be done under a hood with a running exhaust fan. Students should wear gloves, aprons, and goggles.

Questions and Conclusions

Level One

1. What health hazards exist for the art restorer?

2. Discuss reasons for wearing aprons, goggles, and gloves when working in the darkroom and when pouring liquid metals into molds.

3. Consider techniques involving clay, such as glazing and firing, and describe how the materials involved should be handled for safety.

4. Explain how health hazards from paints can be avoided.

Level Two

1. Make a list of several chemical formulas for substances used in painting, photography, clay sculpting, metalworking, and art restoration.

2. Make a list of alternate, less-toxic chemicals that could be used in each of these art disciplines. Explain your choices.

3. Where there is no alternate chemical choice, describe precautions that the artist can take when working with relatively toxic materials.

A REMARRIAGE OF ART AND CHEMISTRY

As with art conservation and restoration, when chemical hazards in art are considered, art and chemistry have again reached a state of matrimonial bliss. The artist needs the chemist and the chemist needs the artist. The artist, with the help of a sound knowledge of chemistry, can substitute less-toxic materials for highly toxic substances. For example, methyl alcohol, toluene, or methylene chloride can be substituted for benzene, which is used as a paint and varnish remover, and boric acid can be substituted for phenol, which is used as a preservative. The chemist needs the artist to shed new light and a new point of view so that the chemist can develop appropriate and better art materials.

REFERENCES

McCann, Michael. *Artist Beware.* New York: Watson-Guptill, 1979.

Rempel, Siegfried, and Wolfgang Rempel. *Health Hazards for Photographers.* New York: Lyons and Buford, 1992.

Rossol, Monona. *The Artist's Complete Health and Safety Guide.* 2d ed. New York: Allworth Press, 1994.

Periodic Table

IA	Alkaline Earth Metals 2A												3A	4A	5A	6A	Halogens 7A	Noble Gases 8A
1 H 1.01																		2 He 4.00
3 Li 6.94	4 Be 9.01												5 B 10.81	6 C 12.01	7 N 14.01	8 O 15.99	9 F 18.99	10 Ne 20.18
11 Na 22.99	12 Mg 24.31	3B	4B	5B	6B	7B		8B		1B	2B		13 Al 26.98	14 Si 28.09	15 P 30.97	16 S 32.06	17 Cl 35.45	18 Ar 39.95
19 K 39.10	20 Ca 40.08	21 Sc 44.96	22 Ti 47.88	23 V 50.94	24 Cr 51.99	25 Mn 54.94	26 Fe 55.85	27 Co 58.93	28 Ni 58.69	29 Cu 63.55	30 Zn 65.39	31 Ga 69.72	32 Ge 72.59	33 As 74.92	34 Se 79.96	35 Br 79.90	36 Kr 83.80
37 Rb 85.47	38 Sr 87.62	39 Y 88.91	40 Zr 91.22	41 Nb 92.91	42 Mo 95.94	43 Tc (98)	44 Ru 101.07	45 Rh 102.91	46 Pd 106.42	47 Ag 107.97	48 Cd 112.41	49 In 114.82	50 Sn 118.69	51 Sb 121.75	52 Te 127.60	53 I 126.91	54 Xe 131.29
55 Cs 132.91	56 Ba 137.33	71 Lu 174.97	72 Hf 178.49	73 Ta 180.95	74 W 183.85	75 Re 186.21	76 Os 190.2	77 Ir 192.22	78 Pt 195.08	79 Au 196.97	80 Hg 200.59	81 Tl 204.39	82 Pb 207.2	83 Bi 209.98	84 Po (209)	85 At (210)	86 Rn (222)
87 Fr	88 Ra	105 Lr															

Transition Metals

Alkali Metals

Inner-Transition Metals

*57 La 138.91	58 Ce 140.12	59 Pr 140.91	60 Nd 144.24	61 Pm (145)	62 Sm 150.36	63 Eu 151.96	64 Gd 157.25	65 Tb 158.93	66 Dy 162.50	67 Ho 164.93	68 Er 167.26	69 Tm 168.93	70 Yb 173.04
**89 Ac 227.03	90 Th 232.04	91 Pa 231.04	92 U 238.03	93 Np 237.05	94 Pu (244)	95 Am (243)	96 Cm (247)	97 Bk (247)	98 Cf (251)	99 Es (252)	100 Fm (257)	101 Md (258)	102 No (259)

* Lanthanides

** Actinides

Materials List

Chemistry Materials

Material and Activity or
Demonstration Where Needed

1 liter beaker: 3.1
1 liter graduated cylinder: 3.1
1 liter volumetric flask: 8.2, 8.5
10 ml. graduated cylinder: 2.1, 2.4, 9.1.
 Demos 1.2, 1.3
100 ml. beakers: 2.3, 3.2, 4.3
100 ml. erlenmeyer flask: 8.2
100 ml. graduated cylinder: 3.2, 6.1, 6.7, 8.2, 8.5.
 Demos 1.3, 1.4
150 ml. beakers: Demo 1.4
2 liter volumetric flask: 8.2
25 ml. graduated cylinder: 2.3, 5.5
250 ml. beakers: 2.4, 3.1, 3.2, 3.4, 4.1, 5.5, 6.4,
 6.7, 8.2, 8.5, 9.1. Demos 1.3, 4.1
50 ml. beaker: 5.5
50 ml. graduated cylinder: 8.2

Acetic acid: 8.2
Aluminum metal: 6.1
Aluminum oxide: 4.3
Ammeter: 6.4
Ammonium carbonate: 2.4
Ammonium chloride: 6.7
Ammonium dichromate: Demo 1.2
Ammonium hydroxide: 9.1
Ammonium sulfide: 6.7
Antimony metal: 6.1
Atomic model kits: 1.1, 5.2, 5.3, 7.1, 7.4
Automatic stirrer: 8.2

Bismuth metal: 6.1
Bunsen burner: 1.4, 2.1, 2.3, 2.4, 3.2, 6.1, 6.2,
 6.7, 9.3. Demos 1.5, 4.1, 6.2

Calcium carbonate: 4.3
Calcium chloride: 3.1
Calcium metal: 6.1
Calcium oxide: 3.1, 4.3
Calculator: 4.2
Carbon powder: 1.16

Carbon tetrachloride: 5.5
Centigram balance: 1.11, 1.12, 2.1, 2.3, 2.4, 3.2,
 3.4, 5.5, 6.1, 6.2, 6.7, 8.2, 8.5.
 Demos 1.2, 1.3, 1.4, 6.2
Chromium oxide: 4.3
Cinnabar or azurite: 2.3
Cobalt oxide: 4.3
Conducting wires with clips: 6.3, 6.4, 6.5
Copper II oxide: 4.3
Copper metal: 6.1, 6.2, 6.3, 6.4. Demo 6.1
Copper nitrate: 6.3, 6.7, 9.3
Copper sulfate: 1.11, 1.12, 1.13, 1.16, 6.4, 6.5,
 6.7. Demos 1.3, 1.4
Copper wire: 6.5, 6.6. Demo 4.1
Crucible: 10.1

Developing tanks: 8.2
Direct current source: 6.5. Demo 1.1

Elon: 8.2
Emery cloth: 6.1, 6.2, 6.4, 6.5, 6.6
Evaporating dish: 1.16, 2.3
Eyedropper: 2.5, 5.5, 6.1, 8.2, 9.1

Filter paper: 2.3, 3.1, 8.2
Fireproof aprons: All activities
Fireproof heat resistant gloves: When handling hot
 materials
Flashlights: 1.7, 1.11
Funnel: 2.3, 3.1, 8.2

Gas discharge tubes (hydrogen, argon, and neon):
 Demo 1.1
Glass stirring rod: 2.1, 2.4, 2.5, 3.1, 3.2, 5.5, 9.1.
 Demo 1.4
Goggles: All activities

Hexamethylene diamine: 5.5
Hot plate: 3.2, 3.4, 5.5, 6.4, 6.7, 8.5, 9.1
Hydrated calcium sulfate: 3.2
Hydrochloric acid: 6.1, 9.1
Hydroquinone (paradihydroxybenzene): 8.2

Iron III nitrate: 1.12
Iron III oxide: 4.3
Iron metal: 6.1

Kodak fixing solution: 8.2

Lead metal: 6.1
Lead nitrate (crystalline): 9.2
Lead nitrate: 2.3, 9.1, 9.2
Lead oxide: 4.3
Litmus paper: 3.1, 3.4

Magnesium strips: Demo 1.5
Matches: 1.4, 2.1, 2.3, 6.1. Demos 1.2, 1.5, 4.1
Mercury I nitrate: 9.1
Methyl alcohol: 10.1. Demo 1.2
Mortar and pestle: 2.3

Nitric acid: 6.1, 9.1

Periodic table: 1.11, 1.12, 4.2, 4.4, 6.1
Petri dishes: Demo 1.2
Pewter metal: 6.8
Phenolphthalein: 6.1
Photography developing trays: 10.1
Phthalic anhydride: 5.5
Potassium aluminum sulfate: 3.4, 4.1
Potassium bromide: 8.2, 8.5
Potassium chromate: 1.11, 1.12, 1.16, 9.1, 9.2
Potassium oxide: 4.3
Potassium thiocyanate: 1.12
Prism: 1.3

Ring and ring stand: 6.7

Sebacoyl chloride: 5.5
Silicon dioxide: 4.3
Silver metal: Demo 6.2
Silver nitrate: 8.2, 9.1. Demo 4.1
Sodium acetate: 2.1
Sodium carbonate: 3.1, 6.7, 8.2
Sodium chloride: 4.1, 8.2, 9.3
Sodium chromate: 2.3
Sodium hydroxide: 3.4, 5.5
Sodium hypochlorite: 3.4
Sodium metal: 6.1
Sodium nitrate: 6.3
Sodium sulfite: 8.2
Soluble starch: 2.4, 3.4
Spatula: 1.16, 2.3, 4.1, 8.2
Spectral line charts (hydrogen, argon, and neon):
    Demo 1.1
Spectroscopes: 9.3. Demo 1.1
Stoppers: 2.5, 8.2
Strontium nitrate or strontium carbonate: 9.3.
    Demo 1.2
Styrofoam balls: 4.1
Sucrose: 2.1

Sucrose: 4.1
Sulfur powder: 1.16
Sulfuric acid: 6.1, 6.4

Test tube holder: 2.1
Test tube rack: 2.1
Test tubes: 1.11, 1.12, 2.1, 2.3, 2.4, 2.5, 6.1, 8.2,
    9.1, 9.2. Demos 1.4, 4.1
Thermometer: 2.1, 5.5, 6.1, 8.2, 8.5
Tin metal: 6.1
Titanium dioxide: 3.2
Tongs: 2.3, 6.1, 6.2, 8.2, 8.5, 10.1.
    Demos 1.5, 6.2
Tweezers: 5.5, 9.2. Demo 6.1

U-tube: 6.3

Voltmeter: 6.1, 6.3

Wash bottle: 2.3, 3.1. Demo 4.1
Watch glasses: 2.4, 3.1, 3.2, 3.4, 4.3, 5.5
Wire or metal cutters: 5.6, 6.6
Wire: 5.6, 5.10

Zinc chloride: 6.7
Zinc metal: 6.1, 6.3
Zinc nitrate: 6.3
Zinc oxide: 3.2, 4.3

Art Materials

Material and Activity or
Demonstrations Where Needed

Acrylic paints: 2.2, 9.2

Beads: 5.6, 6.6
Beeswax: 2.4
Bowl: 7.2
Brush: Demo 6.1

Cardboard box: 6.6
Cardboard: 5.5, 7.2. Demo 6.2
C-clamp: 6.2, 6.6
Charcoal block: Demo 6.1
Cheese cloth: 3.2, 3.4
Clay tools: 7.2
Clay: 4.3, 4.5, 4.6, 4.7, 7.2. Demo 6.2
Colored paper: 1.15, 1.18. Demo 1.5
Colored pencils: 1.2, 1.3, 1.5, 1.6, 1.7, 5.2.
    Demos 1.1, 1.4
Commercial pen cleaner: 8.3
Compasses: 1.10
Construction paper: 3.5
Copper tongs: Demo 6.1

Darkroom safelight or light blocking bag: 8.2
Drawing paper: 1.2, 1.5, 1.8, 5.1, 5.2, 7.4
Dry curd cottage cheese: 3.2

Embroidery hoops: 3.4
Erasers: 1.2, 5.8, 7.4
Exposed black and white film (negatives): 8.2, 10.1

Fettle knife or kitchen knife: 5.4
Fluorescent paints: 9.2
Flux: Demo 6.1
Foam board: 9.2
Food color: 1.11

Glass tubing: Demo 4.1
Glue or rubber cement: 1.10, 1.13, 1.14, 1.15,
    1.18, 3.5, 5.1, 5.6, 5.9, 5.10, 7.4

Hammer: 6.5
Hand drill: 6.5
Hand held hole punch: 5.10
Heavy duty aluminum foil: 5.4
Heavy paper: 1.10, 1.13, 3.5

Ink: 8.3
Iron skimmer ladle: 6.6

Jeweler's saw and blades: 6.2, 6.6

Kiln: 4.3, 4.7, Demo 6.2
Kitchen knife: 5.4, 6.6

Linseed oil: 2.4

Magnifying lens: 4.1
Markers: 1.9, 1.10, 1.13, 1.14, 4.4, 5.9
Masonite board: 3.2
Mixing trays: 1.8, 1.13, 1.14, 2.2, 3.3, 3.4, 3.5.
    Demos 1.4, 3.1

Nail file: 6.6
Needle files: 6.2
Nib straight pen and pen holder: 8.3

Oil paint: 10.1

Paintbrushes: 1.5, 1.6, 1.8, 1.9, 1.10, 1.13, 1.14,
    1.16, 2.1, 2.2, 2.4, 2.5, 3.2, 3.3, 3.4, 3.5,
    9.2, 10.1. Demos 1.1, 1.4, 3.1
Painting paper: 1.10, 1.13, 1.14, 1.15, 1.16, 2.1,
    2,2, 3.5, 10.1. Demos 1.4, 3.1
Paper towels: 1.8, 1.9, 1.10, 3.3, 3.5

Paper: 1.1, 1.3, 1.6, 1.7, 1.9, 1.11, 1.16, 1.17,
    1.18, 3.5, 4.1, 5.1, 5.8, 5.9, 5.10, 6.2,
    6.5, 6.6, 7.1, 7.2, 7.4, 8.3.
    Demos 1.1, 4.1
Pencil: 1.1, 1.2, 1.5, 1.9, 1.13, 1.14, 2.2, 1.15,
    3.3, 4.1, 4.6, 5.1, 5.3, 5.8, 5.9, 5.10, 6.2,
    6.5, 6.6, 7.1, 7.2, 7.4, 8.3, 9.2.
    Demos 1.4, 4.1
Pewter (sheet or ingot): 6.6
Photographic printing paper: 8.2
Pickle solution: Demo 6.1
Plaster files: 5.4, 6.6
Plaster of Paris: 5.4, 6.6, 7.2
Pliers: 5.6, 6.5, 6.6
Poster paints: 1.5, 1.6, 1.8, 1.9, 1.10, 1.13, 1.14,
    1.16, 2.2, 3.3, 3.5. Demo 1.4
Posterboard, illustration board: 1.13, 1.14, 1.15,
    3.5, 5.5, 5.6, 5.10, 7.4
Propane torch: 6.5, 6.6. Demo 6.1
Protractor: 5.2, 7.1
Pumice: 6.7

Rabbit skin glue, animal or hide glue: 3.2, 3.4
Razor blades: 9.2
Ring mandrel: 6.2
Rolling pin: 4.3, 4.6
Rulers: 1.9, 1.10, 1.13, 1.14, 1.15, 2.2, 5.1, 5.3,
    5.6, 5.8, 5.9, 7.2, 7.4. Demo 1.4

Sandpaper: 3.2, 5.4
Scissors: 1.14, 1.15, 1.18, 3.5, 4.4, 5.1, 5.9,
    5.10, 6.2, 7.4, 8.2, 8.3. Demos 6.1, 6.2
Scribe: 6.2
Shelf paper: 1.3, 7.4
Silver solder: Demo 6.1
Soft cloth: 5.4, 10.1
Sponge: 8.2
Sponges: 2.2, 4.7
Spoon: 5.4
Steel block: 6.5
Steel wool: 6.6
Sticks: 4.7
String: 4.4, 4.6

Tape: 3.4, 4.4, 5.9, 7.2. Demo 3.1
Technical pen (Rapidograph): 8.3
Thread: 5.6, 5.10, 6.1
Thread spool: 5.5
Toothpicks: 4.1, 4.5, 4.6
Transparency paper: 1.7, 1.11, 3.5, 5.3
Trays: 3.4, 8.2, 8.5, 10.1
Turpentine: 2.4

Utility knife: 3.2

Varnish: 10.1
Vice and eye screw: 6.5

Water containers: 1.8, 1.9, 1.10, 1.13, 1.14, 2.2, 3.3, 3.4, 3.5. Demos 1.4, 3.1
Watercolor paint and pigment: 2.1, 2.2, 2.5, 3.3, 3.4. Demo 3.1
Wax: 6.4, 10.1

Wire (stove pipe): 6.6
Wooden mallet: 6.1, 6.3

X-ACTO knife: 5.4, 5.10, 6.6, 7.2, 9.2

Index

About the Authors

Barbara R. Greenberg is an intellectual property attorney and retired chemistry teacher in Hinsdale, Illinois. She taught at various schools in New York and Illinois. She was chosen Teacher of the Year at Willowbrook High School in Illinois. Barbara has developed integrated curriculum and taught chemistry at the Illinois Math and Science Academy. Barbara received her Bachelor of Science (chemistry) from the University of Illinois-Champaign, her Master of Arts (guidance and counseling) from Northeastern Illinois University, and a Doctorate in Law from Loyola University of Chicago School of Law.

Dianne Patterson is a retired art teacher in Elmhurst, Illinois. She is past chairperson for the art department at Willowbrook High School in Illinois. She is a current member of the Illinois Alliance for the Arts. Dianne is a former member of Chicago Art Education and the Illinois Art Education Association. She is currently pursuing watercolor painting, creation of wearable art, writing, and travel. Dianne received her Bachelor of Fine Arts (Art Education) from the University of Illinois, and her Master of Arts from the University of Illinois. She pursued post-graduate work in Fine Arts and Art Education at the University of Wisconsin, University of Colorado, and Northern Illinois University.